FOOTBALL'S
GREATEST
STARS

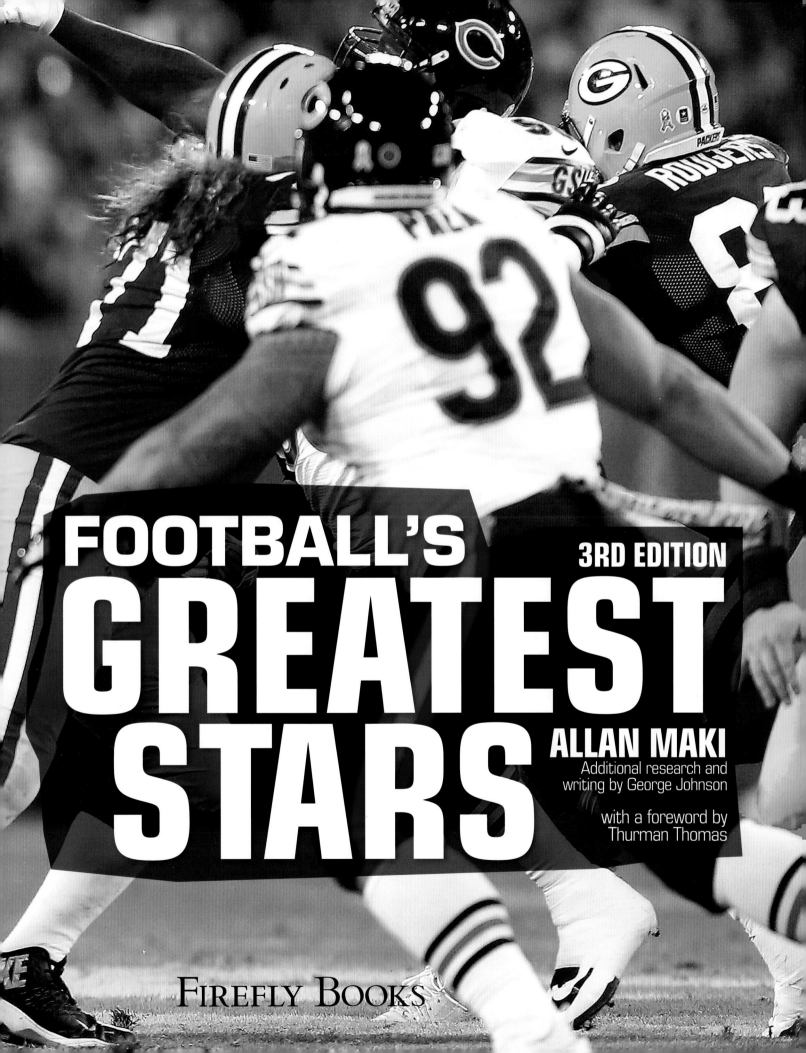

FOOTBALL'S
GREATEST
STARS

3RD EDITION

ALLAN MAKI

Additional research and
writing by George Johnson

with a foreword by
Thurman Thomas

FIREFLY BOOKS

A FIREFLY BOOK

Published by Firefly Books Ltd. 2015

First printing

Publisher Cataloging-in-Publication Data (U.S.)
Maki, Allan.
    Football's greatest stars / Allan Maki.
3rd ed.
[248] pages : photographs (chiefly color) ; cm.
Includes index.
Summary: Profiles of fifty of the greatest and most exciting players in the history of professional football.
ISBN-13: 978-1-77085-595-3 (pbk.)
1. National Football League – Biography. 2. Football players – United States – Biography. I. Title.
796.332/0922 [B] dc23   GV939.A1M354 2015

Library and Archives Canada Cataloguing in Publication
Maki, Allan, author
    Football's greatest stars / Allan Maki ; additional research and writing by George Johnson ; with a foreword by Thurman Thomas. -- Third edition.
Includes index.
ISBN 978-1-77085-595-3 (bound)
1. National Football League. 2. Football players--United States--Biography. 3. National Football League--History. 4. Football--United States--History. I. Johnson, George, 1957-, author II. Title.
GV939.A1M34 2015   796.332092'2   C2015-902804-3

Published in the United States by
Firefly Books (U.S.) Inc.
P.O. Box 1338, Ellicott Station
Buffalo, New York 14205

Published in Canada in 2013 by
Firefly Books Ltd.
50 Staples Avenue, Unit 1
Richmond Hill, Ontario L4B 0A7

Cover design: Hartley Millson
Interior design: Jamie Hodgson | Studio 34
Statistical and team compilations: Derek Iwanuk

Printed in China

The publisher gratefully acknowledges the financial support for our publishing program by the Government of Canada through the Canada Book Fund as administered by the Department of Canadian Heritage.

DEDICATION
For my dad, for teaching me how to laugh,
and for my amazing wife, who keeps me laughing.

KEY TO ABBREVIATIONS
ast = assists
att = attempts
avg = average
comp = completions
FF = forced fumbles
FG = field goal/s
FGA = field goal attempts
FR = fumble recoveries
int = interceptions
KR = kick returns
pct = percent/percentage
PR = punt returns
rec = receptions
TD/TDs = touchdown/s
yd avg = average yards
yds = yards
ypc = yards per carry
XK = extra kicks made
XKA = extra kicks attempted

CAPTIONS
Pg 2–3: Aaron Rodgers looks to throw the ball against the Chicago Bears in 2014. Rodgers threw six touchdowns in the game, helping the Packers win 55–14. Both the Associated Press and the Professional Football Writers Association selected him as the 2014 NFL MVP.

Pg 5: Steve Young and Brett Favre congratulate each other after the hard fought 1997 NFC Championship game. Favre's Packers defeated Young's 49ers 23–10 to advance to the Super Bowl for the second straight year; the Packers would lose the Super Bowl to the Denver Broncos.

Pg 6: Terry Bradshaw in 1979. The Hall of Fame quarterback would lead the Steelers to their fourth Super Bowl in six seasons, and their second in a row, while also winning his second Super Bowl MVP.

CONTENTS

The Deacon was sipping drinks with an inquisitive sportswriter in a Toronto nightclub one evening when the question was raised: What made him one of the NFL's most dominant defensive linemen? Was it his quickness, that quarterback- crippling, inside-outside rush move?

Twenty years removed from his last game, David "Deacon" Jones shook his head and uttered a single word: "Attitude." That was the key that unlocked his greatness, Jones insisted. All those who play in the NFL boast a high degree of talent, he explained. They can run fast, hit hard, throw accurately. But what separates the prime cuts from the herd is how badly they want to succeed: their attitude.

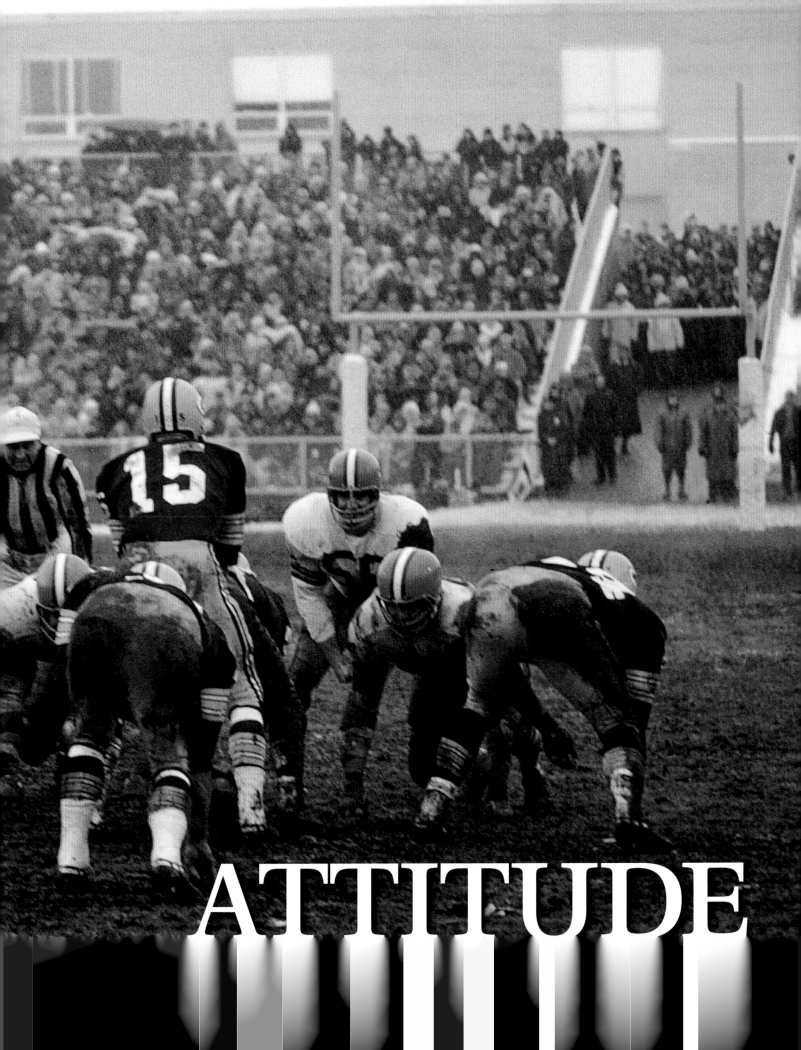

ATTITUDE

SIMPSON AND LEWIS ARE NOT
POPULAR PICKS, BUT AS ATHLETES,
AWAY FROM OUTSIDE TEMPTATIONS,
THEIR WORK HAD THE FOOTBALL
WORLD SHAKING ITS HEAD
IN AMAZEMENT.

That was how the Deacon saw it, and I thought of that conversation with Jones soon after I was contacted by Firefly Books editor Steve Cameron. Steve had asked me to write about the NFL's 50 Greatest Players. The dilemma, aside from a tight deadline, was how to pick the foremost 50. How do you compare players from different eras? How do you value a good offensive lineman as opposed to a good inside linebacker? Do you go by durability? Versatility?

Do you pick an athlete because he took his position and played it like no one else ever had? That worked in a couple of cases (for example, New York Giants linebacker Lawrence Taylor and Baltimore Colts tight end John Mackey), but not for everyone. So how did we come up with our 50?

We used two criteria: only players from the late 1950s and early 1960s up to the present would be included. We wanted a contemporary collection (no offense to Otto Graham or Don Hutson). They also had to pass the Deacon's test, meaning they had to have an attitude about them. That wasn't to say every player had to preen and prance like Deion "Neon" Sanders auditioning for the Rockettes dance troupe. That was his own gimmick, his personal style.

What we wanted overall were players with an unflinching belief in themselves — men whose personal triumphs and attitudes were as impressive as the statistics and records they set.

Green Bay Packers quarterback Bart Starr was a shining example of that. Starr was a late-round draft pick with supposedly limited skills, but his passion for the game helped him to become a master craftsman. Starr's ambition was to execute a game plan to perfection and to do it in the biggest games. In terms of his personality, he was practical and humble.

But make no mistake. Starr was a merciless competitor. He would find the weakness in an opposing defense and exploit it repeatedly. He wasn't in it for the glory. He just wanted the victory. And he collected his share.

Considering the depth of our project — and again, a pressing deadline — *Calgary Herald* sports columnist George Johnson was brought in for his able assistance. Johnson is one of Canada's premier sportswriters and when he began filing his first biographies, he, too, was captivated by the players who had confronted adversity in their lives, if not their careers. His piece on Green Bay linebacker Ray Nitschke captures all the elements we were looking to highlight.

With Johnson aboard, we debated and then settled on our 50 favorites, based on their inner traits and on-field work, and began writing.

A portion of my research came from conversations over the years with some of the NFL's finest minds (coach Marv Levy, who was inducted into the Pro Football Hall of Fame in 2001, and general manager Bill Polian, who built the Indianapolis Colts into 2007 Super Bowl champions), along with some of the game's freest thinkers (NFL assistant coaches Bill Bradley and Fred Biletnikoff, and my long-time source and purveyor of all things NFL, Deep Zone. You know who you are).

Those men provided tremendous insight into the game and helped shape my thoughts as this book was assembled.

When I look back at this endeavor, I realize we excluded many remarkable athletes, for example, Dallas Cowboys defensive lineman Bob Lilly; Oakland Raiders cornerback Mike Haynes; Miami Dolphins receiver Paul Warfield. But I'd argue hard and fast if any of our 50 had to be dropped to make room for someone else.

Some of you may take issue with the inclusion of Buffalo Bills running back O.J. Simpson and Baltimore Ravens linebacker Ray Lewis, both of whom were charged with murder in separate incidents. Simpson was found not guilty; Lewis pleaded guilty to a lesser charge. Simpson's legal battles came after his career; Lewis's came at the height of his playing days. Now retired, he has been able to restore at least part of his reputation through humanitarian efforts.

Simpson and Lewis are not popular picks, but as athletes, away from outside temptations, their work had the football world shaking its head in amazement. They had the gifts. And attitude!

Those same on-field qualities can be found in the stars that populate the Future Greats chapter. We've tagged 20 current players who have pulled away from the herd. They want more and they are primed to get it.

So sit back, relax and marvel at the great players and moments that have shaped the NFL. Where would the game be without them? ▪

FOREWORD

by Thurman Thomas

Reflecting on the stories in this book and the stars that I played with, against, and those who came before me, I can't help but think of my rookie season. It was 1988, and I can remember sitting in the Visitors' locker room at Chicago's Soldier Field on game day, getting ready to play. Our team, the Buffalo Bills, were 4–0 and about to take on the 4–0 Bears. It was our first big test of the season.

I was getting taped, and I heard this voice saying, "Where's that Number 34?" I had no idea whose voice it was. I thought maybe it was a coach looking for me.

But it was Walter Payton, one of my two idols when I was younger — the other was Earl Campbell. Walter had retired from the Bears but he wanted to meet me. I was this 22-year-old kid without a clue, and he was Walter Payton, the NFL's all-time leading rusher. He'd read somewhere that I wore the number 34 because of him, and Earl Campbell, too, and he wanted to talk to me.

I told Walter I had started running up hills as part of my training program because that's what he'd done during his career. He told me it was good for building endurance, and we talked some more and shook hands. After Walter left, Jim Kelly, our quarterback, came up to me and said, "Oh man, that is so cool. Give me a high five."

I said, "Are you nuts? I just shook Walter Payton's hand. I don't want to touch your hand."

My dream was to be like Walter and Earl. Being from Texas, I had followed Earl's career from his days at the University at Texas and then on to the Houston Oilers. Earl and Walter, I wanted to make my game like theirs. I knew I wasn't as physical as Earl or as experienced as Walter, but I wanted to be a great player like them. That's where it probably started for me.

Even as a kid, I used to tell my mom I was going to be a professional football player. And when I made it, I wanted Bills' fans around the world to know that when I was out on the football field, I was doing everything possible to win the game. It didn't matter if I was running the ball or I was catching the ball or I was picking up a blitz. I was a guy you literally had to peel off the football field. I gave it my all on every play.

Personally, I think that's what being a great player is about. It's not just about the winning. I look at other great athletes — Ted Williams, Barry Bonds, Charles Barkley — and they've been in the spotlight and never won a championship. Look at how great a player Barry Sanders was, or Warren Moon, and neither of them won an NFL championship.

In Buffalo, we got to the Super Bowl four years in a row from 1991 to 1994. I look back at that as a remarkable feat, and for sure I wish we could have won one, two or all four of those games. The thing is

if you go to a Super Bowl and lose, it could tear your team apart. To go to four Super Bowls and lose and to keep coming back trying to win, I don't think anyone could fault us for our effort. That's what greatness is about — trying to win and competing hard.

Besides, I say we could have won a Super Bowl if we hadn't played a team from the NFC East — the Dallas Cowboys, Washington Redskins, New York Giants. If we had played the NFC North or South, then we might have won. I've always had a good sense of humor.

When I was coming out of Oklahoma State University, there were questions about me as a running back. A lot of NFL teams passed me up because of my knee, which I injured in my senior year. There were NFL scouts who figured my knee wouldn't hold up for more than three or four years.

Buffalo drafted me in the second round and I always considered myself an every-down back. I worked with Jim Kelly, Andre Reed and the other receivers staying out after practice and running routes with them, just to get some timing down and to let the coaches see I could come out of the backfield and catch the football. I understood that to catch the ball was every bit as important as running it.

Maybe I felt that way because I played in an era when it was Emmitt Smith and Barry Sanders, or Barry Sanders and Emmitt Smith. I was always third, and I understood that. People loved Em-mitt and Barry. Those two were great running backs, and are great friends of mine. I was just a guy in Buffalo trying to do what he could, although I did get my share of attention.

Kids used to always talk to me about Tecmo Bowl. Do you know about Tecmo Bowl? It was a little computer football game. I still have people say to me, "When I played Tecmo Bowl, I was always you. Forget Emmitt Smith or Barry Sanders; I was Thurman Thomas." It was big in 1991, the year I won the NFL's MVP. Apparently I was unstoppable.

I told you I had a sense of humor.

People have asked me what I'm most proud of in my football career. When I look back at my time in the NFL, I'm proud to say I lasted 13 years without having a serious injury. That's probably my greatest accomplishment — playing hard and staying healthy. That's also what I admired about Walter Payton, along with the type of person he was.

For Walter Payton to come into the Bills' dressing room like that before a game, just to say hi, it made a ton of difference, not just for me but for our other players, too. They were so impressed by him. We lost that game against the Bears. The score was 24–3. But meeting Walter and shaking the hand of greatness, that's one of my fondest memories. ▪

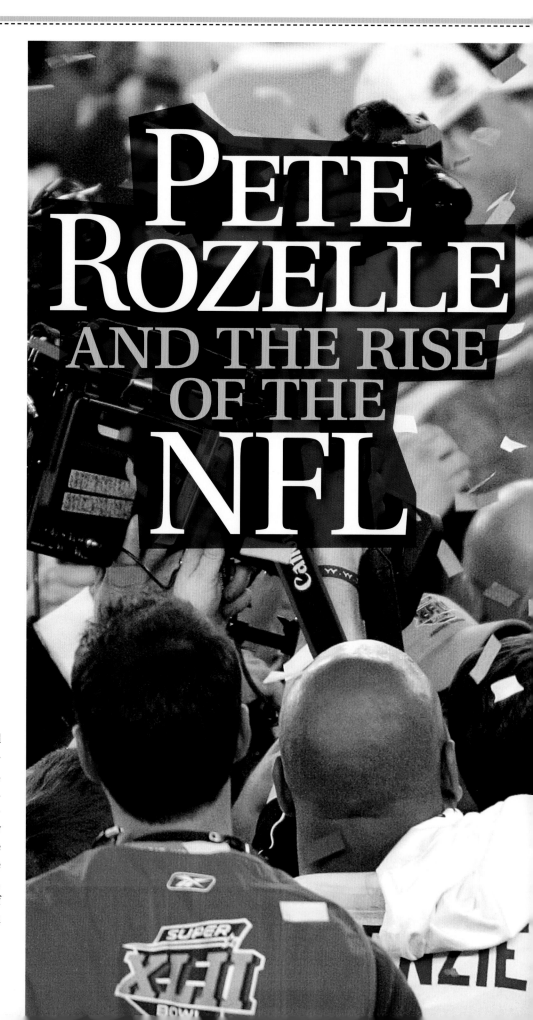

PETE ROZELLE
AND THE RISE OF THE
NFL

"Baseball is what we were. Football is what we have become."

– Mary McGrory,
American journalist

He never really looked the part of a football titan. He was tall and thin with a receding hairline and a fondness for cigarettes, scotch and Drambuie. He smiled a lot. Spoke more about marketing than man-to-man coverage. Couldn't throw like Johnny Unitas or run like Jim Brown. In fact, he never played football. His games of choice were baseball and tennis and, for a time, before he got into the management side of football, he had thought about becoming a sportswriter.

Sid Luckman

Yet Alvin Ray (Pete) Rozelle was the single most influential figure in the rise of the National Football League, and he took it to phenomenal heights: a man who used his salesman's charm and administrative moxie to transform his league into the monster that ate professional sports.

Take a look any Sunday from September to February. All across the U.S., there are 70,000-seat stadiums jammed at or near capacity, with face-painted zealots writhing on every play. Here are multi-millionaire athletes performing for the tens of millions of television viewers around the world. Great plays are highlighted over and over from a dozen different camera angles, helping to add to the anticipation and importance of the next play, the next series.

Then the Super Bowl comes along with its Janet Jackson wardrobe malfunction and its $3.8 million price tag for a 30-second TV commercial and everything goes over the moon. Its New Year's Eve at Times Square times 10.

Rozelle made all this happen. He took the NFL from its lagging position behind major league baseball and college football and maneuvered it to a place other leagues now dream of. National TV rights contracts? Rozelle negotiated those for the owners, always with staggering results. Enforced revenue sharing so the small-market teams could run with their big-market brethren? Rozelle got the New York Giants and Chicago Bears to go along with that, and hence, the birth of parity.

Johnny Unitas sets to deliver a pass in overtime of the "greatest game ever played."

NFL Properties. NFL Films. NFL Charities. *Monday Night Football*. In almost every way, Rozelle's long-range thinking paid off. As *Miami Herald* columnist Edwin Pope told ESPN Classic's *Sports Century* series: "I firmly believe that when the final history of the National Football League is written, the all-time hero of the NFL, the man who contributed most to changing America's Sunday afternoon watching habits, is Pete Rozelle."

Was Rozelle without his faults? Absolutely not. His decision to play games two days after U.S. president John F. Kennedy was assassinated in 1963 was considered a colossal blunder, one that Rozelle came to regret. Late in his 29-year run as commissioner, many players argued Rozelle and the NFL hadn't done enough to take care of the retired players who lacked the pension money to cover the cost of operations for football-related injuries and assisted living. The inference was telling: Rozelle could be cold-hearted and calculating if it suited his interests or the NFL's, which led to his nickname, "the arrogant czar."

But the pluses outweighed the negatives. Rozelle combined his ground-breaking accomplishments with a touch of Madison Ave. As NFL commissioner from 1960 to 1989, he was, as he stated several times, "the right man at the right time."

BEFORE ROZELLE

When Rozelle was named commissioner on Jan. 20, 1960, he replaced Bert Bell, who had suffered a heart attack and died on Oct. 11, 1959, while attending a game between the two teams he had co-founded, the Philadelphia Eagles and the Pittsburgh Steelers.

As the NFL's first commissioner, Bell used to draw up the league's schedule at his kitchen table. He bought his share of the Eagles in 1933 for $2,500. Tim Mara had paid the same amount for the New York Giants in 1925. In essence, the NFL at that time was the domain of seven men — Bell, Mara, George Halas, George Preston Marshall, Earl (Curly) Lambeau, Charlie Bidwell and Art Rooney. Their ambition was to carve out a niche among sports fans who loved college football when they weren't watching baseball playoffs and the World Series. But throughout the 1930s, the NFL did little to excite the masses.

Harold (Red) Grange, known as the Galloping Ghost, helped legitimize professional football when he signed with the Chicago Bears in 1925. But the best thing to hit the game was a change in offensive strategy known as the T-formation. With the quarterback lining up behind the center, and two running backs in the backfield, the pivot had a myriad of options from faking hand-offs to throwing deep downfield. The Bears and quarterback Sid Luckman were so efficient using the T-formation they beat the Washington Redskins in the 1940 NFL Championship game by a score of 73–0. (Yes, you read that correctly.) That was the beginning of the Bears as Monsters of the Midway, the NFL's first dynasty.

While the game was undergoing changes on the field, the NFL was a closed shop that operated solely on the wishes of its owners, particularly the southern-born George Marshall, who wanted nothing to do with black athletes. From 1934 to 1945, not one black played in the NFL. It took the 1946 Los Angeles Rams to change that when they signed former UCLA

Rozelle in New York to announce his appointment as NFL commissioner on Feb. 24, 1960.

star Ken Washington. Soon after, the Cleveland Browns of the All-American Football Conference added Marion Motley and Bill Willis.

Marshall was so against the inclusion of blacks that he uttered his infamous quote, "[The Washington Redskins] will start signing Negroes when the Harlem Globetrotters start signing whites." Marshall stuck to those words until 1962 when he was told by the U.S. Interior Secretary that unless the Redskins signed a black player, the government would revoke the team's lease at D.C. Stadium (now Robert F. Kennedy Stadium). Marshall responded by drafting Syracuse running back Ernie Davis, who promptly said, "I won't play for that S.O.B." And he didn't. He was traded for another black offensive talent, Bobby Mitchell.

NFL EXPLODES INTO THE MAINSTREAM

What saved the NFL from its parochial thinking and lack of pizzazz in general was the Dec. 28, 1958, championship game. On that day, the NFL exploded into the mainstream with what is still referred to as the greatest game ever played — the Baltimore Colts against the New York Giants. The on-field theatrics were spectacular, and it was full of seminal

moments, future Hall of Famers and the first overtime in NFL history. The game was also televised nationwide (watched by more than 40 million people) and it had Johnny Unitas, the first idol of the NFL's modern era.

The pressure-treated Unitas, who operated with a surgeon's precision, engineered two dramatic scoring drives, including the winning march, and thus was springboarded into the limelight. He became the focal point of an emerging game, one that was taking hold of a new generation of Americans, the post-World War II boomers whose changing lifestyle included eating TV dinners on TV trays while flipping through the *TV Guide* and watching the quintessential TV sport: football.

As the game moved toward the Swinging Sixties, Rozelle began his rise to prominence. He had had a series of public relations jobs before joining the Los Angeles Rams as its PR specialist in 1952, and after a brief hiatus to help promote the 1956 Melbourne Olympics, the 33-year-old Rozelle became general manager of the Rams — a franchise that had, up till then, been losing fans almost as quickly as it was losing money.

Rozelle gave the Rams purpose and professionalism. He established a Rams store near the team's offices on Beverly Boulevard, where fans could buy all manner of merchandise, including Rams bobblehead dolls. But the California son of a depression-era store owner couldn't do enough to make the Rams a winning team and so, after three seasons as GM, as he was contemplating a change, he was asked if he'd let his name stand as a candidate for the commissioner's job.

Finding the late Bert Bell's replacement had turned into a colossal stand-off. Some of the owners wanted to stick with Austin Gunsel, the former FBI agent and NFL treasurer, who had been serving as acting commissioner. Others preferred west-coast lawyer Marshall Leahy, who wanted the league offices moved to San Francisco from Philadelphia.

After 22 ballots and seven days, on Jan. 26, 1960, Rozelle left the conference room so the owners could debate his merits. He stayed in a men's room to kill time. Whenever someone came in to use the facilities, he would straighten his tie and wash his hands. Finally notified that he'd been approved as commissioner, Rozelle displayed his gift for the appropriate quip. "At least I'm taking the job with clean hands," he said.

He had no idea how messy things were going to get.

THAT UPSTART — THE AFL

"I wonder if that S.O.B. Tex Maule is watching?"
— NBC broadcaster Curt Gowdy commenting on-air about the *Sports Illustrated* writer who had written nary a good word about the AFL

Lamar Hunt never looked the part of a football titan, either. He, too, was tallish but with a knobby chin, a round face and horn-rimmed glasses.

Hunt was born into enormous wealth, yet wanted little to do with the family oil business. He wanted to own a football team, and after trying unsuccessfully to buy his way into the NFL fraternity, he came up with a solution: he would start his own league. And so, on Aug. 14, 1959, Hunt announced the formation of the American Football League, which was to begin play in 1960.

At first, it seemed as if Hunt and his sev-

Legendary coach Sid Gillman congratulates offensive stars Lance Alworth and John Hadl in 1965.

en associates (jokingly known as the Foolish Club) had the blessings of the NFL and its commissioner, Bell. But when the NFL began granting expansion teams to the very cities the AFL had intended to cultivate, the tone was set and the battle was on. Not that the AFL was fighting from anything resembling a position of strength.

Early on, almost everything about the new league had a hand-me-down, garage-sale feel to it. The Oakland franchise fumbled its first attempt at naming the new team: a local newspaper held a name-the-team contest and for reasons never quite understood, "the Senors" won by a landslide. (Team officials later switched the name to Raiders rather than have a public address announcer say, "First and 10 for the Senors.") The New York Titans didn't even have a playbook. Head coach Sammy Baugh kept everything recorded in his head. The Denver Broncos may have been the AFL's cheapest-run organization. At the first training camp, the players slept in army-style barracks and were fed poorly. The exception was Friday when everyone was served steak. The idea was to offer meat on Friday because the Catholic players wouldn't eat it. As for the Broncos' uniforms, they were the height of ugliness, including socks with vertical stripes.

At least the Broncos had uniforms for their debut, whereas the Houston Oilers didn't. When the Oilers hit the field, most of the players wore blue and white while 14 others were outfitted in red practice jerseys. Apparently, thieves had made off with the rest of the Oilers'

Broadway Joe Namath

blue-and-white uniforms. "We looked like a bunch of rinky dinks," recalled Oilers' owner Bud Adams. True enough, they did.

History shows the AFL's first regular-season game was played on Sept. 9, 1960, with the vertically-striped-challenged Broncos taking on the Boston Patriots. The game drew 21,597 spectators, and the AFL was off and bumbling. It had few established star players and lacked the NFL's crisp professionalism. Knowing that, the AFL opted for a more wide-open brand of play. Offense was the name of the game and offense is what the AFL sold. Coach Sid Gillman saw to that.

With the Chargers, first in Los Angeles and then in San Diego, Gillman brought a meticulous, inventive mindset to a league that desperately needed both. He didn't like the short passing game that dominated the NFL. He believed in throwing the ball downfield and exciting the fans. The Chargers also had Al Davis and Don Klosterman as scouts. They would eventually bring in the likes of college stars Ron Mix, Paul Lowe, Keith Lincoln, Lance Alworth and John Hadl. The Chargers became regulars in the AFL championship games, twice losing to Houston before crushing the Boston Patriots 51–10 in 1963.

The NFL was convinced all it had to do was sneeze and the AFL would be scattered to the four corners whence it came. But the junior circuit embraced the newness of the

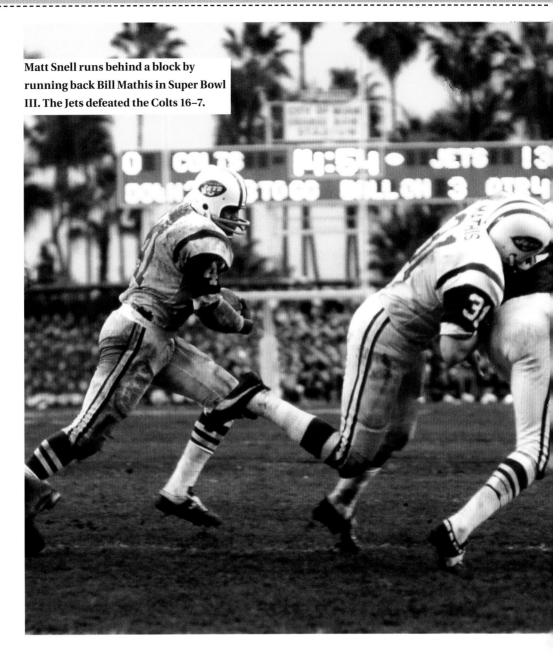

Matt Snell runs behind a block by running back Bill Mathis in Super Bowl III. The Jets defeated the Colts 16–7.

LIFE ON THE SUPER STAGE

QUIRKS AND QUOTES

Now entering middle-age, the Super Bowl has provided many a bad game, some good ones, some great games and a list of characters longer than Ben Davidson's handlebar mustache in the 1968 AFL–NFL championship.

One of the early stars of the Super stage was Dallas Cowboys running back Duane Thomas, who had a Rubik's Cube personality. The more you worked with it, the more confusing it got. Thomas was equal parts strange, belligerent, brilliant and infuriating. During the week leading up to 1972's Super Bowl VI, he was required by the NFL to meet with the media. He did so by sitting in the stands with several scribes clotted around waiting for the great man to speak. For several minutes, Thomas sat there without saying word. When he spoke, it was to ask, "What time is it?" He eventually got up and left. Apparently, it was time to go.

Thomas, however, did serve up two of the finest Super Bowl quotes ever uttered. Asked on national TV by Tom Brookshier if he was as fast as he looked on the field, Thomas replied,

decade by using two-point converts, having the players' names on the back of their jerseys and the official time on the score clock. Fans began to take to an old game made livelier. The 1962 AFL championship clash between Houston and the Dallas Texans, won by Dallas in overtime, drew 56 million television viewers.

The off-field drama was compelling, too. The AFL began to snap up collegiate stars such as Buck Buchanan, Bobby Bell, Pete Beathard and Matt Snell. The entire football community was rife with tales of intrigue about what teams were doing to ensure they got their player before the other league did. The NFL even had a clandestine procedure, dubbed Operation Hand-holding, to stand guard over prized recruits and ensure they signed with "the right league." NFL team officials and scouts were involved in the ploy while Rozelle, as commissioner, offered no public knowledge of its existence.

> NAMATH GAVE THE JETS $427,000 WORTH OF INSTANT PUBLICITY. HE HAD THE LOOKS, THE CHARISMA AND A FOOTBALL PEDIGREE.

Then came the day the AFL arrived in the minds of the American sporting public: the day Joe Namath agreed to sign with the New York Jets.

Right from the snap in 1965, it was clear the Jets wanted to make a splash with Namath. They drafted him first overall compared to the NFL's St. Louis Cardinals, who took him 12th overall. The Jets offered Namath a three-year deal worth a record $427,000. The Cardinals and the NFL thought Jets owner Sonny Werblin had flipped his lid. Werblin's background in the entertainment business had convinced him that his team, and the AFL too, needed a star and Namath, as Rozelle had said of himself, was the right man at the right time.

Namath gave the Jets $427,000 worth of instant publicity. He had the looks, the charisma and a football pedigree, having led the University of Alabama to a U.S. college championship under coach Bear Bryant in 1964. The Jets began selling out at home and on the road. Before 1965 ended, the AFL had entered into a five-year, $36 million TV agreement with NBC, with veteran announcer Curt Gowdy calling the games. That same year, the Kansas City Chiefs signed Heisman Trophy-winning running back Mike Garrett. The NFL retaliated by signing a player (Buffalo Bills kicker Pete Gogolak) who was already under contract in the AFL.

One of the first to grasp the magnitude of the NFL/Gogolak move was Al Davis, the former Charger scout who had gone on to run the Oakland Raiders and was now AFL commissioner. "I guess [the AFL owners] thought I'd be a catalyst," Davis said of his appointment. "It was a situation that called for some constant pressure to be put on the other side."

The squeeze-happy Davis applied more pressure than a pair of vice grips. He signed eight NFL quarterbacks, including Roman Gabriel and John Brodie, to AFL contracts. Davis wasn't interested in negotiating peace. He wanted a fight to the finish.

With Davis in office for two months, a series of back-channel meetings were held between the NFL and AFL to discuss the possibility of a merger. The two leagues had been locked in an escalating bidding war for players. Together, they had spent $7 million on their 1966 draft picks — an unheard of amount for player salaries and bonuses. Something had to give.

At first, Rozelle wasn't interested in a merger but the NFL's owners wanted to end the spending spree. Rozelle negotiated the

---

"Evidently." And when asked if winning the Super Bowl was the ultimate, Thomas responded with a question of his own. "If the Super Bowl is the ultimate game, how come they're playing it again next year?" Good point.

Dallas linebacker Thomas (Hollywood) Henderson, who said of Pittsburgh Steelers quarterback Terry Bradshaw, "He's so dumb he couldn't spell cat if you spotted him the 'c' and 't'." After the Steelers beat Dallas, Henderson had to backpedal furiously. "I didn't say he couldn't play, just that he couldn't spell."

Russ Grimm of the Washington Redskins said he'd run over his own mother to win the Super Bowl. Oakland linebacker Matt Millen concurred: "I'd run over Russ Grimm's mother to win the Super Bowl, too."

HEROES AND ZEROES

You can't miss much at the Super Bowl. Under the media's unforgiving eye, stars become heroes and the mistake-prone become scoundrels. Joe Montana drove his San Francisco 49ers for a late, game-winning touchdown in Super Bowl XXIII. Prior to that game, Cincinnati Bengals running back Stanley Wilson was suspended after being caught in a bathroom using cocaine. In Super Bowl XXXIII, John Elway retired in style winning his second consecutive Lombardi Trophy. Prior to that game, Atlanta Falcons defensive back Eugene Robinson was arrested for soliciting a female undercover police officer who was posing as a prostitute. Robinson had just received the Bart Starr Award from the Christian group Athletes in Action for his "high moral character."

best deal he could. He sent Tex Schramm of the Dallas Cowboys to talk with Hunt, who seemed the most agreeable of the Foolish Club members. As part of the merger, 10 AFL teams were accepted under the NFL banner. Two (Oakland and New York) had to make indemnity payments to the NFL teams in their area. It was agreed the two leagues would officially unite in 1970, with three NFL teams: the Pittsburgh Steelers, Baltimore Colts and Cleveland Browns moving to what would be called the American Football Conference. However, an annual AFL–NFL Championship game would be played starting January 1967.

Ironically, it was Lamar Hunt, the man who wanted to own a football team so badly that he started his own league, who gave the AFL–NFL championship game its lasting moniker. After watching his daughter play with an incredible bouncy toy, the Super Ball, he thought, "the Super Bowl"? Some said it sounded too hokey. Hunt thought so, too. But the name stuck. The first thing Rozelle did was sell the broadcasting rights to the Super Bowl to both CBS and NBC. The two networks paid $1 million each for the one game. That Rozelle was able to play the two networks against each other, for the good of the NFL, was further proof of his negotiating skills.

SUPER BOWL MADNESS

"If there had been a Super Bowl back then, Nero wouldn't have burned Rome. He'd have been too busy schmoozing with corporate chieftains who arrived by sedan chair and reclined under purple robes as grapes were dropped into their mouths."

– Sports writer Dave Kindred on the Big Game

The Super Bowl is the perfect American institution: pomp and pageantry, celebrities and newsmakers and, occasionally, an entertaining football game, although that's hardly necessary. So majestic is the Super Bowl that it no longer requires breathtaking action. Just start the countdown to kickoff and the show promotes itself. It is a rolling, rollicking bit of overindulgence you don't want to miss out on. The game has become so grandiose, so ingrained, that it has evolved into a world phenomenon and a parody of itself. How many media-day spoofs have you seen or read? Or Super Bowl TV commercials that never fail to amuse? It's all part of the package now.

Back in 1967, the first AFL–NFL Championship game between the Kansas City Chiefs and the Green Bay Packers was hardly the hottest ticket in Los Angeles. The Packers carried the NFL's expectations as the superior league and were aware of their responsibility. The Chiefs had some outstanding players, but were overwhelmed by the enormity of the challenge and Vince Lombardi's unstoppable Packers' power sweeps.

Ironically, Lombardi wanted no part of hyping the game and sequestered his team in Santa Barbara, 90 miles north of L.A. It was left to the likes of Kansas City defensive back Fred (The Hammer) Williamson to fire up the media with talk of how he was going to flatten Packers' receivers Carroll Dale and Boyd Dowler with his mind-numbing kung-fu karate chop "delivered perpendicularly to the earth's latitude." Late in the second quarter, Williamson was knocked cold trying to tackle Green Bay running back Donny Anderson. Asked why it took the Packers so long to get to Williamson, safety Willie Wood replied, "It took him that long to make a tackle."

Despite The Hammer's best trash-talking efforts, most everything about the first title game was pedestrian. The final crowd count of 61,946 looked small inside the mammoth L.A. Coliseum. Ticket prices were $12. The game ended with the Packers winning by 25

Then there was the case of the stolen wristwatch. When the Miami Dolphins won Super Bowl VII to go 17–0 on the year, the players hoisted head coach Don Shula on their shoulders and carried him off the field. Before he reached the dressing room, Shula noticed someone, a fan, had stolen his watch right off his wrist. Shula spotted the thief and ran after him. The coach got his watch back; the perfect ending to a flawless season.

The Super Bowl is so powerful it can even elevate the stature of a losing player and ennoble him in defeat. Don Beebe of the Buffalo Bills earned lasting notoriety in Super Bowl XXVII for chasing down Dallas Cowboys defensive lineman Leon Lett in the fourth quarter and punching the ball out of his hands before Lett could showboat his way into the end zone. Dallas won the game anyway, 52–17. Beebe won a lot of fans.

And let's not forget Carolina Panthers quarterback Jake Delhomme, who in Super Bowl XXXVII passed for 323 yards and three touchdowns only to be beaten by the New England Patriots on a last-minute field goal. As the Patriots celebrated, Delhomme stood on the field as long as he could to capture the disappointment. "I just wanted to watch and let it sink in and hurt a little bit," he explained afterward. "When I have a tough day, I'll just think about that feeling and it will make me dig down just a little deeper."

Delhomme won a lot of fans that day, too. Chances are he would have ditched them all for a chance to hold the trophy. ◾

The 1983 *Monday Night Football* crew: Frank Gifford, Howard Cosell and O.J. Simpson

a larger-than-life form that was part sport, part business, all entertainment. University marching bands gave way to Carol Channing, Up With People, New Kids on the Block, Michael Jackson, Janet Jackson, Paul McCartney, the Rolling Stones and Prince. Anthem singers ranged from Anita Bryant to Diana Ross, Billy Joel, Cher, the Dixie Chicks, Beyoncé and back to Billy Joel. The most unusual Super Bowl halftime theme? The XXVIII tribute to Indiana Jones and the Temple of the Forbidden Eye produced by Disney.

The Forbidden Eye? Why not?

"The Super Bowl is like the last chapter in a hair-raising mystery," Rozelle said. "No one would dare miss it."

THE MOVE TO PRIMETIME

"Everything … everything is magnified by television."

– TV sports guru Roone Arledge

Through the early 1960s, Rozelle had a vision. It was a good vision and he wanted to share it with the NFL's owners. "Let's play a regular-season game on a week night," he said. "How about Fridays?" The owners said no. That night was reserved for high school football, they argued.

So Rozelle rejigged his proposal and had a 1964 game scheduled for Monday night in Detroit between the Lions and Green Bay. It drew more than 59,000 spectators. By the time the 1969 season ended, the NFL had played six more Monday nighters and had enough faith in Rozelle's vision to allow him to sell it to a major U.S. TV network.

"There were a lot more TV sets in use on Monday night than on Sunday afternoon," reasoned the commissioner, who rightly deduced that a prime-time presence would expand the brand and attract more viewers and those all-precious advertising dollars.

CBS and NBC passed on the idea but ABC, which trailed its small-screen rivals, took the chance only after knowing Howard Hughes' sports network was ready to

points. The NFL's honor had been preserved and not much more happened the following year when the Packers won again, this time by 19 points over Oakland.

With the NFL's showcase event in danger of becoming a non-event, it was Namath who rode to the rescue with a pre-game boast that left The Hammer Williamson sprawled in its wake. With the Jets about to face the all-powerful Baltimore Colts in the Super Bowl, Namath predicted, "We're going to win on Sunday. I guarantee it."

This was akin to saying the Mona Lisa wasn't much of a painting. The Colts had obliterated their foes and crushed Cleveland 34–0 in the NFL championship game. Sports writers of the day, particularly Tex Maule of *Sports Illustrated*, wrote that the Jets would lose by 30 points or more. The official betting line had the Jets as 18-point underdogs.

Enter Namath, stage right. He not only backed up his prediction by leading the Jets to a 16–7 upset, he put the "super" in the Super Bowl. He made it matter and, in doing so, he became the idol of football's new era much the same way Unitas had done a decade earlier.

"Standing in the press box and watching Namath unravel the NFL myth was a thing to behold," said broadcaster Howard Cosell.

That myth was further unraveled when Kansas City whipped Minnesota in Super Bowl IV, giving both leagues a pair of championship wins before their official merger in 1970 — the same year Vince Lombardi died of cancer. Rozelle had the good gumption to name the Super Bowl trophy in honor of the venerable coach; the commissioner knew how to keep the calliope playing by cultivating captains of industry with one hand and playing to the masses with the other.

In the years following, the big game began to expand like a hot-air balloon. It took on make a deal with the NFL. ABC producer Roone Arledge, a pretty fair visionary himself, was given the Monday Night assignment and opted for a bolder, more stimulating approach to broadcasting NFL games. His innovations came at viewers like an unblocked defensive end.

First, there was the theme music, the instrumental intro by Johnny Pearson that became a recognizable call to the couch. More TV cameras were used to give fans a vibrant look at the action with the stadium lights glimmering off the players' helmets. There was the increase of on-screen graphics, instant replays and three announcers in the booth. One of those announcers was Don Meredith, the former quarterback who had joined the expansion Cowboys in 1960 when the NFL was doing its best to thwart the AFL. He got to do the color commentary on *Monday Night Football*'s first game, featuring Joe Namath, the AFL icon who super-sized the Super Bowl.

Within a year, Meredith was joined on *Monday Night* by Frank Gifford, who had played for the New York Giants in the first nationally-televised championship game in 1958 that brought the NFL to the mainstream. It was a mix of personalities and possibilities; past participants forming new elements.

But the man who gave the show its tone, its swagger, its feeling of uniqueness was Howard William Cosell. No one ever loved the sound of his own voice more than Cosell. After listening to him for five minutes you either wanted your ears cut off with a rusty saw or hear another five minutes of Cosell's soap-box ramblings. Either way, he garnered reaction and that's what ABC and the NFL wanted.

Cosell's shtick was his punctuated, verbose style of announcing. He could make something as simple as a pregame coin toss sound like the lead up to the Civil War. He didn't know the x's and o's of football, but he understood story lines and he delivered them while playing off the rigid Gifford and fun-loving Meredith, who would warble "Turn Out the Lights, The Party's Over" whenever a game got out of reach.

"We were desecrating something," ABC's Arledge told *Sports Illustrated*. "CBS had Ray Scott, and now we had this loudmouthed Cosell on TV questioning everything, yelling about what a dumb trade that was, and asking, 'Don't football players have rights?' And a lot of the owners just couldn't deal with it."

Viewers kept tuning in either to laud Cosell's clout or dismiss him as a clown. After its debut season, enough viewers had tuned in to make *Monday Night Football* the third highest-rated TV program behind *The Flip Wilson Show* and *The Mary Tyler Moore Show*. And still the innovations kept coming. At halftime, *Monday Night Football* showed the highlights from all of Sunday's games, with Cosell providing the breathless voice-over.

Then there were the guests, the visitors who dropped by the booth to share a few words, usually with a star-struck Cosell (who could curb his yapping tongue when he wanted to). Beginning in 1973, the cast of droppers-by included politicians Ronald Reagan, Henry Kissinger and Ted Kennedy, musicians John Lennon and John Denver, actor Burt Reynolds and even Kermit the Frog. Sadly, it was during a Dec. 8, 1980, Monday night game that Cosell announced to the world that Lennon had been shot and killed in New York.

"This, we have to say it, is just a football game, no matter who wins or loses," Cosell said to the nation in the wake of Lennon's death — much to everyone's agreement.

Winners and losers all had their moments on Monday night. One of the best featured a close-to-retiring Joe Montana leading Kansas City to a 31–28 win against John Elway and the Denver Broncos. Another had Green Bay quarterback Brett Favre playing the day after his father's death and throwing for 399 yards and four touchdowns. One of the worst showings? The Pittsburgh Steelers over the winless Miami Dolphins by a final score of 3–0 in 2007.

THE REST OF THE STORY

With Sundays and Mondays locked up as the sole sporting domain of the NFL, the biggest challenges for Rozelle next came from within the organization itself. Labor strife was inevitable as revenues grew and the players demanded their share. There were two player strikes in the 1980s. The first, in 1982, lasted 57 days. The 1987 strike wiped out one week of games before the NFL brought in replacement players to play the next three weeks. There were also issues over franchise relocations. Rozelle fought long and often with his former AFL peer, Al Davis, who moved the Raiders out of Oakland to L.A. when the Rams left the L.A. Coliseum to play in Anaheim.

As the 1980s wound down, so did Rozelle. He had fought off both the upstart World Football League and the U.S. Football League to maintain the NFL's dominance of the pro-football market. He had moved the game "from the back page to the front page," said New York Giants owner Wellington Mara. "From daytime to prime time." It was time to retire, which he did in 1989.

Before he died of a brain tumor in 1996, Rozelle said he wanted to be remembered most for developing the Super Bowl into one of the biggest sporting spectacles on the planet. He'll be remembered for that and more.

"Pro football was taking off when I became commissioner," he said, "and when a sport's successful, and you're its chief executive officer, much of the credit flows to you and you develop a good track record."

You become a football titan, as much as Unitas, Brown, Lombardi and Montana. Different, for sure, but no less important. ▥

THE
TOP 20

Terry Bradshaw
Jim Brown
Dick Butkus
John Elway
Brett Favre
Forrest Gregg
Deacon Jones
Dan Marino
Joe Montana
Walter Payton
Jerry Rice
Barry Sanders
Deion Sanders
Gale Sayers
Emmitt Smith
Roger Staubach
Fran Tarkenton
Lawrence Taylor
Johnny Unitas
Reggie White

12 TERRY BRADSHAW

QUARTERBACK

THIS GOOD OL' BOY'S NOBODY'S FOOL

Don't for an instant let that folksy charm and the good-ol'-boy demeanor con you. The Smoky and the Bandit schtick that he has transformed almost into an art form on Fox NFL Sunday broadcasts is part Terry, surely.

But the kid from Shreveport, Louisiana, was, and is, nobody's fool.

In his day, his Pittsburgh Steelers had it all. They had the rampaging Mean Joe Greene, snarling Jack Lambert and the unassailable Steel Curtain defense. They had the Mikhail Baryshnikov of wide receivers in Lynn Swann. They had a workhorse tailback in Franco Harris carrying the overland mail, and they had coach Chuck Noll pulling the strategic strings along the sidelines.

But most of all, they had a director fully equipped to draw the very best out of his ensemble cast.

"Imagine yourself sitting on top of a great thoroughbred horse," Terry Bradshaw would later say in describing the experience. "You sit up there and you feel the power. That's what it was like, playing quarterback on that team. It was a great ride."

At 6-foot-3 and 215 pounds, Bradshaw would never be confused with a jockey. But no one could argue that he wasn't the man in the saddle, driving the big, fast, unbeatable stallion relentlessly forward.

Today, he is one of the most amiable sports personalities in America. Funny. Self-deprecating. As at home in a TV booth at Lambeau Field as he is guesting with Jay Leno on *The Tonight Show*. Football fans love him for his wit, his candor and, naturally, for the four Super Bowl championships he directed in only six years.

What many conveniently forget now is that the Terry Bradshaw legend was painfully slow in developing.

In the formative years of his career (and after), Bradshaw was derided as a bumpkin, a rube. Every time he opened his mouth, it seemed, he stuck a cleat in it. His sound bites were peppered with phrases such as: "We had 10 turnovers in one game, seven fumbles and four interceptions." Or, "I may be dumb but I'm not stupid." His critics lapped it up.

Bradshaw arrived in Steeltown from Louisiana Tech as the first player select-

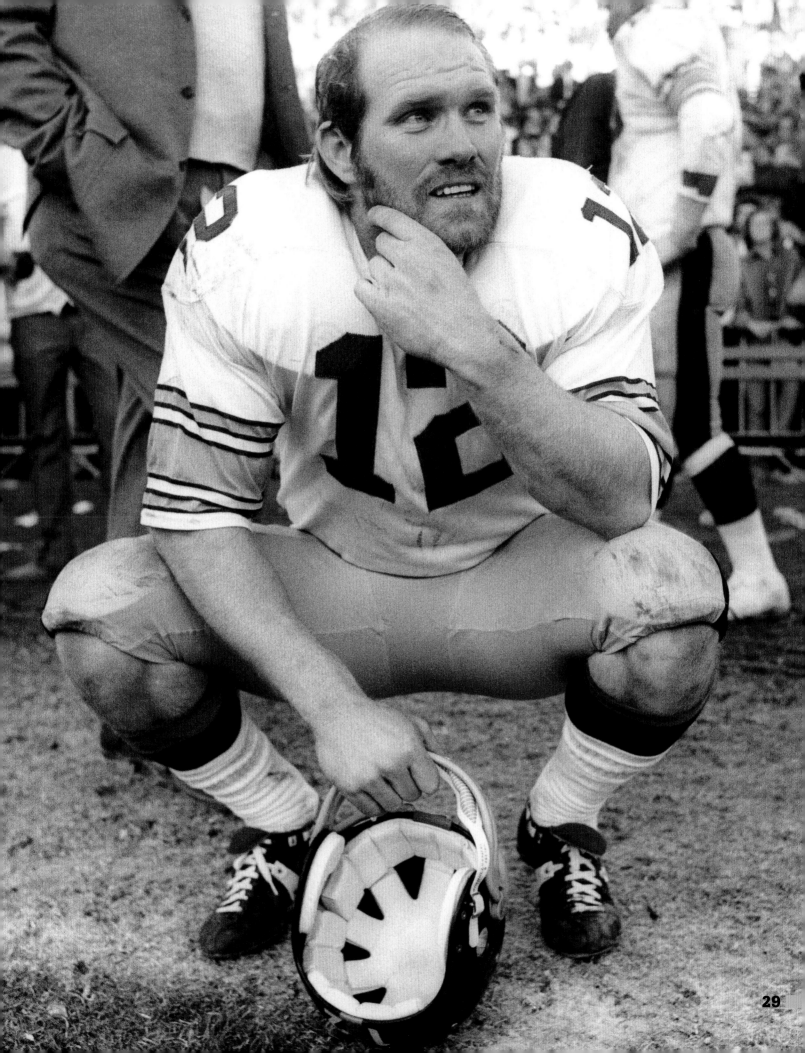

ed in the 1970 draft. In his first five seasons, he threw 48 touchdown passes — and 81 interceptions.

In his second autobiography, *No Easy Game*, he recounted how much he had to endure to win over a city, establish a reputation, and find his feet in the pro ranks. "I always wanted everyone to like me," he wrote. "I wanted the city of Pittsburgh to be proud of me. But my first few seasons, I could count the number of people on my bandwagon on one finger.

"I had people call me a dummy and a hick. I had a lady stop me outside the stadium and tell me I stunk. I heard the people cheer when I got hurt. Rub up against enough briar patches and your hide will get pretty tough. Mine did."

Bradshaw even lost the starting quarterbacking spot to Joe Gilliam in 1974 for a short time. But by the end of that season he had regained control of the offense, and the Steelers were on their way to Super Bowl IX, a 16–6 verdict over the snake-bitten Minnesota Vikings.

It would be the first bold step in an unparalleled march to greatness.

The next year, Bradshaw and Co. were back at the big dance again, Super Bowl X. The man at the helm threw for 209 yards, including the now legendary 64-yard toss to Swann late in the fourth quarter to ice a 21–17 win over the Dallas Cowboys.

As proficient as he was in directing his offense, utilizing its assets to the fullest measure, there was a streak of the riverboat gambler about him, too. One of the characteristics that made him such a perfect fit for this nearly perfect team was his unshakable confidence.

"My nature," he explained once, "was attack. Throw it deep. Anybody can throw wide. Let's go deep." The air-out to Swann remains the most memorable example of that go-for-broke mindset.

Three seasons later in 1978, the Steelers were once again back in the title hunt. Bradshaw produced his finest regular season, and was named Associated Press NFL MVP for 2,915 passing yards and 28 touchdowns. There wasn't much more he could do professionally to convince people. Still, the snide remarks would not die.

Before Super Bowl XIII, mouthy Dallas linebacker Thomas (Hollywood) Henderson famously ratcheted up the rivalry between America's Team and the NFL's best team by saying of Terry Bradshaw, "He couldn't spell 'cat' if you spotted him the 'c' and the 't'."

Bradshaw didn't much care about spelling bees, but he certainly knew how to spell W-I-N. His 318 yards and four touchdown tosses earned him the Super Bowl MVP as Pittsburgh claimed its third championship in five years, 35–31.

Hollywood Henderson offered only a lame rebuttal.

No one knew it at the time, of course, but the 1979 season would be the swansong of that legendary Pittsburgh run. Another Super Bowl, this time a 31–19 shutdown of the Los Angeles Rams, and another MVP for the guy behind center.

Terry Bradshaw would soldier on for another four seasons, through injury and disappointment, finally retiring in 1983. He'd be a first-ballot Hall of Famer, naturally. And although the Steelers do not make a habit of retiring numbers, no one in his right mind would be daft enough to ask for No. 12. So consider it unofficially retired.

Over 14 seasons, he threw for 27,989 yards, and his touchdown-to-interception ratio is only 212-to-210, hardly impressive by conventional "great quarterback" standards. But then, Terry Bradshaw was never a conventional quarterback. Merely a great one. He just won, long before the Nike ads coined the phrase, "Just do it." ■

	Gms	Att	Yds	Avg	TD	College
TOTAL	118	2,359	12,312	5.2	106	Syracuse

32 JIM BROWN

RUNNING BACK

IF SUPERMAN WAS A RUNNING BACK

Jim Brown and Sam Huff: the unstoppable force vs. the immovable object.

Their confrontations were the stuff of legend: Brown, the greatest running back of his age — arguably of any age — and Huff, the Hall of Fame-bound middle linebacker of the Washington Redskins. One particular duel stands out in Huff's mind. It encapsulates the rivalry and respect between the two men, as well as Jim Brown's brilliance.

On Brown's first carry of this particular game, Huff plugged the hole with his usual ferocity and stopped his adversary for no gain. As Brown picked himself up off the turf and hauled himself back into the huddle, Huff hollered, "Brown, you stink!"

The next time Brown got his hands on the ball, same result. Negligible pick-up. Again, a taunting, "Brown, you stink!"

"The third time Jimmy carried," Huff would recall years later, "he drove into the middle. But nobody stopped him. He got a couple of key blocks, exploded past me and the secondary and raced 65 yards for a touchdown. Trotting back to the Browns' bench, he turned toward me and I could see he had a big grin on his face. Then he shouted, 'Hey, Huff, how do I smell from here?'"

Long before there was Sweetness or Barry or LaDanian or Tony D, there was Jim Brown. He was the prototype NFL running back: strong, powerful, fast. Gone from the game for over five decades now, his name still resonates whenever people speak of the top players of all time. Huff once said that the only way to handle Jim Brown was "to grab, hold, hang on and wait for help."

The image of him hitting the line and powering past is what lingers — the pure, raw brute force of it all. Brown left such a legacy that he was voted the best football player ever by *Sporting News* in 2002. A quote attributed to an unnamed defender, perhaps merely fanciful, but nonetheless dead accurate, gives a fair impression of the man's impact: "That Jim Brown. He says he isn't Superman. What he really means is that Superman isn't Jimmy Brown!"

This was a pile driver of a back, legendary for brushing off tacklers and taunts alike. He was one of the few in his sport who wasn't tied to numbers, as unparalleled as they were. He played only nine seasons

Brown runs against the Giants in 1963 on his way to the NFL MVP.

before retiring in the summer of 1966 to pursue his ambitions as an actor and devote more time to the racial struggles of African Americans, but he led the league in rushing in eight of those seasons. Naturally, he was a Pro Bowl selection every year.

"You gang-tackled him, did whatever you could, give him extracurriculars. He'd get up slow, look at you, and walk back to the huddle and wouldn't say a word, just come at you again, and again," said Chuck Bednarik of the Philadelphia Eagles. "You'd just say 'What the hell? What's wrong with this guy for heaven sake? When is he gonna stop carrying the ball? How much more can he take?'"

The answer: Anything any defender had to give.

Brown gave this bit of advice to Baltimore Colts tight end John Mackey: "Make sure when anyone tackles you, he remembers how much it hurts."

"He lived by that philosophy," said Mackey, "and I always followed that advice."

Brown hit. People hurt. And they remembered. At 6-foot-2 and 228 pounds, he could run around you, past you or through you.

"I always made it a practice to use my head before my body," Brown once said in an interview. "I looked upon playing football like a businessman might. The game was my business, my body and my mind were my assets, and injuries were my liabilities."

Brown spent his youth on St. Simons Island, off the Georgia coast, being raised by his great-grandmother. His father, a gambler called "Sweet Sue," had run off. His mother had gone north to look for work. When the young Jim Brown rejoined his mother, who was doing housework for a family in Manhasset, Long Island, he got involved with a gang called the Gaylords.

Football pulled him out of trouble. "It changed my life," he said. "Otherwise, I could have been some kind of gangster."

Brown could certainly dish it out on the football field, but off the field he has spent a lifetime giving back to the community. These days, he works with kids caught up in a gang lifestyle through the Amer-I-Can program, which he founded in 1988.

His almost superhuman exploits on the field as well as his social conscience made him an idol to millions.

"I had two heroes growing up, John Wayne and Roy Rogers," former heavyweight champ George Foreman admitted. "Then one day I saw Jim Brown."

Anyone who saw him play could never forget him. In 1965, his last season, Brown piled up 1,544 yards, and the Browns reached the championship game against Green Bay. At that time, he held NFL records for most seasons leading the league in rushing (8), most lifetime carries (2,359), most yards (12,312), highest average gain (5.2 yards per carry) and most TDs rushing (126). And he had propelled Cleveland to the 1964 title.

No one had, or has, done more in less time. Jim Brown walked away leaving fans begging for more.

During a lifetime spent in the public eye, he made the cover of *Time* magazine in 1964 and posed nude for Playgirl a decade later. He's been enshrined in the Pro Football Hall of Fame, the College Football Hall of Fame and the Lacrosse Hall of Fame. Director Spike Lee made a documentary on his career and life called *Jim Brown: All American.*

As an actor, Brown was certainly never All-Pro. No Laurence Olivier or Spencer Tracy. There were relatively small but memorable turns in such films as *The Dirty Dozen, Rio Conchos, Any Given Sunday, tick, tick, tick …,* and others. Undoubtedly his greatest role was as Jim Brown, pile driver without peer. That part was worthy of an Oscar. That part, he was born to play. ▪

51

DICK BUTKUS

MIDDLE LINEBACKER

BORN TO BE A BEAR

"I wouldn't ever set out to hurt anybody. Unless it was, you know, important — like a league game or something."

– Dick Butkus

The ferocity, the anger, that unparalleled rage to be the best and to get it done at any cost, long ago passed into the realm of sporting legend. The story of Dick Butkus apparently trying to bite Miami guard Larry Little in a pileup and then take a nip at an official, whether true or not (Butkus denies it, Little affirms it and the official never gave his view of the situation), has taken on almost mythic proportions. In another game, against Detroit, he was accused of provoking three on-field fights and poking a finger through the facemask and into an eye of Lions tight end Charlie Saunders.

If the name Johnny Unitas embodies cool efficiency, Lynn Swann balletic grace and Brett Favre inspirational toughness, only one word comes to mind when you mention Dick Butkus: Pain.

"It makes me mad sometimes," Butkus once complained. "Some people think I have to get down on all fours to eat my couple pounds of raw meat every day. Nobody thinks I can talk, much less write my name."

Oh, but he left his signature on the NFL in the 1960s. He could hit like an ornery mule, fill a gap in the defensive line and strike fear in the heart of anybody daft enough to hold onto the football for any significant length of time. His image, that of the wild man with a moustache in the dead-of-night Chicago Bears' No. 51 black jersey, defined an era.

Some memorable quotes have been uttered about Butkus's play over the years: Detroit Lions GM Russ Thomas called him "an annihilating SOB," while Green Bay running back MacArthur Lane once said, "If given a choice I'd rather go one-on-one with a grizzly bear. I pray that I can get up every time Butkus hits me."

Pittsburgh quarterback Terry Hanratty summed up his play when saying, "If he doesn't tackle you, you can still hear him coming. You know he's going to be there eventually. It's savage." While teammate Ron Smith said of Butkus, "He'll be all right as soon as he has his couple cups of blood."

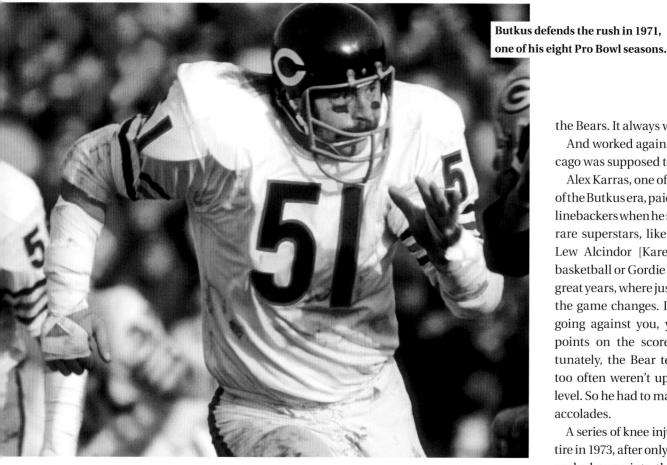

Put simply, Dick Butkus made brutality attractive. He is the gold standard: every linebacker who has come after him is subject to comparison, and every linebacker has ultimately been found wanting.

Born and raised in the Roseland section of the south side of Chicago, from Lithuanian stock, one of nine kids, Dick Butkus was seemingly born to be a Bear. Butkus has always credited his hunger to succeed on being a poor kid who wanted more.

Eventually, he and his city would become synonymous. Inseparable in the public consciousness.

At 6-foot-4 and 245 pounds, Butkus could not only roam from sideline to sideline, but also possessed superb instincts for reading a play, skills he was never given full credit for. Drafted in the first round by his hometown team, handed a reported $235,000 contract to keep him away from the rival AFL, he led the Bears in tackles, interceptions, forced fumbles and fumble recoveries during his rookie season. Not only did he inspire the Bears' defense, he *was* the Bears' defense.

Baltimore Colts veteran offensive lineman Jim Parker called Butkus "the best rookie I've ever seen in my time in the league." Countless others agreed.

During his career, the big Bear would make 22 interceptions from the position and recover 27 fumbles. What set him apart from virtually every other linebacker (with the exception of Green Bay icon Ray Nitschke) was a voracious appetite for physical contact — for confrontation. He absolutely loved to be challenged to one-on-one battles.

"Some people," admitted Butkus, "think I'm kept in a cage and let out on Sundays."

To stoke the inner fire, he would use an old, but effective, parlor trick.

"When I went on the field to warm up," he recalled, "I would manufacture things to make me mad. If someone on the other team was laughing, I'd pretend he was laughing at me or

the Bears. It always worked for me."

And worked against whatever team Chicago was supposed to play that afternoon.

Alex Karras, one of the meanest hombres of the Butkus era, paid homage to the king of linebackers when he said, "He's one of those rare superstars, like Wilt Chamberlain or Lew Alcindor [Kareem Abdul-Jabbar] in basketball or Gordie Howe in hockey in his great years, where just by being on the field, the game changes. If you had 11 like him going against you, you wouldn't get any points on the scoreboard. Ever." Unfortunately, the Bear teams that Butkus led too often weren't up to his extraordinary level. So he had to make do with individual accolades.

A series of knee injuries forced him to retire in 1973, after only nine seasons. But he'd packed more into those years than lesser-motivated men had in 15. He's been inducted into the College Football Hall of Fame and joins the legendary Red Grange as one of only two players whose jersey numbers have been retired at the University of Illinois.

The Pro Football Hall of Fame was, of course, a lock, in 1979, in his first year of eligibility. And in 1985, the Downtown Athletic Club of Orlando, Florida, created an award in his name for the country's top collegiate linebacker.

More than the accolades and the honors, though, we are left with the visceral memory of No. 51, eyes ablaze, arms flying, looking like a madman escaped from the asylum, putting his body on the line to lay another thunderous smack on a ball carrier. That image is the essence, the spirit of the indomitability of pro football.

"With the highest respect," said teammate Mike Ditka on one occasion, "I've got to say that Dick is an animal."

The quintessential Monster of the Midway. ∎

	Gms	Att	Comp	Yds	TD	Int	College
TOTAL	234	7,250	4,123	51,475	300	226	Stanford

7 John ELWAY

QUARTERBACK

THE SENTIMENTAL FAVORITE

"You learn a lot more from the lows because it makes you pay attention to what you're doing."

– John Elway

If ever there was a sentimental favorite, someone for the fence-sitters to root for, it had to be John Elway on the afternoon of Jan. 25, 1998, at Qualcomm Stadium in San Diego. The toothy, bashful, matinee-idol Bronco quarterback who, in 15 seasons, had accumulated everything a man could want in his chosen profession — wealth, fame, the devotion of a city and the respect of his peers … everything, that is, but one thing. That day, Elway shed the title of lovable loser forever. That day, he took the Mile High City higher than it had ever been before. That day, the demons were exorcised and the growing whispers of all heart and no head were forever banished.

The Denver Broncos, after all, had a history of spectacularly melting in the Big One — three Super Bowl appearances for Elway, four for the Broncos: three losses for Elway, four for the Broncos.

Quarterback Brett Favre and the defending champions, the Green Bay Packers, were favored in that afternoon in January at Super Bowl XXXII. True to form, Favre marched the Pack for a touchdown on the game's opening drive. It seemed that fate would spit derisively in the face of John Elway and his compatriots yet again. But this time, the script turned out differently. This time, Elway simply refused to roll over and play dead. In a back-and-forth contest, the old pro directed two fourth-quarter TD drives, and the Broncos held on to win 31–24.

Running back Terrell Davis may have scooted for three touchdowns and gone home toting the MVP honors, but there was no doubt who had been the inspiration behind the renaissance. The fans in San Diego chanted him into the dressing room in tribute. The sound of "El-way! El-way!" reverberated around the stadium. "John left it out on the field tonight," praised Broncos' linebacker Bill Romanowski. "He played his heart out. He left his soul on that field."

"This guy is almost 40 years old," echoed linebacker John Mobley, "and he is laying his life and body on the line." For John Elway, a quest that for so long seemed

Elway celebrates after his last NFL game, a 34–19 victory in Super Bowl XXXIII.

tantalizingly out of reach had finally come to an end.

"I've experienced the highest of highs and lowest of lows," he said. "I think to really appreciate anything, you have to be at both ends of the spectrum. I've always joked about Joe Montana not appreciating his Super Bowls nearly as much as I do because he never lost one. We lost three before we won one."

And it felt so damn good, the Broncos went out and did it again the next season. In what was to be Elway's swansong in professional football, he steered the only team he'd ever played for to another title, throwing the ball for 336 yards and touchdown while scoring one himself along the ground, as Denver blew away the overmatched Atlanta Falcons 34–19 at Pro Player Stadium in Miami. Elway was named MVP of Super Bowl XXXIII. It would be his last game.

One of the most highly-publicized players ever to enter the NFL, following a stellar collegiate career at Stanford (as well as two summers of minor-league baseball for the New York Yankees' organization), Elway was chosen first overall by the Baltimore Colts in 1983. He balked, convinced that the Colts offered him no chance to compete on a successful team, and used his baseball option as leverage. If Baltimore wouldn't trade him, he'd take his chances on the diamond. He held firm.

In this game of blink, the Colts eventually relented, dealing Elway's rights to Denver in exchange for quarterback Mark Hermann, offensive lineman Chris Hint and a first-round draft choice in 1985.

The Broncos were, naturally, ecstatic. In sports parlance, this big, rawboned kid had everything you could want from a competitive and a marketing standpoint. A gun for an arm. Size. Toughness. And that Ultra Brite smile aligned with a boyish charm. In fact, Elway had everything an organization dreams for when looking to anchor a franchise. It would turn out to be one of the most lopsided trades in memory.

Almost immediately, Elway began to pay dividends. He became not only one of the great quarterbacks of an era, but he also morphed into the face of his franchise. For a decade and a half, he was Denver's favorite adopted son. Professionally, he had grown up in front of their eyes. They considered him one of their own.

When John Elway retired, on top — a place many doubted he'd ever reach — he ranked second all-time in passing yards (51,475), attempts (7,250) and completions (4,123). He had engineered 47 come-from-behind victories for the Broncos and had won five of the six AFC championship games he took part in. His record of 148–82–1 is one of the finest ever by a quarterback. He finished tied (at nine) for the second most Pro Bowl selections at the position, and only one man, Tom Brady, has since lined up at quarterback in more Super Bowls than John Elway's five.

History would, doubtlessly, have looked slightly more ambiguously on the Elway legacy had he not corralled those two late Super Bowl titles. Regardless, the statistics and the impact he made on the Broncos, and the league as a whole, stand on their own. With his induction to the Hall of Fame, Elway joined the likes of Johnny Unitas and Bart Starr, Roger Staubach and Terry Bradshaw, Joe Montana and Dan Marino, as a quarterback for the ages.

"I don't know if I like being the sentimental favorite," the man who had almost everything protested uneasily, on the eve of what would turn out to be his first taste, Super Bowl XXXIII in San Diego.

By that time, John Elway had little choice. ∎

4 BRETT FAVRE

QUARTERBACK

FOOTBALL'S ANSWER TO THE PONY EXPRESS

In an era of transience, of quick fixes and fleeting fads, he had been a welcome constant. Game in and game out. Season in, season out.

In Green Bay, he was the Packers' answer to the Pony Express. "Through wind and sleet and hail and dead of night …" And don't forget those snow-cone frosty December afternoons at legendary Lambeau Field.

"You're never guaranteed about next year," Brett Favre was famous for saying. "People ask you what you think of next season … you have to seize the opportunities when they're in front of you."

When he finally retired at the age of 41, Favre had done virtually all he could for the Packers and seized every opportunity as a New York Jet and Minnesota Viking before admitting it was time to leave, as hard as that was to do.

In his run with the Packers, it was impossible to think of a quarterback with a greater capacity for competition than the No. 4 in green and gold. He loved the game. He embraced it like few others. He was a gunslinger, a riverboat gambler, a throw-

back to the days of Slingin' Sammy Baugh. A man of action.

He never had the Super Bowl ring collection of Joe Montana or Terry Bradshaw or Tom Brady, but no one in the history of the NFL has done more at the position. Look it up. The man played in 321 consecutive games including playoffs in 20 seasons. His 10,169 pass attempts, 6,300 completions for 71,838 yards and 508 touchdowns all set NFL records (the last of which being broken in 2014).

So are the 336 interceptions, but that statistic only serves to underline Favre's willingness to take chances. That earned him both love and infamy in Green Bay. As a Packer, his life was an open book. Fans lived through not only the wins and losses on the field, but also the death of Favre's father, the death of his brother-in-law, his wife's breast cancer and the destruction of the Favre family home when Hurricane Katrina stormed through Mississippi.

For 17 years, the Favre faithful followed his story. He was on television longer than Bonanza. The peak of his career came in 1996, the year he led the Pack to a 13–3

Brett Favre calls an audible at the line of scrimmage during a game against the New England Patriots in 2010.

record and playoff wins over the San Francisco 49ers and Carolina Panthers. In Super Bowl XXXI at the Louisiana Superdome, Favre threw for 246 yards and 2 touchdowns as Green Bay blitzed New England 35–21.

There would be one more trip to the Big Dance and a slew of individual honors, but the one Super Bowl title would be all Favre would win. And that would have been fine for Green Bay fans. But then he retired in 2008, only to say months later he wanted to come back. Packer management was ready to turn the page and go with backup passer Aaron Rodgers. Favre insisted on playing and was traded to the Jets for a conditional fourth-round draft pick. He lasted one season in New York, and then signed as a free agent with the Vikings, Green Bay's divisional rival.

That didn't sit well with Packer backers. They got to watch Favre add to his legacy by becoming the first quarterback in NFL history to defeat every one of the league's 32 franchises. They saw him set the NFL record for the most four-touchdown-pass games. They also got to see him named to his 11th Pro Bowl while taking the hated Vikings to the 2009 NFC championship game before losing to the New Orleans Saints.

He returned to the Vikings in 2010 and topped the 70,000-yard mark for his career, but the season did not end well. A right shoulder injury ended his ironman streak, while a concussion playing against the Chicago Bears ended his career. Unable to play in Minnesota's final regular season game, Favre announced his retirement and this time it stuck.

Asked a year later how he was faring away from the game, the old gunslinger replied, "It went a lot smoother than the previous three or four years. I'd said in years past that I knew [I was done]. I really knew this time. I got beat up a little bit physically, but I still felt like I could do it. But I just felt like it was time. Mentally, I was just burned out."

He needn't concern himself. Even Packer fans understood. No player ever earned the rest more. ∎

75

FORREST GREGG

TACKLE/GUARD

THE QUINTESSENTIAL FOOTBALL PLAYER

It's a photograph that says a thousand words, all of them about the man in it. Standing there, his football helmet and face mask caked with mud, his face bathed in dirt, his football uniform soaked to the point where you can barely see his jersey number 75, is the 27-year-old offensive tackle Vince Lombardi would eventually call "the finest football player I've ever coached."

In that photo, taken in 1960 during a Green Bay Packers–San Francisco 49ers game, Forrest Gregg is on the sidelines, shouting something (to teammates, the referee, who knows?) and looking every bit what a football player is supposed to look like. Tough. Gritty. A guy wanting to get back into the action so he could dirty himself up some more.

Of all the star players Lombardi coached in tiny Green Bay, Wisconsin — Paul Hornung, Willie Davies, Bart Starr, Ray Nitschke, Herb Adderly, Willie Wood — Gregg earned the highest praise, despite playing one of the more anonymous positions: right offensive tackle. Left tackles garner their share of notoriety because most

quarterbacks are right-handed throwers, which means they need someone sizeable and skilled to protect their blind side. And in Green Bay, all the offensive line publicity went to Jerry Kramer, Fuzzy Thurston and later Gale Gillingham, the pulling guards who cleared the way for the Packers' fabled power sweep.

But Gregg was so good at what he did that he neutralized defensive ends all by himself without much help, if any, from additional blockers. That's saying plenty, since the defensive ends of Gregg's day included Gino Marchetti of the Baltimore Colts, Carl Eller of the Minnesota Vikings and Deacon Jones of the Los Angeles Rams, three of the best to ever crunch a quarterback.

"Forrest, at right tackle, and I played next to each other for most of my 11 seasons," recalled Kramer in his book *Distant Replay*. "He was a master of technique, of position. He would shield, slide, maneuver, and almost always get the job done … When we lined up for a play, and the defense suddenly shifted, we would never have to adjust. I'd say, 'Forrest,' and he would say, 'Yeah,' and I'd know exactly what he was going to

Gregg watches from the sideline during a 27–23 win over the Los Angeles Rams in 1966.

do and he'd know what I was going to do."

Gregg came out of Southern Methodist University in 1956 as a second-round draft pick by the Packers. (In that same draft, the Packers selected Starr in the 17th round.) He cracked the starting lineup as a rookie and set what was the iron-man record of his era, playing in 188 consecutive games all the way to 1971. In Green Bay, Gregg was one of the leaders on a football team that won five NFL championships, including the first two Super Bowls. While the Packers were never the most imaginative team offensively, they were nearly flawless in their execution, all of it beginning up front along the line, a position Lombardi had once played himself. In their 1966 NFL championship win over the Dallas Cowboys, the Packers' game plan consisted of just 14 plays, eight running, six passing. Gregg and his blocking partners did their job to perfection.

In fact, Gregg was so good, so light on his feet at 249 pounds, he became known as "the best dancer since Fred Astaire," and the accolades followed. He played in nine Pro Bowls and was voted to both the 1960s All-Decade Team and the NFL's 75th anniversary team. He finished his career with the Dallas Cowboys and earned a third Super Bowl with the team's victory over the Miami Dolphins. He retired soon after, at age 38, having won six NFL championships. And then he went to work as a coach. He began as an assistant with the San Diego Chargers and Cleveland Browns before taking over as Cleveland's head man in 1974. Gregg coached the 1979 season with the Toronto Argonauts of the Canadian Football League, who won only five of 16 games, and was succeeded by Willie Wood, a former Green Bay teammate. He

returned to the NFL and guided the Cincinnati Bengals to Super Bowl XVI where they lost, 26–21, to the San Francisco 49ers.

After Cincinnati, Gregg agreed to coach the Packers, where he replaced former teammate, Bart Starr, who had held the position for nine years. The Green Bay media wanted to know if Gregg, who had greatly admired Lombardi, would be as tough as his former coach. "That's impossible," Gregg answered. "I can be demanding, but not that demanding."

In his four seasons with the Packers as coach, the best Gregg could produce was a pair of 8–8 seasons. He returned to his alma mater, Southern Methodist, to revive a football program that had been suspended for two years due to NCAA violations. He later returned to the sidelines in the CFL with the short-lived Shreveport Pirates and was the vice-president of football operations for the Ottawa Renegades before they folded in 2006.

"I think it's tougher to retire from playing," Gregg said in an interview with profootball-hof.com. "There's a time for everything and things must come to an end. You have to accept that both as a player and a coach. In coaching, you're not limited in age — although people think you go brain dead after 60."

Asked if he thought the 1960s Packers are the greatest football team of all time, Gregg replied, "Absolutely and without a doubt. You know how that old saying goes, 'Look at the scoreboard.'" Gregg embodied the Packers of the 1960s. He was an efficient player who was as smart as he was talented. He practiced hard and studied harder and was driven by a sense of fair play. Once, someone told Gregg that if he went low on Carl Eller, his Minnesota nemesis, he could "tear him up" since Eller had bad knees. Gregg wouldn't go for it. "[Eller] is a helluva guy. He's such a good clean competitor, I wouldn't do anything like that."

Ah, but battle him one-on-one for two-and-a-half hours in the cold and the mud, Gregg loved that. He loved it like few others and did it better than most. ■

75

DEACON
JONES

DEFENSIVE END

THE MAN WHO NEVER SACKED

According to the NFL, David "Deacon" Jones spent 14 years in the trenches, appeared in eight Pro Bowls, was named to the league's 75th-anniversary team and was inducted into the Pro Football Hall of Fame in 1980 — and not once did he sack a quarterback.

Oh, he did a few things — scored two safeties, made two interceptions, recovered 15 fumbles, ran back two kickoffs and kicked an extra point. But tackle a quarterback?

Nope. Never happened. Not even for the man who invented the term "sack" and a nasty helmet-rattling technique known as the head slap, which begs the question: If Deacon Jones is considered one of the most dangerous pass rushers the NFL has ever seen, just how revered would he have been had the league recorded quarterback sacks as an official statistic back when he played in the 1960s and 1970s?

It wasn't until 1982 that the NFL began keeping tabs on sacks. Anyone who played prior to that year was left with a collective zero next to his name, even if his name was synonymous with terrorizing offensive lines from New York to Los Angeles.

"Since when does 'all-time' begin in 1982?" Jones has asked repeatedly, claiming his sack count was over 200, the all-time career count set by Bruce Smith.

Unofficially, NFL fans and researchers have pegged Jones's total at 173.5. The Los Angeles Rams' organization is believed to have kept at least a partial log stating that in 1964 Jones broke the 20-sack barrier (with 22 in 14 games), and then upped the count to 26 sacks, along with 100 tackles, in 1967.

"Deacon Jones is one of my really good friends, and like my mentor," said former New York Giants defensive end Michael Strahan, who holds the acknowledged record of 22.5 sacks in a 16-game season. "According to Deacon, he has like 3,000 sacks. And it grows each year. Those guys who played before they had all the stats, they do have some kind of legitimate gripe."

Anyone who played against Jones would agree that he was a man ahead of his time. He stood 6-foot-5, weighed 272 pounds and had the quickness of a leopard. He could make tackles from sideline to sideline, all over the field. On top of that, he was part of what was the first dominant defensive line

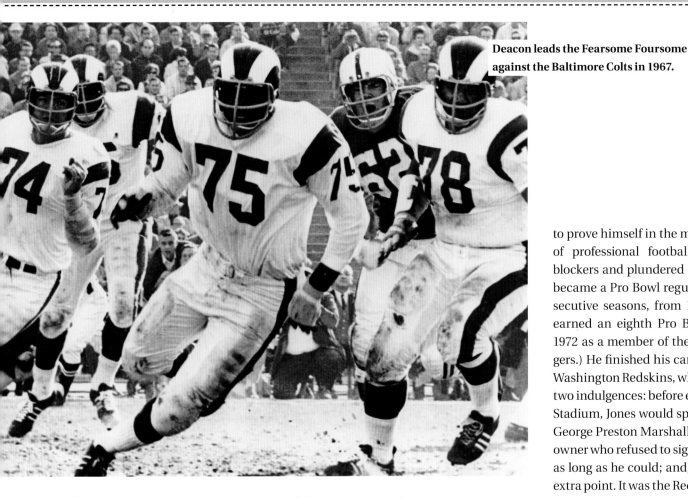

to prove himself in the mostly white world of professional football, Jones pillaged blockers and plundered quarterbacks and became a Pro Bowl regular for seven consecutive seasons, from 1964 to 1970. (He earned an eighth Pro Bowl invitation in 1972 as a member of the San Diego Chargers.) He finished his career with the 1974 Washington Redskins, where he partook in two indulgences: before every game at RFK Stadium, Jones would spit on the statue of George Preston Marshall, the former team owner who refused to sign black players for as long as he could; and, he got to kick an extra point. It was the Redskins' George Allen, who had coached Jones with the Rams, who let the veteran attempt a convert, and it was good.

Before his death in 2013, the culmination of Jones' life experience was something he used to help young students from inner-city neighborhoods succeed. The Deacon Jones Foundation's seven-year program gives under-privileged teenagers an opportunity to get to university and become leaders and volunteers in their community, so they can give back and help the next generation succeed. It was a project that Jones, in retirement, tackled as hard as he had any quarterback.

"I'm probably the toughest [expletive] here," he once said. "Ain't no question about that with me. I'm the toughest guy here … I'm clean. I mean, I ain't got no marks on me. I don't know nobody else who can say that who came out of any sport. I ain't got no marks on me so I've got to be the baddest dude I know of."

Officially or unofficially. ■

in NFL history, the Fearsome Foursome, which included Lamar Lundy, Rosey Grier and Merlin Olsen in its heyday.

"We started the trend. We proved that defensive lines can control the game," Jones said in an interview with ESPN.com. "I don't think you'll find, even now, four men who had as much talent and doled out as much damage and devastation as our group. After our group came the Purple People Eaters, the Steel Curtain, Dallas's Doomsday team and that Baltimore [Ravens] team. The dominant teams all had great defensive lines, and we had something to do with that trend. That's why they've changed so many rules. They don't want games controlled by defensive lines."

Jones, who was hailed as the Secretary of Defense, was never shy about highlighting his abilities. What was far more remarkable was everything he endured to make it as a pro football player. Growing up in Florida in a family of 10, Jones picked watermelons and pitched them into trucks to earn money. In town, he couldn't drink from the same water fountains as whites. He couldn't use the same restrooms as whites. He had to sit in a blacks-only section in restaurants. He had to stay in the black wing of the local hospital when he needed an operation. When Jones enrolled at South Carolina State, he took part in a march protesting the treatment of black youths who had been arrested for eating at a lunch counter. Jones said the police and fire department dispersed the marchers with hoses and dogs, and that he was pinned against a wall by a blast of water. For taking part in the march, Jones lost his football scholarship and enrolled at Mississippi Vocational, where he and others were later rounded up by the police and told to leave the state and never come back. The players' participation in the protest march at South Carolina State was the reason for their expulsion.

The Rams were only so-so on Jones and drafted him in the 14th round. When he got to training camp, he knew he had to make an impression. Fueled by an overwhelming desire

13 DAN MARINO

QUARTERBACK

THE PURITY OF THE PASS

There are, in sport, a rare few blessed with gifts so sublime that they captivate us by their sheer maddening effortlessness, their purity of line. For close to two decades of unrivaled passing opulence in Miami, there was Dan Marino's release: quick and accurate. He delivered the ball crisply — like the snap of a wet towel being cracked in the wind — with the precision of a watchmaker's hand: quite simply, a thing of beauty.

"I know I've got to just keep throwing the ball," Marino said. "That's what I do best."

Better, arguably, than anyone ever has.

Nurtured by the ideal coach in Don Shula, and blessed with an array of game breakers at receiver that included Mark Duper and Mark Clayton, Marino didn't merely play quarterback, he redefined the position, taking what quarterback Dan Fouts and Don "Air" Coryell had in San Diego and expanding on the premise that the best, quickest way to move the football was by throwing it.

"Sure, luck means a lot in football," Shula acknowledged. "Not having a good quarterback is bad luck." If so, Don Shula

was the luckiest man in the NFL.

Other quarterbacks have left their legacies: Brett Favre is legendary for his toughness, Joe Montana for dramatics, Johnny Unitas for his reading of a game. But throwing the ball? That was Marino's domain. Only Joe Namath could rival him for purity in that department. Interceptions didn't faze him. He never shied away from a mistake. Caution was for losers. Marino kept throwing the ball, undeterred, until he finally rammed it down your throat.

Remember the movie, *The Matrix*? Keanu Reeves' character Neo studies and studies until he is mentally able to slow everything around him down to a standstill — until he can catch the bullets. Dan Marino could catch the bullets. And — this is the most amazing part of it — he could catch them right away. He would become the first rookie ever to start in a Pro Bowl.

"You were basically at Dan's mercy," said defensive back Ronnie Lott of the 49ers. "All the great ones see the game so quickly that when everybody else is running around like a chicken with his head cut off, they know exactly where they want to go

with the ball. It's like they see everything in slow motion."

Precisely.

Marino adjusted his game over 17 seasons, alternating between long-ball thrower, precision mid-range passer and proven leader, all with the same franchise. When talk surfaced near the end of the road that he might consider joining another organization to prolong his playing career, the possibility was met with disbelief. The Pope is Catholic, Dan Marino was a Dolphin. End of story.

The one sticking point in the vast Marino legacy is that he never piloted a Super Bowl winner. He didn't need to, at least not to validate his brilliance as a quarterback. He made the cover of *Sports Illustrated*, the front of a Wheaties box and kept the deep blue south-Florida sky filled with tight spirals.

"There are times on the field," he once wrote, "when I feel like I can't miss, when I'm in complete control and everything just clicks. The ball is always on time, it's always catchable, and I'm making the right decisions on who to throw to. Those are the times when I want to pass on every play because I feel like we're unstoppable."

Growing up in a working-class neighborhood in Pittsburgh, where his father, Dan, would get up at 3 a.m. to deliver bulk copies of the *Pittsburgh Post-Gazette* newspaper, Marino learned the value of hard work. Like Wayne Gretzky, Marino let his skills do the talking. In an age of non-conformity where others would generate headlines with their mouths and their antics, Marino took the high road, working hard for everything he earned.

In 1984, the hard work continued to pay off. In his second year after replacing David Woodley as Miami's starter, Marino was close to unstoppable, as he put together one of the greatest individual seasons in history, on the way to being named the NFL MVP. He broke no fewer than six passing records that year, including touchdown tosses (48) and yards (5,084). The Dolphins finished the regular season 14–2 and reached Super Bowl XIX against Joe Montana and the San Francisco 49ers.

Marino would finish that game 29 out of 50 for 318 yards, one touchdown and two interceptions. The Dolphins lost 38–16. It would, sadly, be Dan Marino's only Super Bowl appearance.

"I am extremely proud of the fact that I was able to play 17 years for the Miami Dolphins," he said in announcing his retirement before the 2000 season began, the dream of that elusive title worn away by the onslaught of time. "And I'm going to miss it. I'm going to miss everything about it. I'm going to miss the relationships with the players, I'm going to miss the fans, I'm going to miss the great friends that I have made over this time. I am going to miss all the good times that we've had together. But most of all, I'm going to miss Sunday afternoons."

Sunday afternoons miss Marino, too.

Over the years other premier gunslingers, like Brett Favre, Drew Brees and Tom Brady, have chiseled away at his all-time and single-season records, but none of that matters — especially to Dolphins fans.

On Sunday, Sept. 17, 2000, at halftime of a home game against the Baltimore Ravens, Marino's signature No. 13 was the second jersey number ever retired by the Dolphins. The other? Bob Griese's No.12. A life-sized bronze statue of him was erected at Pro Player Stadium, and Stadium Street was rechristened Dan Marino Boulevard.

He is irreplaceable. Since Marino retired, the Dolphins have auditioned more starting quarterbacks than any fan would care to remember. All have been found wanting.

Many copies. One original. ■

16 JOE MONTANA

QUARTERBACK

THE COMEBACK KID

Most of all, he had cool. Steve McQueen in a battered bomber jacket astride a '37 Crocker motorcycle sort of cool. Naturally cool, without trying. He was that guy in school everyone gravitated to because it didn't matter how hard the test or how pretty the girl — you just knew. And you just knew he knew, too.

He was Joe. The Comeback Kid. Believer in lost causes.

"He's like Lazarus," San Franciso 49ers teammate Tim McKyer said one time. "You roll back the stone, Joe limps out — and throws for 300 yards."

What sets Joe Montana apart from virtually every other quarterback before or since was his flair for the dramatic, the theatrical. His face should've been plastered on the cover of *Playbill* as often as *Sports Illustrated*.

There isn't an illusionist alive who wouldn't kill to know Joe Montana's secret. He convinced his audience that he could, in fact, manipulate time. Take it in his hands, turn it over, bend it, shape it, and make it do his bidding — quite a trick.

In Joe's mind, nothing was out of reach.

No deficit too great. No mountain too daunting. He gave the impression that he could climb Everest in trainers and a windbreaker.

His amazing 31 fourth-quarter comebacks are why *Sports Illustrated* voted him its all-time clutch quarterback in 2006. Attempting to find consensus on the best Montana comeback is like trying to find common ground on the best Beatles tune, or the best actor to portray Bond; everyone has an opinion, and seldom is it the same.

In four Super Bowl appearances — all victories, by the way — Montana completed nearly 70 percent of his passes and didn't throw a single interception in 122 attempts. In three of those games he was named MVP, stepping back only once to allow his favorite receiver, Jerry Rice, to command the spotlight.

Beyond the cool and the list of accomplishments, early on there was something of the underdog in the cowboy who would go on to conquer the City by the Bay, and that was appealing, too.

He began his collegiate career at Notre Dame, listed seventh on the quarterback

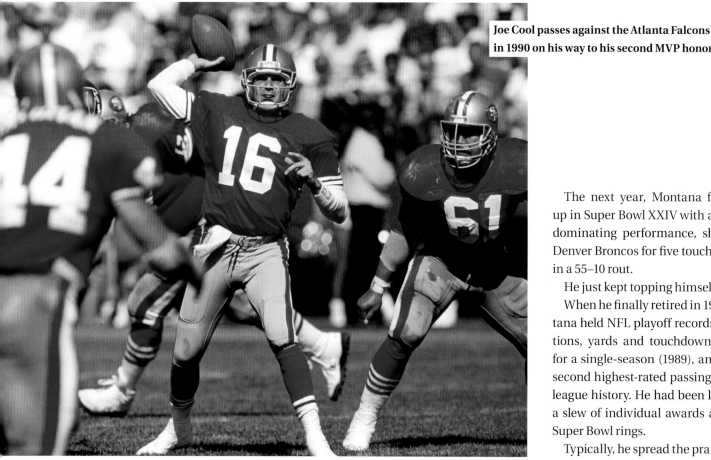

depth chart. In 1977, only three years later, he led the school to a national championship.

It seems ludicrous now, but Montana was considered too slight and his arm strength rated only "average" by NFL scouts, who'd charted his days with the Fighting Irish. Even a wild comeback win in the '79 Cotton Bowl, Montana completing the winning TD pass with two seconds to play — a foreshadow of things to come — wasn't enough to completely convince the skeptics.

He lasted until the third round in his draft year, chosen 82nd overall by the 49ers. The rest, as they say, is history.

With Bill Walsh's legendary West Coast Offense, the kid from New Eagle, Pennsylvania, took over control of the team in 1981 and efficiently went about setting a new standard for the position. Ironically, the play that began the Montana legend, the six-yard pass to Dwight Clark in the Dallas Cowboys' end zone with less than a minute to play that thrust the 49ers into Super Bowl XVI, wasn't planned. The moment remains an image frozen in time: Clark leaping high in the air to snare the ball, forever to be remembered by NFL fans as simply The Catch. Montana later admitted he'd been trying to heave the ball out of the end zone so he could regroup on the next snap. If that isn't being touched by the heavens, nothing is.

Exactly how anointed Joe Montana was would be all too apparent in 1989. In the closing moments of Super Bowl XXIII, Montana drove the 49ers an improbable 92 yards, threw a 10-yard touchdown pass to John Taylor with 34 ticks left on the clock, to give the 49ers a 20–16 win over the Cincinnati Bengals. The man himself endeavored to explain his knack in the clutch:

"It's a blur," he admitted. "I hyperventilated to the point of almost blacking out. I was yelling so loudly in the huddle that I couldn't breathe. Things got blurrier and blurrier."

The next year, Montana followed that up in Super Bowl XXIV with an even more dominating performance, shredding the Denver Broncos for five touchdown passes in a 55–10 rout.

He just kept topping himself.

When he finally retired in 1995, Joe Montana held NFL playoff records for completions, yards and touchdowns, as well as for a single-season (1989), and owned the second highest-rated passing efficiency in league history. He had been lavished with a slew of individual awards and had four Super Bowl rings.

Typically, he spread the praise around as easily as the football. "The beauty of Bill's system was that there was always a place to go with the ball," Montana said, with typical humility. "I was just the mailman, just delivering people's mail. And there were all kinds of houses to go to."

When he walked away from the game he had come to embody, after a swan song two seasons in Kansas City, Joe Montana cited his young family as a major reason. These days, he owns horses and produces wine under the label Montagia.

"When I was playing, I missed my two girls' [activities]," he explained at the time. "They look up, and myself and my wife are not there. To me, it's more important to be home with my boys. The Super Bowl is a great event, but I've moved on with my life. I want to be there for the boys."

He'd spent enough years being there for his other boys; for coach Bill, for Jerry, Roger, John, Dwight and the rest. Fifteen years was enough. In the end, you could say, Joe Cool just ran short of urgency. He never ran out of time. ■

	Gms	Att	Yds	Avg	TD	College
TOTAL	190	3,838	16,726	4.4	110	Jackson State

34 Walter PAYTON

RUNNING BACK

SWEETNESS AND THEN SOME

An infectious joy of being, the possibilities of life itself, combined with a relentless pursuit of excellence. They are only part of why so many were so moved, so stricken, took the loss so personally, when Walter Payton died of a rare liver disease, primary sclerosing cholangitis, at age 45. It was as if we'd lost a member of our own family.

As quarterback Jim Harbaugh, a rookie with the Bears in 1987, said upon Payton's passing, "Sweetness … there may not have been a better nickname for a player."

The sight of him near the end, a man once so in command of his physical prowess, now so gaunt and frail, at an overwhelmingly emotional press conference to discuss his illness, shocked many.

But it gave strength to just as many more.

Out of the skeletal frame, an immense bravery shone brightly. A bravery beyond running between the tackles on fourth down and a yard when everyone in the stadium knows the quarterback is handing you the ball.

"Am I scared?" Walter Payton said that day early in 1999. "Hell, yeah, I'm scared. Wouldn't you be scared? But it's not in my hands anymore. It's in God's hands."

Nine months later, he was in God's hands.

At his memorial service held at Soldier Field, his family and hundreds of friends turned out to say goodbye to a legend.

"Many of you knew my father as a football player and as a business man," said his son Jarrett, then 18, who now runs the Jarrett Payton Foundation to help support Chicago's youth. "I knew him as my dad, and he was my hero.

"My mother, my sister and I will miss him, but we know he's in a place where there's no sickness, no pain."

The emotional service lasted for more than two hours.

"I've got a little girl, she's four years old," defensive tackle Dan Hampton, a teammate of Payton's for nine years, said then. "Ten years from now, when she asks me about the Chicago Bears, I'll tell her about a championship.

"And I'll tell her about great teams and great teammates and great coaches and how great it was to be a part of." Hampton's voice began to quaver. "But the first thing

Payton goes over the top against the Bucs in 1981.

I'll tell her about is Walter Payton."

Not big, at 5-foot-10 and 200 pounds, he was blessed with tree trunks for legs, soft hands, a hide as tough as old shoe leather (he missed only two games in 13 seasons) and an indomitable will. The sight of his patented high kick as he ripped opposing defenses apart remains one of the iconic images of the game.

Amazingly, Payton was as good a blocker as he was a runner, and as good a receiver as he was a blocker. He could throw the ball as a change of pace and, in a pinch, punt. He could, to use a well-worn phrase, do it all.

Payton was tagged with the nickname Sweetness in college while playing at Jackson State and finishing fourth in Heisman Trophy balloting in his senior year. Jim Harbaugh was right — it simply could not have been more appropriate.

A sweetness of style, a sweetness of spirit, a sweetness of philosophy — that's what set Walter Payton apart.

In *The Football Book*, Paul Zimmerman of *Sports Illustrated* recalled an astonishing feeling he had while interviewing Payton one unforgettable night. "His eyes sparkled in that half light," Zimmerman wrote, "and I got this weird feeling there was a glow around him, that he was giving off sparks, that there was some kind of fire burning inside, lighting him up. It was the fire of pure energy."

On the field, Payton towered above the pack: he was a two-time league MVP, a nine-time Pro Bowler, the 1977 Pro Bowl MVP and a 1985 Super Bowl champion with the Bears. He ran for 16,726 yards during his career, a record at the time. Ten times he lugged the ball for 1,000 yards or more in a season. Caught 492 passes, too. One amazing afternoon against the Minnesota Vikings, Payton ran riot, for 275 yards, a record that lasted until Viking rookie Adrian Peterson broke the pinball machine with 296 in 2007.

Typical of Payton's insatiable drive to achieve professionally, when he eclipsed Jim Brown's career rushing mark, he sent up a flare for all those who would follow.

"I want to set the record so high that the next person who tries for it," he said, "it's going to bust his heart."

Nothing could bust Walter Payton's heart. Everything else might wear out, eaten insidiously away by the ravages of disease. But not the heart. That stayed strong until the last.

Off the field is where Payton carved his most extraordinary niche. A quiet, gentle man, unshakeable in his faith and unlimited in his caring for his community, everyone was drawn to Sweetness. It sounds trite in these jaded times, a cliché almost, but he knew the secret of life.

Since his death in 1999, the Payton legend has only grown stronger. His popularity in Chicago and fame nationwide are undiminished. In the pantheon of immortal Chicago athletes, Sweetness ranks with the deities, up there on a par with Bobby Hull, the Golden Jet; Ernie Banks, Mr. Cub; and His Airness, Michael Jordan. That glow, those sparks, the energy Paul Zimmerman wrote of, can never be extinguished.

Sweetness, and then some.

"He was the best football player I've ever seen," said his longtime coach, Mike Ditka, in summation. "And probably one of the best people I've ever met."

As an epitaph, a man could do worse. ∎

80

JERRY RICE

WIDE RECEIVER

THE BEST THERE EVER WAS

Joe Rice didn't stand for excuses or even a few minutes of sleeping in. Every summer morning come 5 a.m., he'd be up and hauling his boys out of bed so they could go to work with him.

Joe was a mason and young Jerry's job was to catch the bricks his brothers tossed at him so he could hand them to his dad for placing. Sometimes Jerry stood on a wooden scaffold two stories high and caught bricks until his hands were calloused but sure. A typical day went to sundown in the unforgiving heat of a Mississippi July and August.

That was how it began for Jerry Rice, the greatest football player of our time. Without knowing it, everything he learned and did as a child, everything he yearned to perfect as a teenager was the foundation for what he would accomplish in the NFL. It was all laid out in Crawford, Mississippi, just like the bricks his father used to set row by row, one on top of another.

There have been hundreds of great football players over the decades, men who aspired and inspired with equal fervor. Rice was one of those who kept doing his best game after game, season after season, until he retired and the numbers showed that he had accomplished what no other receiver or football player had ever done.

The sixth son of Joe and Eddie B., Rice didn't just set records; he etched them in granite. He didn't just outdistance his closest challengers, he humbled them. In every offensive category, he sits at the top, hopelessly out of reach for the next-best player, as good as that player is. From his 208 career touchdowns (Emmitt Smith is second with 175), to his 274 consecutive games of catching at least one pass (Art Monk is second at 183), Rice defied his defenders with seldom seen splendor and style.

For his efforts, he won every award that mattered — NFL MVP, Super Bowl champion and Super Bowl MVP. Once, when asked to comment on his many achievements and accolades, Rice insisted they were only part of the narrative.

"To me it was never about what I accomplished on the football field," he explained, "it was about the way I played the game. I played the game with a lot of determination, a lot of poise, a lot of pride and I think

23 touchdowns for the season.

The next season, in Super Bowl XXIII, he caught 11 passes for 215 yards and a touchdown and was named MVP. In Super Bowl XXIV, he caught seven passes for 148 yards and scored three touchdowns. In Super Bowl XXIX, he caught 10 passes for 149 yards and scored three touchdowns again, this time with a shoulder he had separated earlier in the game.

Rice never stopped working on his game with more practices, more time studying game film, more drills aimed at exploiting the weaknesses in the defensive backs assigned to cover him. When Montana moved on, Rice and quarterback Steve Young kept the show rolling. When Rice left for the Oakland Raiders, he maintained his expectations with a high level of consistency. In his three seasons with the Raiders (2001–2004), Rice averaged 79 catches for 1,078 yards and six touchdowns. As sure as the sun sets in the west, Jerry Rice can catch a football.

He joined the Seattle Seahawks four games into the 2004 season, and attended the Denver Broncos' training camp in 2005 before choosing to retire. By then, the name Jerry Rice stood for unbridled excellence. He set the bar so high it may never be cleared.

From making the hardest catches look easy, to forcing himself to run more sprints because he had to be better than everyone else, Rice proved to be a hard-working stickler. He had no choice, he insisted. That was the way it had to be for him, the way he was raised as the country kid who caught bricks before galloping after his ambitions with a football tucked under an arm.

In Jerry Rice, what we saw was an individual who really just loved the game, and played it like no other. ▪

what you saw there … was an individual who really just loved the game."

The love of football came to Rice early in his childhood. He and his brothers played sandlot games the way they chased the horses that ran wild in the countryside — for fun, with reckless abandon. His first taste of organized football came in Grade 10 after he was caught skipping school. The story goes that Rice played hooky one day, only to be caught by his high school principal, Ezell Wickes. When Rice saw the principal, he took off like a frightened colt.

The next day, Rice was called into Mr. Wickes' office and strapped for his transgression. Still, the principal was so impressed with Rice's running ability that he talked to the school's football coach, who convinced Rice to play.

Rice relied on his natural gifts and capacity for work to become an all-state receiver, but attracted no interest from the major universities. Only one school offered him a scholarship, so he went to Mississippi Valley State, a Division 1-AA school. There, he became one of the most prolific players in the U.S. by starring in coach Archie Cooley's run-and-shoot offense that averaged more than 55 points per game in one season. It was Cooley who said of Rice, "He can catch a BB on a dead run at night."

The San Francisco 49ers were so taken by Rice's catching ability that they traded up in the 1985 draft so they could select him as a target for quarterback Joe Montana. It was a decision that paid off many times over, especially in the critical games where Rice rose to new heights and so did his numbers.

In 1987, Rice caught 22 touchdown passes, a record that was broken in 2007 by Randy Moss of the New England Patriots. But here's the catch: Moss scored his 23 touchdowns in 16 games. Rice did his 22 in just 12 games (the 1987 season was shortened by a players' strike). Not only that, Rice's 22 touchdowns came off 65 catches, which meant one of every three receptions went for a major. For good measure, he scored on a short run, giving him

20 BARRY SANDERS

RUNNING BACK

THE BEST TEN YEARS OF FOOTBALL

It was never enough to know what made Barry Sanders run. What people wanted to grasp was what made him quit? How could he walk away from the game at age 30? What about the records, the fortune and adulation?

He wasn't hurting physically. Certainly, he wasn't hurting for money, not with $20.9 million left on a four-year deal with the Detroit Lions. How could he retire without really explaining why? Where was his loyalty, his sense of responsibility?

"I tell you what I heard from 'Ol Blue Eyes one time — Frank Sinatra," Sanders said, five years after his retirement shocked the football universe. "He said the same question was put to him, 'What do you owe the fans?' And he said, 'First of all, I owe them a good performance.' I really listened to that and really took a hold of that.

"First and foremost, I owe people everything that I was as a football player when I stepped onto the field … and I think I did that. Once I left the field, I've never been good or comfortable with all the other stuff, of what you owe everyone else as far as the media and fans and people like that, and

I may have been clumsy with those things at times. But none of my actions have been intentionally directed towards the fans or the city of Detroit."

No NFL running back has been more exciting to watch and less understood than Sanders. He didn't just perform in shoulder pads, he conducted recitals. He didn't run, he accelerated and exhilarated; a master showman who made opponents wish they had taken up another occupation — anything besides playing defense.

Sanders was a uniquely built, stunningly gifted athlete. He stood 5-foot-8, weighed 203 pounds. As fast as he was running a straight line, it was his ability to maneuver without losing top speed that allowed him to out-distance his adversaries. And strength? Even as a pick-up basketball player, Sanders could dunk the ball from a standing position. He had it all.

He set all kinds of records in college, where he produced five consecutive 200-yard games and scored at least two touchdowns in 11 consecutive games; and the NFL, where he rushed for more than 1,500 yards five times in his career and scored 15

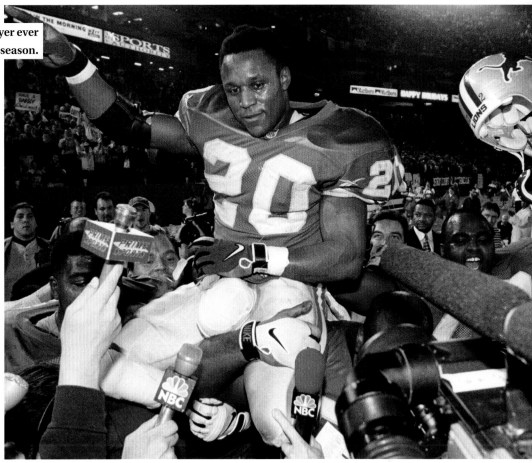

Dec. 21, 1997, Sanders became the third player ever to rush for more than 2,000 yards in a season.

touchdowns on runs of 50 yards or more.

"If there was ever an artist, he was a Picasso," Hall of Fame running back Marcus Allen said of Sanders. "He was one of the few that would make other athletes' jaws drop. You'd go, 'Oh man, did you see that?' You'd call up another top running back and go, 'Yo, [Eric] Dickerson, did you check that out?'"

It was impossible to keep tabs on Sanders' highlights. Picking out his best run was like trying to name your favorite Beatles' song. There was that amazing recovery against the Buffalo Bills, the one where he was in the clutches of a tackler and falling when all of a sudden he stuck out his left arm, pushed himself off the turf, regained his balance, cut back and raced away in the opposite direction.

Or the one where he froze that Minnesota Vikings defensive back with an outside-inside juke en route to a long gain. Or the one where he had the New England Patriots defender turning in circles trying to locate his man, let alone tackle him. Or the one where he exploded through the right side of the Indianapolis Colts defense as if it were nothing but party streamers. Or the one …

There were so many "ones."

But while Sanders reveled in personal triumphs, his Detroit Lions team was hard-pressed to be average. The Lions during Sanders' years (from '89–'98) were 78–82, and made the postseason five times. Only once did they win a playoff game. In that 1991 contest, a 31–6 trouncing of the Dallas Cowboys, Sanders scored on a 47-yard run in the final minutes. The following week, Detroit was crushed 41–10 by the Washington Redskins with Sanders kept to 44 yards on 11 carries.

The Lions' shoddy postseason record, combined with Sanders' drop in yardage, opened the doors for critics to claim the Hall of Fame running back was largely overrated. Their argument was based on Sanders playing the bulk of his career inside a domed stadium and that once outdoors, in the playoffs, he was far less effective. (Statistical note: Sanders scored a touchdown for every 35 touches in his 153 career regular-season games while averaging a touchdown for every 112 touches in his six career playoff games.)

Sanders left himself wide open to detractors when he retired late in July 1999. It happened in the most unanticipated fashion with Sanders faxing a letter to his hometown newspaper, the *Wichita Eagle*. In his statement, Sanders said, "The reason I am retiring is very simple. My desire to exit the game is greater than my desire to remain in it."

Sanders declined to elaborate, which prompted a run of conspiracy theories. Sanders wanted more money, wanted to be traded, hated his coach Bobby Ross, hated the Lions for releasing his friend Kevin Glover two years earlier and not doing enough to field a winning team.

Sanders said little even when the media argued he owed his teammates a definitive explanation, especially with him only 1,457 yards shy of breaking Walter Payton's then record for most career rushing yards.

It took Sanders time to articulate his reasons for quitting: "I'm very competitive when it comes to winning and losing and playing well," he said. "And I did put up big numbers. There were some times in 1997 when I could have gone back in to pad my numbers, but I wasn't as competitive with the numbers as I was about winning and losing."

There was always talk Sanders would return to the NFL, but he never did. Like Jim Brown, Sanders stepped away from the field ensuring a life-long debate that he could have played longer and done more amazing things had he chosen to stick around.

"Ten years is a lot of football," he said. It was enough for him and much too little for his fans. ▪

21 Deion SANDERS

DEFENSIVE BACK

COUNTDOWN TO PRIME TIME

He was a left-handed, spray-hitting, base-stealing Mr. Virtuoso, who played in a World Series, a Super Bowl, and could cover 40 yards in 4.57 seconds running backwards.

He was Neon Deion, Prime Time. A two-sport attraction who hit a home run with the New York Yankees the same week he scored his first NFL touchdown as a member of the Atlanta Falcons.

Some loved him, others hated him, but there was no denying Deion Sanders was a monstrous talent who could do it all, make any play, steal any thunder. But in 1997, Sanders tried to end it all by driving his black Mercedes over a 30-foot cliff. Why? Because nothing mattered to the game's biggest showman, not the fame, not the money. Sanders' life was a bottomless pit he couldn't fill with the richest contract or the hottest car.

"When I hit bottom," Sanders wrote in his autobiography, *Power, Money & Sex: How Success Almost Ruined My Life*, "the car started sliding awkwardly, rocking back and forth, until I came down hard and slid to the bottom of the hill. Miraculously, I walked away without a scratch."

He was not, however, unchanged.

Sanders considers himself a happy man these days, more relaxed and fulfilled. His faith has given him the depth of character to match the many feats he accomplished as his era's greatest two-sport athlete.

As the trash-talking, bandana-wearing, brash and bejeweled Prime Time, Sanders was larger than life. In his major-league baseball career, he played for four teams, including the 1992 Atlanta Braves, who made it to the World Series. In the Fall Classic, against the Toronto Blue Jays, Sanders batted .533 with eight hits, two doubles, four runs and an RBI, all while playing with a broken bone in his foot.

In football, he was vastly, outrageously superior. He ran back kicks and punts, intercepted passes and was as dangerous a scoring weapon as any of the Falcons' receivers. In fact, Sanders would occasionally line up at wide receiver and race downfield to catch passes. In his five years in Atlanta, Prime Time scored 10 touchdowns — three on defensive plays, three on kick-off returns, two on punt returns and two on pass receptions.

He over-celebrated every one of them.

"How do you think defensive backs get attention?" asked Sanders, who had drawn plenty of attention in his days as a baseball-football-track star at Florida State University. "They don't pay nobody to be humble."

Sanders was equally a braggadocio when he high-stepped his stuff for the San Francisco 49ers and Dallas Cowboys. He won Super Bowl XXIX with the 49ers and Super Bowl XXX with the Cowboys, and all along the way he was to rival receivers what a detour sign is to frustrated motorists.

"When we played against him last year, we talked about not even bothering to throw his way," New Orleans Saints receiver Michael Haynes said at the time. "It was part of our game plan to keep the ball away from him. There were routes we wouldn't run toward Deion. He can take away that much."

With the Cowboys, Sanders continued to strut and be well-paid for his bravado. He could shut down entire offenses, intercept passes, then taunt his former teammates as he ran down the sidelines en route to an easy touchdown, as he did against Atlanta. He was living the dream life, even performing rap songs entitled, "Must be the Money." Everywhere you looked in 1997, there was Neon Deion, smiling, shilling, primping, playmaking. He was a one-man corporation. Who could have asked for more?

Then came the fall. His wife sued him for divorce and refused to bring their children to Cincinnati, where he was playing baseball for the Reds. Suddenly, the money no longer mattered. Not even an outstanding year — one that saw him on the field for 50 percent of the Cowboys' offensive plays and 80 percent on defense — could fill the void within him.

"I had just had the best season of my career. Everything I touched turned to gold," he wrote in his autobiography. "But inside, I was broken and totally defeated … I remember sitting at the back of the practice field one afternoon, away from everybody, and tears were running down my face. I was saying to myself, 'This is so meaningless. I'm so unhappy. We're winning every week and I'm playing great, but I'm not happy.'"

After driving his car over a cliff and surviving, Sanders began to reshape his life through religion. He learned to separate Prime Time from real time. He left Dallas and signed with the Washington Redskins. A year later he retired, then un-retired to join the Baltimore Ravens for the 2004 season. That year he intercepted a pass and returned it for a touchdown, the 12th of his career, tying a league record.

After re-retiring, this time for good, Sanders worked as a football commentator before finding some solace in charitable deeds. He mentored two young football players: Devin Hester, the Chicago Bears high-speed kick returner, and U.S. college running back Noel Devine. He raised money for victims of Hurricane Katrina by challenging professional athletes in football, baseball, basketball and hockey to donate to relief efforts.

He also stuck his foot in it by supporting former Atlanta quarterback Michael Vick, who pleaded guilty to funding an illegal dog-fighting operation in 2007 and was sentenced to 23 months in jail. Sanders wondered, "Are we using him to bring an end to dog fighting in the United States? The only thing I can gather from this situation is that we're using Vick."

Still, the new Deion Sanders is happier than he's been in more than a decade. His life isn't a mix of conflicting sports, juggled schedules and empty desperation. It's calmer.

And Sanders can handle that. ∎

	Gms	Att	Yds	Avg	TD	College
TOTAL	68	991	4,956	5.0	39	Kansas

40

GALE SAYERS

RUNNING BACK

THERE'S MAGIC IN THE AIR

Gale Sayers didn't merely run with a football, he slalomed. He was a restless wave of a running back, shifting to and fro, weaving in and out, until he at last found an open portal in the defensive line, and then he was gone.

"He's the only guy I think could be running, stop on a dime, tell you whether it was heads or tails and not even break stride," marveled Green Bay Packers defensive back Herb Adderley.

Apparently hemmed in, changing direction, slithering out of the desperate grasp of tacklers, making his cut at precisely the right instant, Sayers left bamboozled defenders clawing at air. Pro football had not seen his like before. Watching old film of Gale Sayers today, he gives you, more than anything, this exhilarating sense of … freedom.

To defenders, he must have seemed an almost ghostly presence: an apparition clad in white or black, wearing No. 40. As difficult to contain as a drop of mercury. Sayers could run with power and purpose, certainly, but what we remember most is his speed and elusiveness. It sounds ab-

surdly simple and clichéd, but it was nonetheless true: he just made people miss. Sayers once said he could instinctively "feel" defenders getting close to him. Certainly, there seemed to be some form of special intuitive power at work. Magic, they came to call him in Chicago. The legendary Papa Bear, coach George Halas, dubbed him the greatest back since Red Grange. Although their styles were different, Sayers in a heartbeat became heir apparent to the great Jim Brown.

He had come out of the University of Kansas, nicknamed the Kansas Comet, a fourth pick in the 1965 NFL draft, snubbing a more lucrative offer from the Kansas City Chiefs of the upstart AFL, to join the Chicago Bears.

In his second regular-season game, Gale Sayers touched the ball once. And scored a touchdown. By game five, he couldn't be kept out of the starting lineup. That day, one screen pass, in particular, trumpeted the arrival of a new star in the pro football firmament: An 80-yard touchdown ramble after latching onto the ball, shedding Los Angeles Rams along the way. "I hit him so

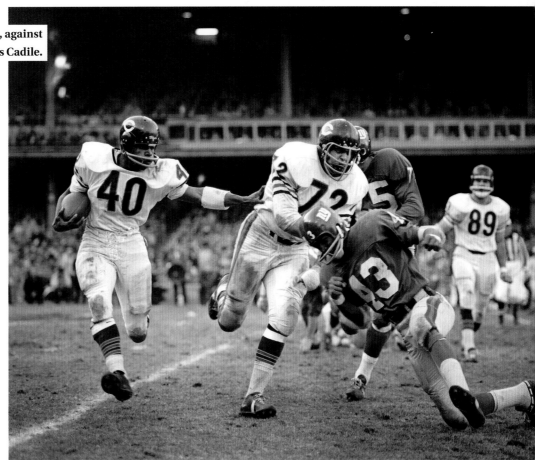

Sayers runs in his rookie season, 1965, against the Giants with a block from James Cadile.

hard," said the Rams All Pro defensive tackle Rosey Grier of that play, "that I thought my shoulder must have busted him in two. I heard a roar from the crowd and figured he'd fumbled, so I started scrambling around looking for the loose ball. But there was no ball and Sayers was gone."

The rookie also threw a touchdown pass that day from an option play. The Bears won, 31–6. Gale Sayers had arrived. But there was more to come. The afternoon of Dec. 12, 1965, was a cold, wet day at Wrigley Field. Some people have labeled the game that day as "the greatest individual game ever played." In the bog of Wrigley, Gale Sayers piled up 336 all-purpose yards and scored a phenomenal, record-tying six touchdowns, despite being pulled by Halas for most of the fourth quarter with the Bears comfortably in front.

"I think in the mud I ran more flat-footed, made my cuts not on my toes but on the balls of my feet and my heels," he recalled. "That kept me on balance."

Sayers captured Rookie of the Year honors in 1965 for his 867 yards rushing, 507 yards receiving and 22 touchdowns, a league record. His second season was no less spectacular. Sayers rushed for 1,231 yards, caught passes for 447 more and scored 12 touchdowns — eight via the run, two through the air and two more on kickoff returns. His stats dipped in 1967, mostly because the Bears were a team in decline. Then, the next season, the unthinkable happened. After nine games, Sayers had amassed 1,463 yards rushing, and was averaging 6.2 yards a carry. But on Nov. 10, 1967, in mid-cut, he was tackled by the 49ers' Kermit Alexander. Sayers crumpled to the field in pain. He'd torn multiple ligaments in his right knee.

Surgery ended Sayers' season, and at that time, cast doubt on his career. But if he was a man of few words, he was also nothing if not incredibly courageous and single-minded. A punishing rehabilitation followed. Looking back on that time, he said, "I learned if you want to make it bad enough, no matter how bad it is, you can make it." When Gale Sayers returned to the Bears the next season, he wasn't the same player. Oh, he could still "feel" the defenders, yes. Avoiding them proved a far greater challenge, though. That electric speed, the impossible-to-explain elusiveness, had been compromised. More and more yards had to be won down in the trenches, between the tackles, in the tough areas.

Sayers still led the league in rushing. It was arguably his greatest accomplishment in the game. A second knee operation, in 1970, did what few defenders had been able to in four and a half unforgettable seasons: cut down Gale Sayers in his tracks.

In 1970, he published his autobiography, *I Am Third*, in part detailing his friendship with teammate Brian Piccolo, who had lost a courageous battle against cancer. The book inspired a made-for-TV movie, *Brian's Song*, starring Billy Dee Williams as Sayers and James Caan as Piccolo. When Sayers accepted the NFL's Most Courageous Player Award that year, he dedicated the tribute to his friend. His words of that night, repeated by an actor after Piccolo had passed away, touched an immediate, emotional chord in a nation: "I love Brian Piccolo, and I'd like all of you to love him. When you hit your knees to pray tonight, please ask God to love him, too."

The Comet, they had christened him in his prime. And a Comet he proved to be, flashing across the sky, burning oh-so brightly, taking our breath away, only to fade from view too soon, leaving us awed and unfulfilled at the same time.

Only 34 when enshrined, Gale Sayers remains the youngest man ever voted into the Pro Football Hall of Fame. ▪

22 Emmitt SMITH

RUNNING BACK

EVERYTHING THAT'S GOOD ABOUT FOOTBALL

Play-by-play man Brad Scham's call of the moment, Oct. 22, 2002, is as instantly familiar to Texans as Al Michaels' call of the Feb. 22, 1980, "Miracle on Ice" is to the nation.

"I-formation, two receivers right. Second and seven from the Dallas 30. [Chad] Hutchinson hand-off Smith — 35, 40-yard-line! Right on the mark! That should do it! Move over, Sweetness! Make a place for Emmitt!"

Nobody had to make a place for Emmitt Smith. He made his own.

"Thirteen years ago," recalled wideout Michael Irvin during an emotional post-game celebration, marking running back Smith's passing of Walter Payton atop the NFL's all-time rushing list. "A rookie walked into my room. He was my roommate. We talked about the things we wanted to accomplish on the field.

"The first thing he said to me — and we were not a good team at the time — was that he wanted to win Super Bowls for you guys. And he did that. He said he wanted to win rushing titles, and he did that. He said he wanted to win MVPs, and he did that. His last goal, which I thought was fantasy,

was to become the all-time leading rusher in the NFL.

"And today he did that."

On that afternoon, in front of the home fans at Texas Stadium, Emmitt Smith ran into the record books.

What people conveniently forget now, in the soft glow of hindsight, is that he was, by that point in his career, generally thought to be a spent force. Observers had begun wondering aloud if Emmitt Smith hadn't stayed too long at the fair. As he reached out to history that Oct. 22, he was en route to the lowest rushing total in his career, a count below the Herculean standards he'd set with 11 consecutive years of 1,000 yards or better. There were opinions voiced that maybe he should've had the good sense to retire. Lucky thing Emmitt Smith hadn't the sense to listen to others.

If he had, he might've also believed the scouts who had written him off as too small and too slow when he came out of the University of Florida. He could've subconsciously agreed with all those teams that so cavalierly bypassed him in the 1990 draft. If he had had that kind of sense, Smith

Smith gains yards against the Bills in Super Bowl XXVIII. He was named MVP in the 30–13 victory.

Bowls and win the 1993 NFL MVP Award. Like his hero, the man he supplanted at the summit of football's Olympus, Walter Payton, Smith did it all with class and distinction. Here was someone who had his head screwed on right.

For instance, he came out of Florida early for the NFL draft, but having promised his mother he'd get an education, returned to school during the offseasons, earning his Bachelor's degree in Public Recreation in 1996.

"He personifies everything that's good about football," said Seattle Seahawks coach Mike Holmgren.

Appropriately, after spending 2003 and 2004 with Arizona to close out his career, the Cardinals released Smith and he signed a one-day, no-pay contract to retire as a Dallas Cowboy.

Deep inside, Emmitt Smith, the guy many believed was too slow and too small, never wavered in his conviction that he had a date with destiny.

"I think about it all the time," Smith once told *Sports Illustrated* as he closed in on the man they called Sweetness. "I'm chasing after legends, after Walter Payton and Tony Dorsett and Jim Brown and Eric Dickerson. After guys who made history. When my career's over, I want to have the new kids, the new backs, say, 'Boy, we have to chase a legend to be the best.' And they'll mean Emmitt Smith."

The 18,355 yards he amassed in 15 seasons remains the touchstone figure they're all still trying to catch. ■

could never have passed Payton, would never have left an indelible mark on pro football.

What Emmitt Smith had, in abundance, was more powerful than sense. It was self-belief, an inner faith that if a person wanted something badly enough, he could get it.

"For me," Smith once said, "winning isn't something that happens suddenly on the field when the whistle blows and the crowds roar. Winning is something that builds physically and mentally every day that you train and every night that you dream."

As philosophies go, that carries a powerful motivational punch.

Smith thrived in a decade that also included the phenomenal Barry Sanders. Just as Ali had Frazier, Wilt had Russell and Nicklaus had Watson, Emmitt had Barry. The two men differed stylistically, and arguments raged through the '90s about who was the better back. But there's little doubt that the greatness of one drove the greatness of the other.

In the final analysis, though, Emmitt Smith was the one to persevere. The one to pass Payton.

"You can just look at my age and say, 'Yeah, he's 33, he should go,'" he told S.L. Price of *Sports Illustrated* as he approached the iconic figure of 16,726 yards accrued in a career. "Yeah, I'm 33. But have I lost my step? Have I lost my vision? Have I lost my power? Have I lost my ability to make a person miss? If I answer yes to all those questions you might be right. But don't tell me I should quit just because of my age. That's what makes this frustrating. You have to know who you are. I know who I am."

When Smith arrived in Big D, the Cowboys were hardly America's Team. They weren't, in fact, much of a team at all. Coach Jimmy Johnson had the gargantuan task of trying to rebuild a 1–15 loser.

With Smith running and Troy Aikman playing catch with Irvin, the Cowboys would go on to glory. In his career, Emmitt Smith would win three Super Bowls, play in eight Pro

	Gms	Att	Comp	Yds	TD	Int	College
TOTAL	131	2,958	1,685	22,700	153	109	New Mexico Military Institute, Navy

12 ROGER STAUBACH

QUARTERBACK

CAPTAIN COMEBACK WAS A COWBOY

In an era of change and rebellion, Staubach was a welcome, old-fashioned super hero, representing less turbulent times. Genial. Straitlaced. Rigidly conservative. Devoutly Catholic. To push the theme you might almost say "prim." He came to symbolize those great Cowboy teams that went to four Super Bowls in an eight-year span.

Somehow, Roger Staubach seemed above it all.

In an interview aired on CBS in 1975, though, he showed he wouldn't let the image compromise his sense of humor.

"Everyone in the world compares me to Joe Namath, you know," he told interviewer Phyllis George. "As far as off the field, he's single, a bachelor, a swinger; I'm married with a family and he's having all the fun. I enjoy sex as much as Joe Namath, you know, only with one girl. It's still fun."

The remark, coming from Staubach the Square, had all of America talking. Just as the man's quarterbacking had all of the NFL talking through 11 seasons of excellence.

As conventional as he was outside the white lines in his personal life, Roger Staubach could be considered a bit of a hell-raiser on the football field. He wasn't christened "Roger the Dodger" for nothing. His ability to avoid trouble netted him 2,264 rushing yards and 20 touchdowns during his seasons in Texas.

Armed with a dizzying array of offensive weapons — former Olympic gold medal sprinter Bob Hayes, Drew Pearson on the outside; pocket-sized dynamo Robert Newhouse, Calvin Hill and the sublime Tony Dorsett charging out of the backfield — Staubach was the choreographer of a brilliant ensemble.

His uncanny knack for bringing the Cowboys back from the abyss transformed the son of a Cincinnati salesman into NFL royalty. He directed 23 come-from-behind victories in the fourth quarter during his career, 14 of those in the final two minutes or overtime.

"Roger," said Dallas tight end Billy Jo Dupree, "never knew when the game was over."

Staubach's Hail Mary pass to Drew Pearson with the Cowboys trailing the favored Minnesota Vikings in the 1975 NFC Divisional tilt with virtually no time left on the score clock has gone into the realm of legend.

Staubach set for the snap in 1977 against the 49ers; Dallas won the Super Bowl that year.

But as Staubach knew, the last-minute theatrics were born not so much out of inexplicable inspiration as through preparation, repetition and the readiness to hold his nerve in any situation. As a field general, he was tough, single-minded, commanding and innovative. Tom Landry, the taciturn coach of the Cowboys, called Staubach the greatest leader he had ever had the good fortune to come across.

"Confidence," Staubach once said, "doesn't come out of nowhere. It's a result of something … hours and days and weeks and years of constant work and dedication. Spectacular results come from unspectacular preparation."

Roger Staubach certainly arrived in the NFL prepared. His path to football immortality was hardly a conventional one, but that makes the story all the more compelling. Originally selected by the 'Boys in the 10th round of the 1964 draft as the reigning Heisman Trophy recipient, he was unable to play pro football until his Naval commitment, including a voluntary one-year tour of duty in Vietnam, had ended.

In his junior year, he had led the Naval Academy's Midshipmen to a 9–1 record and the No. 2 ranking in the nation. Coach Wayne Hardin called him the finest quarterback the Navy had ever seen.

So the talent was obvious. The timing was troublesome. Undoubtedly, that's why he went so late in the draft. The wait was ultimately worth it for the Cowboys.

When Staubach left the Navy in 1969, he was a 27-year-old rookie. By 1971, he was the starter in Big D, taking control from incumbent Craig Morton after Dallas sputtered out of the gate 4–3.

Staubach guided the Cowboys to 10 consecutive regular-season victories, and culminated an astounding NFL debut as a starter by beating the Miami Dolphins 24–3 in Super Bowl VI. His 119 yards passing and two TDs at the New Orleans Superdome that afternoon earned Roger Staubach MVP laurels. He'd taken his sweet time getting there, but he'd arrived in style.

The next decade would see Staubach and the Cowboys set standards for other quarterbacks, other franchises, to emulate.

Staubach would engineer Dallas's marches to three more Super Bowl appearances, beating Denver 27–10 in 1978, back in New Orleans, while losing a pair of title clashes to the Terry Bradshaw-led Pittsburgh Steelers, both times at Miami's Orange Bowl, in 1976 and 1979.

Upon retiring at the close of the 1979 season, in part over concerns of possible lingering aftereffects from a series of concussions, Staubach became more engrossed in a business he'd begun while still playing: real estate. In that, like anything else he has ever thrown his energies into, Staubach made a rousing success.

During his years at the helm of "America's Team," Captain America had thrown for 22,700 yards and 153 touchdowns. His career passer rating of 83.4 was, at the time, the highest career mark ever. He had played in six Pro Bowls (although, ironically, was never chosen All-Pro), led the league in passing four times and took home the NFL Players Association MVP Award in 1971.

He'd proven his versatility a hundred times over, winning games and championships with his arm and his feet and his head. In his first year of eligibility, 1985, to no one's surprise, Roger the Dodger took his place in Canton, Ohio, alongside the greatest in the game.

Roger Staubach may have gotten a late start, but it'd be difficult to argue that he hadn't made up for lost time. ■

10 FRAN TARKENTON

QUARTERBACK

BLOOD, SWEAT AND RECORD BOOKS

It'd be too convenient, too clichéd, to make the claim that Fran Tarkenton reinvented the quarterbacking position. However, it would by no means be out of line to say he stretched its limits, in much the same way he stretched the defenses of his day.

Before him, the overwhelming majority of quarterbacks dropped back in the pocket to throw the football. And stayed there, come hell or high water. That was the accepted way to play. The pocket was their womb, their cocoon. Inside it, they felt safe and protected. Tarkenton changed all that. He broke containment. He created chaos. He gave defensive coaches new, multiple dangers to consider.

"People looked down on scrambling quarterbacks when I broke in," Tarkenton noted ruefully, later in his career. "Now those who can't scramble are at a disadvantage."

The son of a preacher, born in Richmond, Virginia, Fran Tarkenton was drafted in the third round of the 1961 draft by the Minnesota Vikings, coming off a fine college career at Georgia, where he was mentored by the legendary coach Wally Butts.

Right from the get-go, he showed vast potential. His first pro start resulted in a 250-yard passing day and a 35–13 upset of the Chicago Bears.

He'd spend six seasons with the Vikings at old Metropolitan Stadium in Bloomington, bickering with head coach Norm Van Brocklin about the effectiveness of his scrambling style before requesting — and receiving — a trade to the New York Giants in time for the 1967 campaign. In the Big Apple, he provided an interesting contrast to the brash, outspoken quarterback of the other team in town, Joe Willie Namath.

The Giants, though, were no powerhouse. Still, in 1970, Tarkenton had them fighting, unsuccessfully, for a playoff spot. They wound up 9–5. It would be his high-water mark in New York.

By 1972, Tarkenton was back in the Twin Cities. But these weren't the same sad-sack Vikings he'd left in '67. A steely-eyed coaching recruit from the Winnipeg Blue Bombers, Bud Grant, had been installed on the sidelines and Minnesota was putting the pieces in place for a concerted championship push.

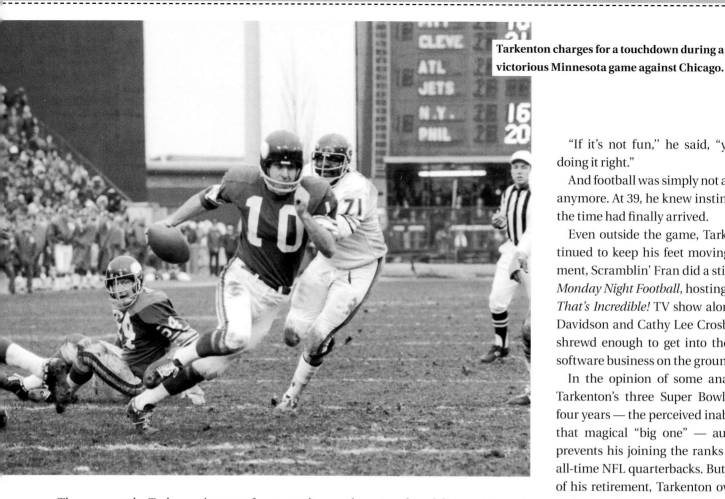

These were to be Tarkenton's years of greatest glory, and most profound disappointment. Always a bridesmaid, never a bride, the Vikings were among the regular-season elite over the next few seasons. But they could somehow never hit pay dirt come Super Bowl time. In one stretch of inexplicable agony, Minnesota lost three Super Bowls in a four-year span: In January of 1974, the Vikes were paddled 24–7 by the Miami Dolphins in Houston. The next year, in Super Bowl IX, 16–6 by the Pittsburgh Steelers at New Orleans and two years later 32–14 by Oakland, in Pasadena, California.

In three trips to the Big Dance, Tarkenton's offenses had delivered a paltry 27 points. Not good enough.

The most punishing, non-Super Bowl disappointment of Tarkenton's career came squished in between all those title challenges, in the 1975 season. The Vikings finished with a chart-topping 12–2 record that year. The Purple People Eater defense, headed by Carl Eller, Allan Page and Jim Marshall, was at its ravenous best. And the elusive Fran Tarkenton had never been more effective, winning the MVP award for his brilliance during the year.

But the Minnesota dream, riding hot on the heels of their stellar regular season, came cruelly undone during the NFC Divisional Playoff, when a controversial Roger Staubach-to-Drew Pearson touchdown pass — controversial because to this day Vikings' partisans claim Pearson interfered with defensive back Nate Wright while running his pattern — helped Dallas slip past the Purple Gang 17–14.

The play would only add to the image of Tarkenton as quarterback of the damned and the unluckiest man in pro football.

Tarkenton would play two more seasons following his final Super Bowl shot, walking away from the game at the close of the 1978 campaign after prepping his successor, Tommy Kramer.

"If it's not fun," he said, "you are not doing it right."

And football was simply not as much fun anymore. At 39, he knew instinctively that the time had finally arrived.

Even outside the game, Tarkenton continued to keep his feet moving. In retirement, Scramblin' Fran did a stint on ABC's *Monday Night Football*, hosting the cultish *That's Incredible!* TV show alongside John Davidson and Cathy Lee Crosby, and was shrewd enough to get into the computer software business on the ground floor.

In the opinion of some analysts, Fran Tarkenton's three Super Bowl defeats in four years — the perceived inability to win that magical "big one" — automatically prevents his joining the ranks of the elite all-time NFL quarterbacks. But at the time of his retirement, Tarkenton owned every major passing record of worth, with 47,003 yards passing, 3,686 completions and 342 touchdowns. Add to that his 3,674 yards rushing, 125 regular-season victories, six All-Pro selections and nine Pro Bowl appearances — and the stats make a mighty persuasive counter-argument in his favor.

This is a Hall of Famer, never forget, someone whose jersey, that famous No. 10, has been retired by the Vikings.

"Success, in my view," Tarkenton once said, obviously alluding to the one blemish on his résumé, "is the willingness to strive for something you really want. The person not reaching the top is no less a success than the one who achieved it, if they both sweated blood, sweat and tears and overcame obstacles and fears. The failure to be perfect does not mean you're not a success."

Fran Tarkenton may have never won a Super Bowl. But, hey, neither did Dan Marino. If success were to be solely measured in blood, sweat and tears, Fran Tarkenton would be as successful as they come. ■

56 LAWRENCE TAYLOR

LINEBACKER

SEX, DRUGS AND FOOTBALL

Say L.T., and everyone, particularly those poor souls in the quarterbacking fraternity, knows exactly who you are talking about.

The No. 56 in New York Giants blue, shedding his block from the outside linebacker position the way a snake sheds its skin, exploding into the backfield, drawing a bead on some poor unsuspecting guy with a Sack Me! sign taped to the back of his jersey. Then … impact! Followed by the aftermath.

The Lawrence Taylor saga, so familiar to football followers, is symbolic of our age: full of controversy, suspensions, sex and self-destructive drug use. It's also overflowing with exponential impact and achievement. Not that L.T. ever did things the easy way.

During a 1993 interview on TV newsmagazine *60 Minutes*, Taylor admitted to sending prostitutes to opponents' hotel rooms the night before games in order to tire them out. He confessed that he had used samples of teammates' urine to beat league drug tests, and to being hooked on cocaine.

But if L.T. couldn't seem to get out of his own way beyond the white lines, no one seemed able to get in his way when he was on patrol between them. He was arguably the most dominant single defensive player the league has ever known.

Double-teaming Lawrence Taylor seldom, if ever, worked. More than dominating his side of the ball, he actually dictated the way offenses lined up. He was a force of nature more than anything. He never felt beaten on a play. Teams were forced to make special provisions for him. Bill Parcells called Taylor the greatest player he ever coached.

"You try to stay within the rules for the sake of the game," said Taylor one time, "but you can always turn up the intensity."

Intensity was never an issue for Lawrence Taylor. He always seemed stuck on maximum overdrive. The title of his autobiography — *LT: Over the Edge* — pretty much summed it all up. His life. His game. His persona.

Taylor and New York took a shine to each other the moment the raw but gifted linebacker was drafted out of North Carolina, second overall in 1981 (the New Orleans Saints, unfortunately, had opted

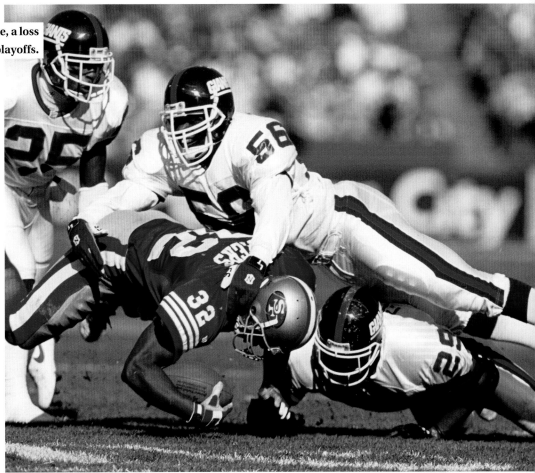

L.T. makes a stop in his last game, a loss in the 1993 NFC divisional playoffs.

for University of South Carolina Heisman Trophy-winning running back George Rogers with the top pick).

Giants general manager George Young was so taken by Taylor's abilities that even before the draft he predicted Taylor would be better than NFL legend Dick Butkus.

"Sure, I saw Dick Butkus play," Young said. "There's no doubt in my mind about Taylor. He's bigger and stronger than Butkus was. On the blitz, he's devastating." L.T. and his new city had much in common: Both were bigger-than-life, badder-than-bad, exhilarating, intoxicating, and infested with a wild, self-destructive streak. It was love at first sight.

Not one to ease into anything, the new kid in town proved to be an immediate sensation, being named the league's 1981 Defensive Player of the Year in his rookie season — his first of three nominations. In 1986, he upped the ante by being named NFL MVP. Only two other defensive players have been so honored. The NFL didn't start recording sacks until Taylor's second season, in 1982. So if you factor in the 9½ sacks he was unofficially credited with in his rookie year, he amassed 142 in 184 games, an incredible ratio.

That he lasted 13 years and was so productive, given his drug and alcohol problems, is nothing short of astounding. In a perverse way, it served to underscore what a giant talent fans in New York had been privileged to watch.

A 1988 game against the New Orleans Saints is widely remembered for personifying Taylor's almost fanatical competitive attitude. Suffering from a torn pectoral muscle, the single-minded linebacker, putting aside the pain, wore a sling/harness to keep his shoulder in place.

He only recorded seven QB sacks that day.

The year Taylor became eligible for Hall of Fame induction (1999), debate sprang up that perhaps his bad-boy image, and all those indiscretions he so readily admitted to, should keep him out of Canton. The shrine of the game, they argued, was reserved for immortals, not immorals.

"If they don't vote me in the Hall of Fame," Taylor countered defiantly, "then they need to close that place down."

They did. They don't.

They might have argued all day long and into the night about Lawrence Taylor's off-the-field misdeeds, but there was simply no way around all those sacks, the 10 Pro Bowls, the individual awards and two Super Bowl rings. His career, however compromised by his off-field actions, screamed out for such recognition.

No one could dispute that he had established a new standard for the linebacker position.

Ever the rebel, L.T., now drug-free and living clean, arrived for induction in Canton decked out unconventionally in a black T-shirt under his yellow Hall of Fame sports jacket, instead of the customary shirt and tie. Oh, and he was wearing sandals — with no socks. But when the time came to speak, the longtime annihilator spoke eloquently, and from the heart.

"It's a great honor to be here," said the man who was so good at his job that he was known far and wide simply by his initials. "I think what I want to leave the people is that life, like anything else, can knock you down.

"You know, anybody can quit. Anybody can do that. A Hall of Famer never quits. A Hall of Famer realizes that the crime is not being knocked down. The crime is not getting up again." ▪

19 JOHNNY UNITAS

QUARTERBACK

THE GOLDEN ARM

Perhaps tight end John Mackey summed up the man and his aura best: "It's like being in the huddle with God." Johnny Unitas, the kid from the tough streets of Pittsburgh, made something of an unlikely deity.

Those sloped shoulders. Crooked legs. Shy grin. Bowed right arm from throwing so many passes. The high-topped black football boots and that trademark crew-cut. So iconic was Johnny U that in one episode of *The Simpsons*, more than two decades after he had retired, grandpa Abe Simpson exclaims, "Now, Johnny Unitas … there's a haircut you could set your watch to!"

Unitas arrived in Baltimore in 1956 after playing for the semi-pro Bloomington Rams. He had been earning six dollars a game, on a field strewn with rocks and shattered glass that had to be sprinkled with oil before every game to keep the dust down. He was also working as a pile driver at a construction company at the time to make ends meet.

The Golden Arm was no stranger to hard work. He grew up in a single-parent home after his father died when he was only five years old. His mother worked two jobs to support four children. Unitas later said he learned more from her than any coach.

After a standout collegiate career at Louisville, he was famously drafted in the ninth round, but then released by the hometown Pittsburgh Steelers in 1955. Apparently, the Steelers had too many quarterbacks to offer him a decent look. After being cut, a downcast Unitas hitchhiked home. "Unfortunately," recalled Steelers owner Dan Rooney, in one of the great understatements in all of sport, "we did not give him a chance." It was an oversight a city and its franchise would long lament. Not that the Baltimore Colts were falling all over themselves to sign some kid named Johnny Unitas. The Colts' coach at the time, Weeb Ewbank, recalled that an anonymous fan sent a letter to the team extolling the virtues of this lanky, rawboned quarterback. Ewbank figured "What the hell!" and offered the guy $7,000 if he stuck around. "I always accused Johnny of writing [the letter]," Ewbank would later joke.

On Oct. 21, 1956, Johnny U tossed his first-ever NFL pass, which was picked off and run back for a touchdown. In the

same game, he then ran into teammate Alan Ameche on the next possession. Chicago recovered the fumble and scored. Another botched handoff later would set up yet another Bears' major. Baltimore lost that day 58–27 — hardly an auspicious debut.

Undeterred, Unitas would go on to lead the Colts to three NFL championships, win three MVP awards, a record 10 Pro Bowl appearances and four All-Pro citations, becoming the quarterback standard for decades. He would be the first man to throw for 40,000 yards in a career. His 47 consecutive games with at least one touchdown toss — a record mentioned in the same breath as DiMaggio's 56-game hitting streak or Glenn Hall's 502 consecutive games tending goal for the Chicago Black Hawks — wasn't broken until 2012, 52 years after it was set.

Johnny U helped usher in the modern, TV-dominated NFL in the so-called "greatest game ever played," the Dec. 28, 1958, championship clash against the New York Giants at Yankee Stadium. With only 90 seconds to work, Unitas completed four passes to set up a game-tying field goal. "We've got 80 yards to go and two minutes to do it in," a teammate remembers him saying on the field to start the march. "We're going to find out what stuff we're made of." Unitas later engineered an 80-yard drive in sudden-death overtime, capped by Ameche's one-yard touchdown plunge. Telecast live and coast-to-coast on NBC, the drama of that game ushered in a new era of mushrooming popularity for the NFL. It also made Johnny Unitas a star from coast to coast. "I don't know what he uses for blood," marveled former quarterback Sid Gillman, "but I guarantee you it isn't warm. It's ice-cold."

To today's football fanatic, the No. 19 in blue might seem something of a relic: the short, slipped steps of a pure old-time pocket passer. Don't be fooled, though. No one tougher, no one smarter, no one more courageous has ever played the position. Johnny Unitas defied eras.

He also defied medical logic. There's something heroic, even romantic, about those who suffer for their art. And Unitas suffered. This was a man as tough as tungsten, just like his hometown. Broken ribs. Punctured lung. Shoulder contusions. Knee surgeries. He ripped a tendon in his right arm almost off the bone and missed most of the 1968 season. He ruptured the Achilles in his right foot playing paddleball with teammate Tom Matte at a YMCA in April 1971 and was supposed to be sidelined for six months. He made it back in half the time. "What made him the greatest quarterback of all time wasn't his arm or his size, it was what was inside his stomach," said former Giants general manager Ernie Accorsi, who worked with Unitas during his final years in Baltimore.

Johnny Unitas retired in 1973, holding 22 records at the time. He'd completed 2,830 passes for 40,239 yards and 290 touchdowns. He was voted into the Pro Football Hall of Fame six years later. In 1999, *Sports Illustrated* voted him the fifth best player of all time, second among quarterbacks only to Joe Montana. But the old-timers, those who'd been there, seen it all unfold and remembered, knew better. On Sept. 11, 2002, while working out, Johnny Unitas died of a heart attack in Baltimore at the age of 69. Baltimore mourned. A nation that had become obsessed with the game, a game he helped reinvent and popularize, stopped to pay tribute. God had left the huddle and gone up to heaven.

"There is a difference between conceit and confidence," Unitas once said. "Conceit is bragging about yourself. Confidence means you believe you can get the job done."

No one did it better — before or since. ■

	Gms	Int/Yds	TD	Sks	Fr	College
TOTAL	232	3/79	0	198	20	Tennessee

92 REGGIE WHITE

DEFENSIVE END/DEFENSIVE TACKLE

SUNDAYS, SACKS AND SERVICE

When the news broke that Reggie White, Green Bay's marauding Minister of Defense, had been found dead of cardiac arrhythmia at his home in Cornelius, North Carolina, on Boxing Day, 2004, it was the world of pro football that was thrown for a substantial loss. He was only 43.

Reggie was the guy who usually did the sacking.

It seemed impossible, though, that arguably the most influential defensive lineman ever was gone long before his time.

Nothing, no one, people thought, could as much as slow Reggie White down, much less stop him from reaching the quarterback; from strapping on the pads, no matter how banged up his body might be; or from voicing his opinion on a wide range of subjects, however controversial.

"He may have been the best player I've ever seen," said Packers quarterback Brett Favre in tribute. "Certainly he was the best I've ever played with or against."

Those sentiments were echoed around the NFL.

Another former quarterbacking teammate (and later opponent), Rick Mirer, remembered his dealings with Reggie. "I had the pleasure of getting hit by him several times. The way he just threw around 300-pound guys, I've never seen anyone do that. He was just head and shoulders above anybody else I saw. He just ... dominated."

For further verification, consult Phil Simms. The one-time New York Giants star was the victim of 15 of the 198 quarterback sacks White administered over 15 glorious seasons. Why, if Simms had been found in bed late at night, perspiring heavily, after experiencing visceral nightmares about Reggie White, he could have been forgiven.

The list of the Minister's quarterbacking victims is extensive. Seventy-five different men in all felt his wrath: the aforementioned Simms, sacked 15 times and Neil Lomax, 13 times, led the way. Over the years, White hunted down great ones, such as Troy Aikman (7 times), John Elway (5.5) and Dan Marino (2), along with the likes of Danny Kanells and Blair Kiels and Anthony Dilwegs, whose main claim to NFL fame is that they made it onto Reggie's list.

The big man from Tennessee, all 6-foot-5 and 300 pounds of him, really was a Chat-

White knocks down Rodney Peete of the Philadelphia Eagles, one of 198 career sacks.

tanooga Choo-Choo. When his train pulled out of the shed and built up a head of steam, nothing could stand in his way. At least, nothing human.

No one who ever played the position instilled quite the same degree of fearful respect. Oh, Bruce Smith of the Bills, unquestionably a wonderful defensive lineman, may have eclipsed White's all-time sack mark, by two. But Smith rang up that total in 19 seasons, four more than the Minister.

Reggie White was such an overwhelming force exploding into the backfield that he could dictate offensive strategy. He collected 23.5 sacks in 34 games for the Memphis Showboats of the United States Football League in 1984 and 1985, and joined the Philadelphia Eagles for the 1985 NFL season when the USFL went belly up, and he quickly became an NFL superstar. During eight seasons in Philly, White piled up 124 sacks. Amazingly, during his time in Eagle green, his sack total eclipsed the number of games he played.

In 1993, White used free agency to move to the Green Bay Packers. In six seasons there, he registered 68.5 sacks and helped the Pack to two Super Bowls, earning a ring in XXXI.

He didn't miss a beat, hadn't lost a step.

In 1998, White played what would be his last season in Green Bay, choosing to retire after being named the NFL's Defensive Player of the Year, and getting selected to his 12th consecutive Pro Bowl. Retirement, which wasn't an easy decision for White (there was much flip-flopping on White's part), didn't last long. He was convinced by the Carolina Panthers to come back and play, but his one season there in 2000 proved to be his last. He then retired from the game with nothing left to prove.

Ordained an Evangelical minister, Reggie White was, to many, a personal and professional contradiction. The relentless Sack Master between the lines, a gentle, peaceful man off the field. Never afraid to voice an opinion, to underline his conviction, White angered and upset many with his outspoken, fundamentalist views on homosexuality. He was accused of being archaic and hate-mongering.

"God," he said once, "places the heaviest burden on those who can carry its weight."

The Minister of Defense could carry plenty, which is what made his death, at the age of 43, so hard to believe. He had, in life, seemed something close to invincible.

In his chosen profession, he remains, quite simply, unmatched. In 1999, *Sporting News* ranked him 22nd on its list of the 100 Greatest Football Players. In 2005, three teams — the University of Tennessee, the Eagles and the Packers — all retired White's famous No. 92.

His nine consecutive seasons with at least 10 sacks remains an NFL record.

At his Hall of Fame induction ceremony at Canton in 2006, White's wife Sara and son Jeremy delivered the acceptance speech for a husband, a father and a football player. Jeremy, echoing the feelings of so many there that day, said in part:

"Reggie will be remembered by some as the man who sacked quarterbacks on Sundays … But to others, he will be remembered for his faith in God. And yet to others he will be remembered, yet again, as a father, a friend and a husband. Even though Reggie is not here to receive this great honor the NFL has allowed him to receive, I know he is with us. He is with us in spirit, but most of all he is with us in our memories. As long as we continue to remember anyone we have lost, they are never completely gone. They are with us."

Amen.

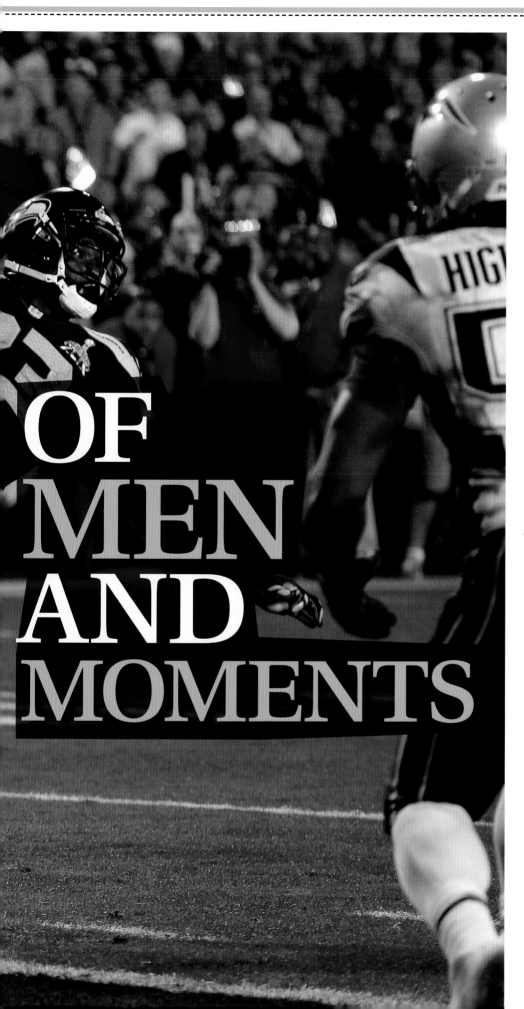

OF MEN AND MOMENTS

"Most football players are temperamental. That's 90 percent temper and 10 percent mental."

– Doug Plank,
Defensive Back, Chicago Bears

Doug Plank didn't say every football player was that way, but he could have. Plank himself was as rough as knotty pine and could hit like a two-by-four. He understood the essence of pro football. He understood just what it took to play a violent game in rain or snow with the clock ticking down and tens of thousands of people cheering against you, and that those people wanted you to be trampled underfoot or, at the very least, humbled and scarred for life.

Jim Marshall defends against the Rams in a 1969 playoff game. The Vikings won, 23–20.

It's no wonder it takes all kinds to play in the NFL. As such, the league has been a clearinghouse for the athletically blessed, the quiet and withdrawn, the loud and petulant, as well as the certifiably loony. Over the years, the game has treated fans to a mixed-nut assortment of characters.

To be clear, the word "character" is used here in its fullest form. We're not just talking about the swift and the strong who can split a pair of tacklers the way scientist Ernest Rutherford split the atom. We're including malcontents and foul-ups, scoundrels and flakes — off-tackle, off-the-wall eccentrics who broke the rules because they insisted there weren't any. They may have given their coaches nuclear ulcers, but those same players produced memorable moments of another kind.

THE MEN

Wrong-Way Marshall

Take Jim Marshall of the Minnesota Vikings. Marshall was a member of the team's fabled defensive front, the Purple People Eaters, who were named after Sheb Wooley's 1958 song, "The Purple People Eater."

Defensive end Marshall was a remarkable talent. Weighing just 235 pounds, he played 21 years in the NFL and started 302 consecutive games. To keep his streak alive, Marshall often played through injuries. Twice he checked himself out of a hospital to suit up on game day. The first time, he was recovering from pneumonia. The second time, he had accidentally shot himself in the side while cleaning a shotgun.

When Marshall retired at age 41, he had recorded 127 sacks, recovered an NFL record 29 fumbles, played in two Pro Bowls and a Super Bowl, and yet, all of that paled in comparison to one moment, one play.

It happened in a 1964 game between the Vikings and the San Francisco 49ers, who were playing at home in Kezar Stadium, nestled in the green confines of Golden

Gate Park. The 49ers were on the move offensively when one of their receivers was hit and fumbled the ball. An alert Marshall scooped it up and ran untouched 66 yards for what he thought was a Minnesota touchdown. But Marshall ran the wrong way and crossed the goal line into his own end zone, where he scored a safety for the 49ers.

Weren't his teammates yelling at him to turn around? (Marshall thought they were simply shouting the encouragement, "Go, Jim, Go.") Did he know something was askew when San Francisco lineman Bruce Bosley walked up to him and said, "Thanks, Jim"? (Oh, yeah. That's when it hit home.)

Marshall's gaffe became not just a running gag, pardon the pun, but the defining moment of his career. Never mind that in the same game, he recorded a sack and recovered a second fumble to help the Vikings to a 27–22 win. Forevermore, he was wrong-way Marshall, the guy who thought all end zones looked alike.

"The No. 1 question is, 'I've always wondered what you thought at that moment,'" said Marshall. "And I say, 'Think of the worst thing you've ever done, the thing you're most ashamed of — and it was seen by 80 million people. Then think of people coming up to you and reminding you of it for the rest of your life.' That gives you a sense of what I've gone through."

Despite the embarrassment, Marshall bore his infamy with grace. He later learned to laugh at its irrelevance after surviving a near-death experience in the mountains of Wyoming.

In January 1971, Marshall encountered a hellacious blizzard while traveling through Beartooth Pass. He was with a party of 16 and was almost killed when he drove his snowmobile over a cliff. The machine came close to rolling over Marshall, who fell 30 feet before climbing back to the top of the cliff with the help of a friend.

That was the start of a 36-hour ordeal that saw Marshall and Vikings teammate

Joe Kapp, under pressure from Deacon Jones, gets set to deliver a "ruptured duck."

Paul Dickson fight to stay awake so they wouldn't freeze to death. At one point, Marshall burned $1 bills and then his checkbook to start a fire.

They eventually saw a rescue party and were told one of the group's members had frozen to death. Marshall never again complained about playing in the cold and snow of Minnesota — or running the wrong way in San Francisco.

Joe Kapp and the Magnificent Seven

One of the NFL's true characters had a day for the ages when he tied a league record by throwing seven touchdowns in a single game. Sid Luckman was the first to do it in 1943. Three others had duplicated the feat since then, but in 1969, Minnesota Vikings Joe Kapp stepped forward and joined the Magnificent Seven club with a showing that defied all logic.

Kapp, you have to understand, was not a great passer. He never threw the ball with his fingers on the laces, a tactic all the winged-arm wonders have used over the decades. His excuse was, "All the laces are different." Sometimes, when the ball was tough to grip, Kapp would wash his hands in mud puddles along the sideline. Even with a good grip and no laces, Kapp's throws fluttered through the air like broken badminton birdies or, as Detroit Lions defensive lineman Alex Karras called them, "ruptured ducks."

And still, Kapp threw for seven touchdown passes in a single game against the Baltimore Colts, who had one of the better defensive units of the time. Did it make sense? Not at all. But Kapp was about winning, about doing whatever it took to get the job done. When told his passing style lacked the classic look of Bart Starr or Johnny Unitas, Kapp snapped and replied, "Classics are for Greeks."

Kapp had won a Rose Bowl and a Grey Cup in the CFL before joining the Vikings. In one of his early NFL games, he lined up under center against the Los Angeles Rams' fearsome foursome defensive front of Deacon Jones, Merlin Olsen, Lamar Lundy and Roger Brown and shouted at them, "All right, let's see how tough you sons of bitches are."

Once, after a heartfelt loss, Kapp later got into a fight with one of his own teammates, linebacker Lonnie Warwick.

"Most quarterbacks like to run out of bounds," said Minnesota coach Bud Grant, who watched Kapp charge into some of the game's toughest tacklers, just to prove a point. "Mine likes to run over people."

The Man Who Hated Rules

For sheer lunacy, no one caused more head scratching than the aptly named Joe Don Looney. Considered "the greatest player who never was," Looney squandered his size, speed and abilities on acts of defiance and strangeness.

Dozens of players and coaches insisted Looney had it all — power, slashing speed, good hands, everything from the neck down. But he could never bend his knee to conformity. He hated rules and being told what to do. He refused to do anything if it didn't feel right.

At the University of Oklahoma, he told coach Bud Wilkinson, "Take me out. My biorhythms are out of sync." Looney sat on the bench, didn't move for several minutes; then jumped up and proclaimed, "Coach, my biorhythms are fine. Put me in." Wilkinson did and Looney scored on a long touchdown romp.

Drafted by the New York Giants, Looney didn't believe in curfews and being told when to go to bed. With the Baltimore Colts, he used to sneak out of training camp and sleep in graveyards and was once fined $100 for being 15 minutes late to a meeting. He asked coach Don Shula, "Why wasn't I paid $100 for being 15 minutes early [the day before]?" With the Detroit Lions, Looney uttered his most memorable quote. Told to run in a play from the sidelines, Looney said to coach Harry Gilmer, "If you want a messenger, call Western Union."

Looney also refused to tape his ankles. When ordered to, he taped over his socks instead.

He didn't stay long in the NFL, just eight seasons, and he didn't accomplish much while he was there. He eventually did a tour of duty during the Vietnam War, converted to Hinduism, and died in a motorcycle crash at the age of 45. His legacy is one of unfulfilled promise and a lot of laughable tales.

Ol' Tooz

John Matuszak was another raging individualist. He stood 6-foot-8, weighed close to 300 pounds, and played for an Oakland Raiders team that got its colors and tackling style from the Hells Angels. Nicknamed Tooz, he was a natural-born partier. *Animal House* on two legs.

As the Raiders prepared to boot-stomp the Philadelphia Eagles in Super Bowl XV, Matuszak vowed he was going to make sure none of his teammates broke curfew, especially with the game being held in New Orleans, where the temptations were as thick as gumbo.

"I'll keep our young fellows out of trouble," he said. "If any players want to stray, they gotta go through the Ol' Tooz." The very next night Matuszak was seen partying into the early-morning hours and fined $1,000 for his troubles.

John Matuszak in 1976, his first season with the Raiders and his first Super Bowl victory.

Matuszak won a pair of Super Bowls, but he is also remembered as an actor. Arguably, his finest performance came in *North Dallas 40* where he played — wait for it — a football player confused by his place within the cosmos. "Every time I call it a game, you call it a business," Matuszak roared at his coaches. "Every time I call it a business, you call it a game."

Matuszak almost died once during his time with the Kansas City Chiefs. Having mixed beer with sleeping pills, the Tooz collapsed at a bar. Chiefs coach Paul Wiggin was called to the scene and accompanied Matuszak in an ambulance ride to the closest hospital. Along the way, Matuszak's heart stopped and Wiggin revived it by thumping on the big man's chest. That was in 1974. Fifteen years later, at the age of 38, Matuszak died from heart complications.

Burning to Be a Success

Tim Rossovich lived his football life to the fullest. He was the Philadelphia Eagles' first-round pick in the 1968 draft, after a stellar career at Southern Cal, where his roommate was actor-to-be Tom Selleck. Rosso, as he was known, had that 1960s style about him. He had a puffy Afro hairstyle, and wore tie-dyed shirts and bell-bottom jeans. He was equal parts free-spirited and nonsensical. Once, he drove a motorcycle off a pier and into the ocean. He used to open beer bottles with his teeth and, when that got a little too tame, he'd grab a glass and start eating it. He'd also munch on cigarettes, paper, insects — whatever suited his fancy, if not his palate.

Rossovich's flair for the unusual is best captured in a 1971 *Sports Illustrated* cover story. On the front of the issue, with the headline "He's Burning to be a Success," was a photograph of Rosso with his Afro on fire.

Rossovich once opened his mouth to say something and a bird flew out. True story.

"You know how I learned to play middle linebacker? From [Chicago's] Dick Butkus," Rossovich said. "Not from him personally, but at the time I was living with Steve Sabol of NFL Films and [Eagles' defensive tackle] Gary Pettigrew, and I said, 'They moved me to middle linebacker. I need to know how Butkus plays middle linebacker.' So Steve would bring all the highlights and I would study Dick Butkus for hours and hours and hours and hours."

Rossovich spent four seasons in Philadelphia and was voted to the Pro Bowl in 1969. He was traded to the San Diego Chargers, where he suffered a knee injury and watched his career fizzle out. He turned to acting where he reunited with Selleck and even appeared in several episodes of *Magnum P.I.* Not once, though, did Rosso upstage his former roomie by lighting his hair on fire.

Owens the Terrible

One of the most audacious characters in the NFL's recent history, Terrell Owens, went by the moniker "Terrible" for good reason. The mercurial former receiver has insinuated that one of his quarterbacks was gay while another wasn't in shape. He fired his agent, demanded his multi-million dollar contract with Philadelphia be renegotiated, and made enough negative comments about the Eagles to finally be suspended.

After being released, he signed with the Dallas Cowboys and the theatrics continued. In one 2006 episode, he was found "unresponsive" in his home. The Dallas police alleged it was the result of an accidental overdose of pain medication. Owens' publicist said it was an allergic reaction to the medication combined with the dietary supplement Owens was taking. Owens eventually fired his publicist for bringing about so much adverse publicity.

His many on-field hijinks also kept Owens in the headlines. His famous touchdown celebrations included pulling a Sharpie marker out of his sock and autographing the football before handing it to someone in the crowd; running to mid-field in Dallas, as a member of the opposition, and celebrating on the team's giant-sized star; lying down in the end zone and using the football as a pillow; and finally, running to the front-row seats where he grabbed a fan's bag of popcorn and poured it through the facemask of his helmet.

"A lot of people think I'm stuck up. Pretty much that I'm arrogant," Owens said of his persona. "I only do that when I'm on the field."

He did it well.

Dallas' Owens takes a nap in the Redskins end zone in 2006. Washington won the game, 22–19.

Just Having a Bit of Fun

Chicago quarterback Jim McMahon had a penchant for fun. In 1985, when the Bears dominated the league with a 15–1 record, McMahon got himself into a pair of controversies. First, he mooned a helicopter hovering over the team's practice session. "I was just showing them where it hurt," said McMahon. He then defied the orders of Commissioner Pete Rozelle by wearing headbands adorned with handwritten messages such as POW–MIA (Prisoners of War–Missing in Action) and Pluto (the name of a friend who was suffering from cancer). "Outrageous is nothing more than a way to wake people up," said McMahon.

Jim McMahon defies commissioner Rozelle's headband orders.

THE MOMENTS

A sure way to wake up NFL fans is to give them a performance they can't possibly forget, and the last 40 years or so have been crammed with remarkable efforts and character games. Some have been so staggering that they evoke instant recall with the mention of only a few words, such as The Drive, The Catch, The Comeback or Hail Mary. Today, you would be hard-pressed to find a football fan who hasn't heard all of these phrases. For example, every football fan knows what a Hail Mary is: the quarterback throws the ball up for grabs, says a prayer, and hopes one of his receivers can make the catch. It's a desperation move. Then again, desperation has been the mother of many a fine invention . . .

The Wrong Call

It seemed such a no-brainer: just keep giving the ball to running back Marshawn Lynch and, as sure as it rains in Seattle, the Seahawks would have scored the go-ahead touchdown and celebrated back-to-back Super Bowls. But none of that happened. Instead, Seahawks' quarterback Russell Wilson threw a pass on second and goal that was intercepted by the New England Patriots' defensive back Malcolm Butler. Final score in Super Bowl XLIX: 28–24 for New England. As for Seattle coach Pete Carroll's explanation as to why a pass play was called: "Really, we just didn't want to run against their goal line [defense] … I told my guys that's my fault totally."

The Weirdest Super Bowl Touchdown … Ever

Maybe it was only fitting that after beating New England in Super Bowl XLII on an amazing one-handed catch by David Tyree, the New York Giants would win their rematch with the Patriots in Super Bowl XLVI on a completely bizarre play.

With a second-and-goal attempt at the Patriots' six-yard line and 63 seconds left in the game, the Giants decided they could force New England to use its last timeout and burn off some valuable seconds if they didn't score too quickly. The Patriots figured the same thing and told their defense to stand down and let New York score a touchdown. That way, the New England offense would get the ball back with time enough to counter.

As Giants' quarterback Eli Manning handed off to running back Ahmad Bradshaw, he yelled, "Don't score. Don't score." Bradshaw, trained to do nothing but score touchdowns, ran through the Patriots' non-existent front only to realize what was going on. When he tried to stop, he turned his back and fell over the goal line like a guy sitting down only to have the chair pulled out from underneath him. The Giants had to sweat out a New England rally before celebrating their second Super Bowl title in five years. As for Bradshaw, he readily admitted, "That was not my finest game ever."

The Hail Mary

The year was 1975 and the Cowboys had to play the Vikings on their frozen tundra in an NFC playoff game. The Cowboys were trailing 14–10, starting at their 15-yard line with less than two minutes remaining in the fourth quarter. Roger Staubach, the Cowboys artful quarterback, got his offensive unit to the 50-yard line with only 24 seconds showing on the clock.

From a shotgun formation, Staubach took the snap, stepped up into the pocket and flung the ball downfield in the direction of receiver Drew Pearson. What happened in the next few seconds was a convergence of fate. Minnesota defensive back Nate Wright tripped over Pearson's leg and fell to the turf. Safety Paul Krause couldn't get over in time to tackle Pearson, who caught the ball on his hip and slipped, untouched, into the end zone for the touchdown.

The Vikings were mortified, then angry.

Steve Watson catches the ball to gain yards in the legendary Bronco drive.

They wanted a pass interference call against Pearson but didn't get it. Spectators littered the field with garbage. One fan flung a bottle that hit field judge Armen Terzian in the head, bonking him for 11 stitches. (The Vikings faithful would later joke that the clink off Terzian's noggin was the real Hail Mary of the day.)

Staubach never saw the touchdown since he had been tackled soon after he released the ball. In the winners' dressing room, he told reporters, "I closed my eyes and said a Hail Mary." A catch-phrase was born.

To this day, Staubach and Pearson are approached by football fans who want to talk about their dramatic completion.

"It's amazing that you find so many Viking fans around the country," Pearson told *The Dallas Morning News*. "Some people bring their ticket stubs from the game for me to autograph. Others tell me, 'I remember exactly where I was when I saw that catch. You ripped my heart out.'"

Dwight Clark cements a 49ers win with one of the most memorable grabs in NFL history.

The Drive

In the 1986 AFC championship game, John Elway's Broncos trailed the hometown Cleveland Browns 20–13 in the fourth quarter with less than six minutes left in the game. Time wasn't the problem, but the Broncos' field position was. They started from their two-yard line with Elway mixing short passes and runs. Faced with third and 18 at the Cleveland 48-yard line, Elway zipped a 20-yard completion to Mark Jackson. Five plays later, Jackson caught the five-yard scoring pass that tied the game and sent it into overtime.

Overall, Elway completed five of eight passes for 73 yards in The Drive. In overtime, he added a 60-yard march that set up Rich Karlis for the 33-yard field goal that won the game and stomped on the souls of Cleveland's fans and players. "I think becoming involved with the Super Bowl quest is a lot like falling in love," said Browns linebacker Clay Matthews. "You dive headfirst and you don't worry about the consequences. It felt so good. But today we broke up."

The Catch

The Catch was San Francisco's joyous version of the Hail Mary. It featured an emerging young star in quarterback Joe Montana, a venerable receiver in Dwight Clark and a 49ers team that was bursting at the seams with greatness in 1982.

With Dallas leading 27–21, Montana directed his offense to the Cowboys' 6-yard line with 58 seconds remaining in regulation time. Rolling to his right, Montana was corralled by three Dallas defenders and, at the last possible second, threw the ball high in the end zone before stepping out of bounds. Clark made a finger-tip grab at the back of the end zone to put San Francisco in front 28–27.

"You just beat America's Team," Dallas defensive end Ed (Too Tall) Jones told Montana.

"Well," answered Montana, "you can watch the Super Bowl on TV with the rest of America."

With 51 seconds left in the same game, Drew Pearson (remember him?) almost scored for the Cowboys on a long pass reception. Unfortunately for the Cowboys, they fumbled two plays later, San Francisco recovered and The Catch was immortalized.

The victory helped the 49ers capture their first Super Bowl title and established them as the NFC's new powerhouse over Dallas. After losing to San Francisco, the Cowboys' fortunes took a turn for the worse. They didn't make it to the Super Bowl even once in the 1980s, which meant they got to watch the game on TV an awful lot.

The Comeback

The Comeback started as the Blow-Out on a cold January afternoon in 1993. The Buffalo Bills were hosting the Houston Oilers after having lost to them the week before. In that game, starting quarterback Jim Kelly suffered strained knee ligaments and was subsequently sidelined for the rematch in the AFC wild-card playoff game.

On top of that, the Bills lost their ace running back Thurman Thomas when he hurt his hip in the first half of their playoff battle with Houston. Left with Frank Reich, their backup quarterback, and Kenneth Davis, their backup running back, the Bills promptly went out and fell behind 28–3 by halftime.

The lead had grown to 35–3 when the Oilers intercepted a Reich pass and returned it for a touchdown in the second half. At that point, a Houston radio announcer said, "The lights are on here at Rich Stadium, but you might as well turn them off … this one is over."

Not so. Buffalo scored on its next possession when Davis ran in from the one-yard line. The Bills recovered the ensuing onside kick and scored again, this time on a 38-yard pass from Reich to Don Beebe. On his next series, Reich tossed a 26-yard touchdown pass to Andre Reed, and Buffalo had sliced Houston's lead to nine points, 35–24. Reich went back to Reed again, connecting on a fourth-and-five completion that covered 18 yards for another touchdown. Then it was Reich to Reed for a third touchdown.

Trailing for the first time, the Oilers fashioned a 63-yard drive capped by Al Del Greco's 26-yard field goal that tied the score at 38–38 forcing overtime. Houston won the toss and went on the attack. On his 50th pass attempt of the game, Oilers quarterback Warren Moon was intercepted. Adding to the damage was a 15-yard penalty against Houston for face-masking, which gave the Bills a first down at the Houston 20-yard line. Steve Christie calmly kicked a 32-yard field goal giving Buffalo the win and the greatest comeback in NFL history. As a tribute, Christie's kicking shoe was enshrined at the Pro Football Hall of Fame in Canton, Ohio.

Other Amazing Comebacks

Perhaps as payback, the Bills took one off the shins in 2007 by being on the other side of an amazing comeback. For much of a Monday night game against Dallas, the Bills had rattled the Cowboys and forced quarterback Tony Romo into throwing five interceptions. The score was 24–16 in favor of Buffalo with 24 seconds left in the game. Romo found Patrick Crayton for a four-yard touchdown pass, but the two-point convert attempt was stopped.

UNFORGETTABLE
SNAPSHOTS

There have been many unforgettable moments in NFL history. Among them:

• Joe Montana's last-minute Super Bowl XXIII winning touchdown pass to receiver John Taylor. Trailing the Cincinnati Bengals 16–13 with 3:10 left in the game, Montana marched the San Francisco offense 92 yards. Taylor's 10-yard catch with 34 seconds left gave the 49ers their third Super Bowl title.

• Tony Dorsett's 99-yard touchdown run for Dallas in a *Monday Night Football* game in 1982. Dorsett took a handoff in his own end zone, ran through the left side of the Cowboys' offensive line, cut right and was off to the races. The best part about Dorsett's record romp? Dallas had only 10 men on the field when it happened.

• Minnesota rookie Adrian Peterson rushing for a record 296 yards in a game in 2007. To underscore just how impressive Peterson was against the San Diego Chargers, he gained the bulk of his yards (253 to be precise) in the second half. His three touchdown runs covered one yard, 64 yards and 46 yards.

• Green Bay receiver Max McGee's relief performance in the first AFL–NFL championship. McGee had stayed out the night before the game because he figured there was no way in the world he was going to play. When an injury to another receiver rushed him into the game, a thoroughly hungover McGee surprised even himself with seven catches for 138 yards and two touchdowns.

• The 1968 "Heidi Bowl" that saw NBC cut away from the New York Jets–Oakland Raider match-up with 50 seconds left, in order to begin the movie *Heidi* at the top of the hour. The Raiders scored two touchdowns in those last 50 seconds to win 43–32. But they were not seen live on TV.

Agony! Kevin Dyson is tackled by Mike Jones one yard shy of the end zone.

The Cowboys successfully recovered an onside kick and appeared to be in excellent position for a game-winning field goal after Terrell Owens caught a 20-yard pass. But the Bills challenged the catch and replays showed that Owens had trapped the ball. That put Dallas back at the Buffalo 47-yard line with 11 seconds to play. Romo completed two passes, setting up rookie kicker Nick Folk for a 53-yard field goal.

Folk's kick was good, but the officials standing in the end zone refused to make a signal. At the last possible second, Buffalo had called a time out in a bid to unnerve Folk. On his second try, the ball sailed straight down the middle. Dallas scored nine points in 20 seconds to win 25–24.

"I haven't been around anything like that," said Dallas head coach Wade Phillips, "and that's 31 years I've been in the league."

Still on the comeback theme, San Francisco pulled a late rabbit out of its helmet in the 2002 NFC wild-card playoff game. The New York Giants were holding a seemingly comfortable 38–14 lead when the second half began at San Francisco's Candlestick Park. But again, things began to change. Jeff Garcia, the 49ers quarterback, opened the third quarter with a 70-yard drive that included a 26-yard touchdown strike to Terrell Owens, who also added the two-point convert. New York 38, San Francisco 22.

Garcia then scored on a 14-yard run and Owens added another two-point convert to make the score New York 38, San Francisco 30, just seconds into the fourth quarter. San Francisco added a field goal and then went ahead, 39–38, with one minute remaining on a Garcia scoring toss to Tai Streets. The Giants attempted a 40-yard field goal for their shot at the win, but blew it with a bad snap.

Monday Night Football put one into the memory bank when the Indianapolis Colts edged the Tampa Bay Buccaneers 38–35 in 2003. Trailing by 21 points at the half, the Colts scored 35 points — including three touchdowns in the final four minutes — to force overtime before winning the game on a 29-yard field goal by Mike Vanderjagt.

The Tennessee Titans could write a book about their come-from-behind sagas and call it *The Ecstasy and the Agony*, a rearrangement of the title of Irving Stone's great novel. The Titans accomplished the Music City Miracle only to end up One Yard Shy of

Glory. First, the Miracle.

With 16 seconds left in their AFC 2000 playoff match-up, the Buffalo Bills kicked a field goal to take a 16–15 lead over the Titans. On the ensuing kickoff, Tennessee's Lorenzo Neal fielded the ball, pitched it to Frank Wychek, who lateraled it to receiver Kevin Dyson, who raced 75 yards for a mind-blowing touchdown. The Bills were incensed and claimed the Wychek lateral was actually a forward pass and illegal. The officials reviewed the play and the ruling stood: touchdown.

That was the ecstasy, especially since the Titans (formerly the Houston Oilers) were able to avenge their loss to Buffalo in The Comeback seven years earlier. And the good times continued for the Titans, who won two more playoff games and earned their ticket to Super Bowl XXXIV against the St. Louis Rams. But that's where the Titans would experience their agony.

Tennessee fell behind 16–0 before someone broke out the smelling salts and revived its offense. By the time the Titans tied the score, there were little more than two minutes left in the game, but the Rams responded with their most explosive outburst of the day, a 73-yard catch and run for a touchdown by Isaac Bruce. When the Titans got the ball back, they had 1:54 to travel 90 yards for the tying touchdown.

Titans' quarterback Steve McNair passed and dashed his way to the St. Louis 10-yard line, where he used his last time out. There were only six seconds showing on the game clock. This was it. McNair completed a short pass to Dyson, who looked as if he had room to score. Instead, Rams linebacker Mike Jones made a textbook tackle stopping Dyson, the Music City Miracle Man, one yard short of the end zone.

"You'd rather get beat by 50 [points] than get beat by inches," McNair said afterward.

The Tour de Force

Kellen Winslow may not have been as flamboyant as some, but he was very much a character player in a 1982 AFC playoff game between his San Diego Chargers and the Miami Dolphins. To this day, some observers rate Winslow's tour de force as the NFL's finest. Here's what Winslow did: He played the game despite suffering a pinched nerve in his shoulder, severe dehydration, cramps and a sliced lip that required three stitches. He caught 13 passes for 166 yards, scored a touchdown and then, with the game on the line, he blocked a Miami field-goal attempt to force overtime.

Then he helped the Chargers win 41–38 before being helped off the field by two of his teammates, an image that was photographed and preserved for eternity.

"I've never felt so close to death before," Winslow said. "That's what Muhammad Ali said in Manila and that's how I felt out there at the end."

The Kick Heard Around the World

Our last look back has to do with the man who first kicked the longest field goal in NFL history. It came, as you might expect, in the final seconds of a close game in 1970, with the home team losing and having but one chance to win. And if having to make a 63-yard field goal from a mucky field wasn't demanding enough, Tom Dempsey had a significant disadvantage to overcome: his right foot, his kicking foot, wasn't really a foot, but a stump. His right hand was also misshapen by a birth defect. Not that Dempsey was troubled by his limitations.

He had cracked the New Orleans Saints roster the year before, in 1969, as their fulltime placekicker and reserve defensive end. Even his nickname, the horribly inappropriate Stumpy, failed to bother Dempsey, who had developed a thick skin to any kind of taunting while playing football in high school and college.

Dempsey had a free-agent tryout with the San Diego Chargers in 1968 and at that time was outfitted with a special boot that was cut-off at the toes, giving his foot a flat edge to drive into the ball. In 1969, his first season with the Saints, he hoofed 22 field goals and scored 99 points. On Nov. 8, 1970, against

Kellen Winslow is helped off the field after an incredible show of heart and determination.

the visiting Detroit Lions, Dempsey had already made three field goals, but his team trailed 17–16 with only seconds remaining. When the New Orleans field-goal team trotted out onto the field for one last kick, several Detroit players started laughing. "We didn't even rush it," Lions tackle Alex Karras said later.

But photographs of the kick show Karras desperately reaching out to block a kick that was perfectly snapped, perfectly held and perfectly propelled 63 yards for a 19–17 New Orleans triumph.

"I thought I kicked it pretty well," Dempsey recalled years later. "I was hoping the winds wouldn't swirl and drive the ball off-course. It seemed like it took forever to get there. I just kept watching it, wondering if it had enough distance. Finally, the referees raised their hands that it was good."

While the kick was good, others around the NFL complained that Dempsey's shoe gave him an unfair advantage. There was even a rumor the boot was reinforced with steel, which allowed him to kick the ball farther than anyone else. There was no steel in that boot, and Tex Schramm of the Dallas Cowboys eventually called Dempsey to apologize for implying that being born without a full foot and hand was an unfair advantage.

"I guess if not having any toes is an unfair advantage, I have an advantage," said Dempsey.

Twenty-eight years later, in 2007, Jason Elam of the Broncos tied the record, kicking his 63-yarder into Denver's thin air. One of the first people to call Elam was Dempsey.

"I wanted to congratulate Jason because when I set the record, Bert Rechichar (who had previously kicked the longest field goal, 56 yards, for the Baltimore Colts), was very gracious to me," Dempsey said of the man he dislodged from the record book. "I told Jason that if someone breaks our record, it would be up to him to do the same thing."

Sebastian Janikowski of the Oakland Raiders and David Akers of the San Francisco 49ers have also been good from 63 yards. But on December 8, 2013, Denver's Matt Prater booted a 64-yard field goal to earn a place atop the greats. And Dempsey would be proud; Elam didn't have Prater's phone number, but the digital age provided him another avenue, a congratulatory Tweet:

"Way to go Matt Prater! Awesome! Way to keep it in the Broncos family! I'm very proud and excited for you!" ▪

THE
BEST
OF THE REST

Troy Aikman
Lance Alworth
Fred Biletnikoff
George Blanda
Mel Blount
Tom Brady
Earl Campbell
Eric Dickerson
Tony Dorsett
Dan Fouts
Darrell Green
Franco Harris
Jack Lambert
Dick Lane
Steve Largent
Ray Lewis
Howie Long
Ronnie Lott
John Mackey
Peyton Manning
Bruce Matthews
Anthony Munoz
Joe Namath
Ray Nitschke
O.J. Simpson
Mike Singletary
Bruce Smith
Bart Starr
Thurman Thomas
Steve Young

8 TROY AIKMAN

QUARTERBACK

BIG IN THE BIG GAMES

Auspicious would hardly be the word to describe Troy Aikman's NFL baptism.

As the Dallas Cowboys surveyed the wreckage of their 1989 season, the prospect of a Hall of Fame career for their rookie field marshal — three Super Bowl rings, half a dozen Pro Bowl appearances and more wins throughout the decade of the '90s than any other quarterback — seemed almost laughable.

Aikman, the boy wonder — their No. 1 pick from the UCLA Bruins, had lost his first 11 games as a starter. The 'Boys flatlined 1–15 that year under a new coach, Jimmy Johnson, who had controversially replaced the legendary and beloved Tom Landry.

The smell of doom hovered over Big D.

"I know how difficult my rookie year in the NFL was," Aikman would say years later, "and I know how competitive the sport is."

But those who wrote off the Cowboys after the horrors of '89 underestimated the ambition of owner Jerry Jones, the savvy of coach Jimmy Johnson and, most foolishly, also underestimated the spirit of Troy Aikman.

In 1990, ignoring the naysayers, Aikman brought the Cowboys back to respectabil-ity and into playoff contention. The next season, despite being injured, he bounced back to start an NFC Divisional postseason game. The Cowboys were beaten 38–6 by the Detroit Lions that day. But the seed of onrushing success had been planted in Irving, Texas.

The golden years of Troy Aikman began in 1992, when the 'Boys won 13 games in the regular season and ran the table come playoff time, brutalizing the Buffalo Bills 52–17 in Super Bowl XXVII in 1993.

The quarterback that the critics had so openly questioned only three years earlier passed for 273 yards and four touchdowns en route to being named the game's Most Valuable Player. No one would ever doubt Aikman again.

Consistency would become his trademark, and he'd retire with a completion percentage of 61.5, the third highest career figure in history at the time, behind only Steve Young and Joe Montana. He may never have put up the same kinds of passing yardage numbers as, say, Dan Marino. But then Marino never had a running back like Emmitt Smith to hand the ball to.

Aikman drops back to pass in 1996; the final of his six Pro Bowl seasons.

For Aikman, running the show, not being the show, was always the priority.

There would be still more Super Bowl glory: in 1994 against the beleaguered Bills again, 30–13, and a 27–17 decision over Pittsburgh in 1996.

By now, Aikman was a star, the toast of Dallas. He exuded a folksy charm. It was impossible not to warm to the man. When asked about being selected as one of *People* magazine's 50 Most Beautiful People, for instance, he was typically self-deprecating: "I thought, 'Well, they don't know that many people.'"

During his final seasons, Aikman absorbed a ferocious physical pounding. In December 2000, while rolling out to throw a pass, Washington linebacker LaVar Arrington drilled the unsuspecting quarterback. That jolt triggered Aikman's 10th concussion, and it would be his final NFL play.

The hit left a dent in his helmet. Its aftermath left a hole in his heart.

Still wanting to play but unable to find a team to take the chance on someone who had given so much, at such great personal cost, Aikman retired the next year.

He left behind him a decade of excellence: 90 wins (the most, to that point, by any QB in a ten-year span), six consecutive Pro Bowl appearances and a place on the Cowboys' Ring of Honor alongside his buddies in the famed Triplets offensive set-up: Emmitt Smith and receiver Michael Irvin.

The once-derided messiah had, in the end, proven a worthy successor to Roger Staubach.

"In my mind," said Jimmy Johnson, "I always judge a quarterback by how he plays in the big games. How does he perform in the playoffs? Troy Aikman always came up big in the big games."

On Feb. 4, 2006, Aikman took his place in the Pro Football Hall of Fame.

Standing at the podium during the induction ceremony, his thoughts must've drifted back to that first season.

"I'd like to share something that a close friend used to tell me back when I was playing," he told the audience. "When times are tough, maybe we'd lost a close game, I'd thrown the deciding interception or the grind and the rigors of the season were beginning to take their toll on me. He would say this: 'Sometimes we have to remind ourselves that these are jobs we've always dreamed of having.'

"For as long as I can remember, all I ever wanted to do was play pro sports. A lot of kids want that, but only a few actually get there. I was able to live a dream. I played pro football." ■

19 LANCE ALWORTH

WIDE RECEIVER

THAT INDEFINABLE QUALITY

"He runs like a deer," blurted one astonished teammate. And so, Lance Alworth became Bambi.

Possessed of a graceful, almost balletic stride, great leaping skills, sure hands and an ability to cover 100 yards in 9.6 seconds, he would leave an indelible mark on the game in only 11 seasons.

Alworth was only 6-feet tall and weighed a scant 184 pounds, but that didn't stand in the way of his partnership with San Diego Chargers quarterback John Hadl, one of the great collaborations of a decade. When the canny Al Davis, then an assistant coach with the Chargers, coaxed Alworth into signing with the AFL club in 1962 rather than the NFL San Francisco 49ers, he knew his franchise had landed more than just a great receiver.

"Lance Alworth," Davis would recall, "was one of the maybe three players in my lifetime who had what I call 'It.' You could see right from the start that he was going to be a superstar."

Smart man, that Al Davis. His prize catch more than justified the hyperbole. He had 'It,' and more.

Fitting perfectly into the west coast, sun-and-surf lifestyle, Alworth flourished. His talents were undeniable, even by those who openly mocked the AFL's overall quality. The slender gazelle from Houston cut across leagues and prejudices.

He was as electrifying as that lightning bolt on the sides of his helmet, and in short order came to symbolize the Chargers franchise. From an All-American halfback at the University of Arkansas to one of the finest receivers of the '60s, he would be one of the few AFL players to be featured on the cover of *Sports Illustrated*. A decade and a half after he exploded onto the scene, he was the first AFL player inducted into the Pro Football Hall of Fame.

He helped San Diego win an AFL title in 1963, hooking up with Hadl on a 48-yard TD pass-and-run to slay the Boston Patriots. He caught at least one pass in 96 consecutive games and still holds the record for most games (five) with 200 or more yards receiving.

Alworth apparently never did like the nickname Bambi. But even he had to admit that Chargers fullback Charlie Flow-

Alworth exhibits why he's called "Bambi" with a spectacular touchdown grab in 1966.

ers caught the essence of his style when he tagged him with the famous moniker. "He looked like a kid of 15," remembered Flowers. "He had real short hair and brown eyes. And he reminded me of a graceful deer when he ran."

Oh, he ran. He ran and ran, superb routes, past opposing secondaries. It seemed as if he never stopped. There was an uninhibited freedom about the way that Alworth flew down a field that caught people's imaginations. Add that to the elegance and the incomparable grace, and his star quality would be difficult to overemphasize.

It'd be difficult to argue that he wasn't the best receiver in all of pro football in 1965. That season he caught 69 passes for 1,602 yards and 14 touchdowns, averaging an astounding 23.2 yards a catch. There was a home run waiting to be hit on every snap of the ball.

In 11 professional seasons, Alworth snared 542 passes for 10,266 yards and 85 touchdowns. More amazing is an 18.94-yard per-catch average, a testament to his dazzling abilities after making the grab.

Bambi finished out the final two seasons of his career in Dallas, and won a championship ring there, catching the first touchdown pass in the Cowboys' 24–3 conquest of the Miami Dolphins in Super Bowl VI. But he only latched onto 49 passes in two seasons in Big D, and wasn't particularly enthralled with the way coach Tom Landry deployed him. He decided to retire, and did so on top.

He left on his terms, with the admiration of his peers and having given more than a decade of keepsake catches to fans of two leagues.

There were, naturally, honors aplenty to come. He would be enshrined in the

Breitbard Hall of Fame at the San Diego Hall of Champions Sports Museum and his No. 19 would be the first number ever retired by the Chargers. To this day, he remains one of the most popular Bolts of all time.

Six years after walking away from the game, Lance Alworth was inducted at Canton, the first player from the renegade league so honored by the football Establishment.

But his heart, his legacy, lay in California, not Ohio.

"This is about as good as it gets," he said about the day of honors bestowed on him in San Diego. "It's a humbling experience. Being inducted into the Hall of Fame was special, but being honored at home means even more."

Lance (Bambi) Alworth: Forever a Charger. ∎

25

FRED
BILETNIKOFF
WIDE RECEIVER

CHEWING GUM, EYE-BLACK AND STICKUM

Before every game, it was the same fastidious ritual: Fred Biletnikoff would examine his football pants and cut every tiny thread hanging from them, probably so they wouldn't slow him down when he was running. He'd cut the back of the pants behind the knees to allow for more flexibility. He'd tie and re-tie the laces on his football cleats before covering them in white tape. He'd tape a crucifix under his shoulder pads and tape his wrists and douse his fingers in Stickum. Then he'd slip on his jersey and his helmet and adjust (and re-adjust) his chinstrap for as long as it took to feel right.

Finally, when he was ready to play, his teammates on the Oakland Raiders would shout, "Hey Freddy, your uniform looks like crap today." And Biletnikoff would take everything off and start all over.

Such was the depth of Biletnikoff's perfectionist nature. Of course, it all paid off on the field, where the sinewy, eye-black-wearing, sticky-fingered receiver ran pass routes so sharp and precise you could have cut a diamond with them.

Biletnikoff was never the fastest receiver in the game, nor the most gifted, but he got the most out of his abilities through tireless effort. For either quarterback Daryle Lamonica or his good buddy Ken Stabler, Biletnikoff was the Raiders go-to receiver.

In his career, he tied Raymond Berry of the Baltimore Colts by catching 40 or more passes in 10 consecutive seasons. Most of Biletnikoff's numbers were fashioned in the shorter, 14-game regular seasons, at a time when cornerbacks didn't have to stop bumping the receiver five yards downfield. He also added 70 catches for 1,167 yards and 10 touchdowns in 19 playoff games. Although he had a meager four receptions for 79 yards in Super Bowl XI, three of his grabs led to Oakland scores and the 32–14 win.

After receiving the game's MVP award, a humbled Biletnikoff quipped, "A stick of gum would have been enough."

To suggest Biletnikoff was quirky, both in how he dressed and how he played, is to say Oakland owner Al Davis used just a little dab of Brylcreem in his hair. Biletnikoff was as unusual as Davis' hair was greasy. No other receiver in the NFL used as much Stickum as Biletnikoff. Eventually, the NFL banned the substance, saying it provided

Biletnikoff runs the ball on his way to MVP honors in Super Bowl XI.

an unfair advantage — not that Biletnikoff needed one, considering how good he was at catching a football.

Along with Stickum, Biletnikoff was addicted to cigarettes. The word was that he smoked heavily while playing for the Raiders and that his socializing, usually with Stabler, was off the charts.

"We lived together for like four years, which really wasn't a great idea," Biletnikoff joked of his friendship with Stabler. "I had a little bar called The Flanker so that's where we were able to eat and go drink and nobody had to pay the tab."

Biletnikoff, whose nicknames were Coyote and Dr. Zhivago due to his Russian heritage, was born into an athletic family. His dad was a regional Golden Glove boxing champion. His younger brother was a quarterback at the University of Miami who left

to sign with baseball's New York Yankees.

In his collegiate days at Florida State, Biletnikoff became his school's first consensus All-American in 1964. That same season, FSU defeated Oklahoma in the Gator Bowl on the strength of Biletnikoff's 13 catches, 192 yards and 4 touchdowns.

Both the AFL and the NFL drafted Biletnikoff, who chose the Raiders and stayed long enough to be named to six Pro Bowls. He spent one year in the CFL with the Montreal Alouettes, and then retired in 1980. Two years later, he began a coaching career that took him from high school to small colleges to the USFL, CFL and back to the Raiders, where he coached their receivers until 2007.

While working for the Raiders, Biletnikoff and his wife Angela suffered a staggering loss. In 1999, their 20-year-old daughter

Tracey was murdered by a man she had met while the two were undergoing drug rehabilitation. The man's arrest created a maelstrom of anger since he was on probation for kidnapping an ex-girlfriend. He was sentenced to 64 years to life in prison for first-degree murder.

Biletnikoff didn't attend the sentencing but a statement was read on his behalf. "You created a hole in my heart and all of Tracey's family's hearts," his daughter's killer heard. "That can never ever be repaired."

The Biletnikoffs established a non-profit foundation for their daughter "dedicated to support young women recovering from substance abuse, and education for the prevention of domestic violence." It's proving to be a new cause for an old perfectionist. ■

16 GEORGE BLANDA

QUARTERBACK/PLACEKICKER

PUNT, PASS AND KICK

Back in 1970, when people were singing "Bridge Over Troubled Waters," watching *Love Story* at the movies and *The Flip Wilson Show* on television, they couldn't help but notice this old guy who kept doing the most amazing things time after time, week after week, for more than a month.

Apparently, the guy was so old that he was born before the Great Depression, in the same year as Charles Lindbergh's historic solo flight across the Atlantic Ocean in 1927.

But for five weekends in the fall of 1970, 43-year-old George "The Fossil" Blanda was cooler than string art, eight-track players, pet rocks and Led Zeppelin. Well, maybe not *that* cool, but certainly close to it.

He didn't just blow the NFL's mind with his last-minute comebacks as the quarterback/placekicker for the Oakland Raiders — he struck a blow for mid-lifers everywhere. He defied his younger opponents. Scoffed at Father Time. Made people believe in the power of positive thinking.

"Can you imagine even playing at 43, never mind doing what he did in the 1970 season?" Oakland teammate George

Atkinson said of Blanda's heroics.

Blanda was rushed off the bench to replace starting quarterback Daryle Lamonica against the Pittsburgh Steelers and responded by throwing two touchdown passes and kicking a field goal in a 31–14 win. The next week, he nailed a 48-yard field goal with three seconds left in the game to break a 17–17 tie with the Kansas City Chiefs and steal the game. The weekend after, against the Cleveland Browns, Blanda again came off the bench and threw a late touchdown pass that deadlocked the score at 20–20. As time ran out, he hoofed a 53-yard field goal to win the game.

Of his winning boot, Blanda said, "I put a little more rear end into the kick than usual."

And he wasn't done.

A week after beating the Browns, Blanda did in the Denver Broncos. Again, he came off the bench, and again he threw a touchdown pass with less than two-and-a-half minutes left in the fourth quarter, this time for a 24–19 decision. The week after that, he kicked a 16-yard field goal in the dying seconds to clip the San Diego Chargers, 20–17.

Blanda looks to throw against the Jets in 1965; he completed a season-high 186 passes.

No one else rocked the NFL's cosmos the way Blanda did that season or since.

The son of a Pennsylvania coal miner, Blanda had a storied football career long before he got to Oakland. After his senior year at Kentucky University, he was signed by George Halas, the crusty owner of the Chicago Bears. The year was 1949 and Blanda received a contract for $6,000 plus a $600 signing bonus. He didn't get a raise for four years.

Used mostly as a kicker by the Bears, Blanda eventually got bored and retired after the 1958 season. He worked as a sales manager with a trucking company, a job he held during 22 of his record 26 seasons in professional football.

When the AFL was formed in 1960, the 33-year-old Blanda dusted himself off and joined the Houston Oilers as a quarterback and kicker. He led the team to the league's first two championships and was named the AFL's Player of the Year in 1961. That season he threw 36 touchdown passes, the most ever in a single season. The record stood until Dan Marino of the Miami Dolphins shattered it in 1984.

Having led the Oilers in passing and scoring for seven seasons, Blanda was thought to be spent, and thus he was traded to Oakland, where he kicked and served as a backup quarterback.

And then in 1970, George got his groove back. Every time the Raiders trotted him out, he moved the ball. Every time people cringed because the old guy was going into the game, he completed a pass or kicked a field goal and his team would win. His teammates were in awe of him.

"George was never gentle," said Raiders linebacker Phil Villapiano.

"There were three people on the Raiders whom you were scared of because you knew if you made a mistake they were really going to get on you —[head coach John] Madden, [center] Jim Otto and George Blanda."

At the end of the 1970 season, after Oakland lost to the eventual Super Bowl champions, the Baltimore Colts, Blanda was presented with the Bert Bell Award as Player of the Year. It was followed by a funny line from Chiefs owner Lamar Hunt, who said: "Why, this George Blanda is as good as his father, who used to play for Houston."

His second retirement, in 1975, was permanent. The NFL record book lists him as the first player to score more than 2,000 points and the first to score more than 500 points for three teams. He was inducted into the Pro Football Hall of Fame in 1981.

He was 54 then, and probably had another season or two left in him. ∎

47

MEL
BLOUNT

DEFENSIVE BACK

THE BUMP AND RUN

Mel Blount had a rule when he played: no free passes. Every receiver he covered had to earn his yards, even when he was running his routes, even if the football hadn't been thrown, especially if the ball hadn't been thrown.

To protect his ground, Blount would "bump" receivers. Bump them like a Central Park mugger. One smack from the 6-foot-3, 205-pound Blount and some pass catchers stopped dead in their tracks. Others went down like a sack of wet towels.

Naturally, the receivers complained, and the NFL put in a rule (the bump-and-run rule), which restricted how far downfield a cornerback could molest a receiver. Offenses were delighted. The Mel Blount rule had saved them from the man who was single-handedly (sometimes two-handedly) rerouting their passing game.

That's how domineering Blount was when he played for the Pittsburgh Steelers. In 1972, his third season in black and gold, Blount played his position to perfection. He intercepted three passes, recovered two fumbles, returned one for a touchdown, and did not give up a single touchdown pass in 14 games.

"When you could nail receivers all over the field before the ball was thrown, pass defenses had a big edge," said former Pro Bowl cornerback Rod Perry, now an NCAA assistant coach. "Mel Blount in Pittsburgh was 6-foot-3, and he just planted and killed guys all over the field on the way to the Hall of Fame."

Blount's role in the fabled Steel Curtain defense cannot be understated. If a ball carrier could slip past Mean Joe Greene on the Pittsburgh defense, and then avoid linebacker Jack Lambert, he was bound to run into Blount, who played the running game the same way he covered receivers — with an edge.

In 1975, Blount intercepted a league-leading 11 passes and was named the NFL's Defensive Player of the Year. It was one of many accolades he would receive over his career.

Hundreds of NFL players have come from humble beginnings. Blount came from a place that made humble beginnings look like the Hamptons. He grew up on a farm in Georgia, the youngest of 11 children. The house had no plumbing or electricity. His first job was stacking tobacco on a wagon in the early morning hours, before going to school.

Blount learned to take pride in the hard work and his father's praise. On Sundays, the Blount boys and friends went to church and then played football. In high school, Blount starred in football, basketball, baseball and track and earned a football scholarship at Southern University at Baton Rouge, Louisiana.

Earning Southwestern Athletic Conference all-star status, Blount was chosen by the Steelers in the third round of the 1970 draft (quarterback Terry Bradshaw was taken in the first). Soon after he arrived in Pittsburgh, Blount settled in at right corner and stayed there for 14 seasons, helping the Steelers win four Super Bowls. His biggest championship moment came in Super Bowl XIII in 1979 when his steal of a Roger Staubach pass led to a key Pittsburgh touchdown in its 35–31 win.

Blount's uncanny athleticism is illustrated in the following 1982 story: When the 31-year-old veteran came across a group of scouts at Three Rivers Stadium recording the vertical jumps of a prized prospect, Renaldo Nehemiah, who happened to be the world-record holder in the 110-meter hurdles. There was a mark on a wall. Blount saw it and was told that it represented how high Nehemiah had leaped. Dressed in street clothes, Blount jumped higher and said, "That's the Steelers' mark."

There's also the story of Blount's moral conviction, when, in 1977, he sued his own coach, Pittsburgh's Chuck Noll. It happened after Noll had accused Oakland Raiders defensive back George Atkinson of being part of the NFL's "criminal element" for using a forearm hit to knock out Steelers receiver Lynn Swan. Atkinson sued and Noll testified that the criminal element included Blount.

Blount's response was to file a $5 million defamation suit against his coach. It was dropped when Blount ended a 56-day

Blount on the sideline in 1980 intently watching his teammates perform.

contract holdout (the Atkinson suit was dismissed). The coach and his cornerback patched up their differences.

"It was never anything personal," Blount told the *Pittsburgh Post-Gazette*. "I showed my character by being the type of player I was after I came back. Chuck showed his character by never holding it against me."

Blount's football accolades came in droves. He was named to the Pro Bowl five times and was MVP of the game in 1976. He was voted to the NFL's 1980s All-Decade Team, the league's 75th Anniversary Team, and was inducted into the Pro Football Hall of Fame in 1989.

Since retirement, he has immersed himself in charity work and horse breeding and competition. In December 2004, he finished third in the National Cutting Horse Association World Championship in Fort Worth, Texas.

No doubt, he treats his horses better than he ever treated the opposition's receivers. ■

12 Tom BRADY

QUARTERBACK

NOT YET DEFLATED

Not exonerated and not proven guilty, Tom Brady exists in football's moral purgatory.

"Deflategate"—as the underinflated ball scandal that followed New England's AFC Championship romp over the Indianapolis Colts was cheekily called — has put the less glamorous side of competitive zeal at the forefront of the national football conversation. And whether or not Brady "was at least generally aware of the inappropriate activities," as the Ted Wells investigation reports, the Patriots gunslinger won't let his detractors take him down.

Pick an accomplishment, almost any quarterback accomplishment, and sooner or later Tom Brady is bound to come up.

Most Super Bowl records set, tied or extended: Nine, by Tom Brady, who went over the top in Super Bowl XLIX with 37 completions and four touchdown passes. Only team to post a 16–0 regular season record: The 2007 New England Patriots *led by* Tom Brady. Most regular season wins, playoff wins and Super Bowl appearances by a head coach–quarterback duo: Bill Belichick *with* Tom Brady.

That's how it is when you're a four-time Super Bowl champion and a three-time Super Bowl MVP. Success breeds success breeds supersized success, and Brady has stretched his prominence to marquee status. He was a cover boy for GQ's 50th anniversary issue, featured in the company of such cultural icons as Muhammad Ali, Johnny Depp and Sean Connery.

The tall, cool Brady has been profiled on *60 Minutes*, lampooned on *The Simpsons* and *Family Guy* and has hosted *Saturday Night Live* as well. His wife is Brazilian supermodel Gisele Bundchen. In this new age of celebrity, he defines what it is to be a star. With his charming persona and model looks, Brady is in a class all his own.

But peel back that layer of fame for a moment and understand it's more about substance than style. Tom Brady is the finest quarterback of his time — deflated balls or not. And when all is said and done, he might arguably be the finest of all time.

"A lot of time I find that people who are blessed with the most talent don't ever develop that attitude," he said of his inner drive. "And the ones who aren't blessed in that way are the most competitive and

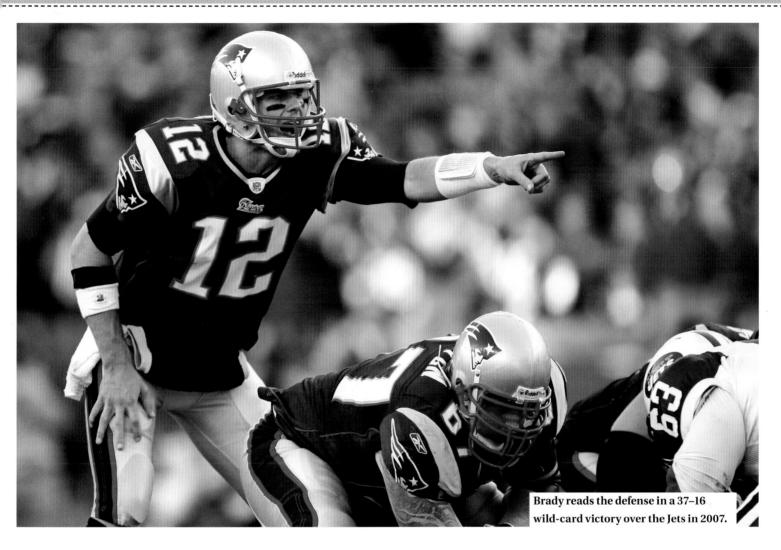

Brady reads the defense in a 37–16 wild-card victory over the Jets in 2007.

have the biggest heart."

Belying his upper-middle-class upbringing in San Mateo, California, Brady developed an almost obsessive desire to succeed, to push for more, early on. "I had the worst temper when I was little," he once said. "I could never stand to lose in anything. I kicked through glass windows and threw video game controllers at the TV and broke more tennis rackets than I could count. It got to where nobody ever wanted to play with me."

Now it's gotten to where nobody would want to play against him. There isn't a coach in the NFL who wouldn't want Brady at the controls with the game on the line, a player who wouldn't want to line up beside him, a fan who wouldn't want to be just like him.

From unheralded NFL beginnings — he was the 199th overall pick in the 2000 draft — to a fortuitous blending of the right tal-

ent, the right coach (Belichick) and the right team, the result is the closest thing to a current-day dynasty.

More than anything else, it's Brady's efficiency that has impressed those of stature within the game. For no small reason did the late Bill Walsh say Brady was as close to a Joe Montana clone as anybody he'd seen.

"I look at the demeanor of a quarterback, and there is such a calm and a confidence about him," marveled Pro Football Hall of Famer Warren Moon. "It's the look of a guy who knows he is prepared."

When he led the Pats to that first Super Bowl in 2001, a huge upset of the favored St. Louis Rams, the question on the lips of all but the most diehard football fan was: Who on earth is this Tom Brady? Only a few years and a couple of Super Bowl wins later, you'd have been hard-pressed to find

anyone in North America who didn't know his name or recognize his face.

Ironically, Brady's finest individual year, 2007 — highlighted by 50 touchdown passes and the Patriots' unbeaten run — ended in defeat in one of the biggest upsets in Super Bowl history. Eli Manning and the upstart New York Giants engineered a Brady-like comeback to win Super Bowl XLII. The same result happened in the rematch four years later. Word was out: Brady was past his prime.

But in Super Bowl XLIX, Brady was dominant. The difference? His defense made the late-game stop they had twice previously failed to make. The goal-line interception by Malcolm Butler ended the Seattle Seahawks chances and returned the Patriots to the top of the NFL. And Tom Brady? He still has a few more cover shoots left in him. ∎

34 EARL CAMPBELL

RUNNING BACK

IN A CLASS BY HIMSELF

Only four men have ever been named an Official State Hero of Texas: Davy Crockett, Stephen F. Austin and Sam Houston, for obvious political and historical reasons. The fourth is a football player, and not just any football player.

Earl Campbell was a star even in high school when he led John Tyler High to the Texas 4A state championship. He was a bigger star at the University of Texas, where he was nicknamed the Tyler Rose and led the NCAA in rushing, en route to winning the Heisman Trophy as the best player in collegiate football. Then he signed with the NFL's Houston Oilers and became an even bigger star. As Oilers coach Bum Phillips liked to say of his 232-pound battering ram, "He may not be in a class by himself, but whatever class he's in, it doesn't take long to call roll."

Squat and muscular, with legs that belonged to a Clydesdale, Campbell was a tough load to topple. His approach to running was straight on, straight ahead. He liked to run into tacklers instead of avoiding them. That was his trademark. That and the fact it usually took two or three men to stop him.

"I always thought if I let one or two guys tackle me, I wasn't doing something right," he said of his wrecking-ball style. "I mean, I didn't think I was part of a game unless I had the ball in my hands 20 or 30 times. I had to get lathered up, you know? And right when the game was over was when I felt like really gettin' it on. Not that I didn't get it on in the middle. But I always thought if there was a fifth quarter, I could really show 'em something, you know?" Campbell showed plenty when he first got to the NFL. In 1978, in a *Monday Night Football* game against the Miami Dolphins, he carried his team to a 35–30 victory by gaining 199 yards and scoring four touchdowns. He was named the league's Rookie of the Year and its Most Valuable Player after rushing for 1,450 yards.

He was again hailed as the NFL's MVP in 1979 and 1980, which proved to be the high-water mark of his career. In that 1980 season, Campbell rolled to four 200-yard rushing games and finished with 1,934, second only at the time to O.J. Simpson's 2,003 yards, which was set in 1973. By the time Campbell said farewell to football in the summer of 1986, he had totaled 9,407 yards and 74 touchdowns in eight seasons and appeared in five Pro Bowls.

In 1991, he was inducted into the Pro Football Hall of Fame, where fans and former players alike regaled others with stories of how Campbell would purposely look for the largest collection of defenders, then charge headlong into them. Campbell's success had NFL coaches searching for bigger, bolder runners or, as *Sports Illustrated* once described them, "beefy, big-butted backs who could both bowl over and blow past the opposition." Consider the likes of Jerome Bettis, Eddie George, Jamal Anderson and Craig (Ironhead) Heyward as those whose styles were allowed to rumble down a path blazed by Campbell.

"One time," said former Dallas Cowboys' running back Tony Dorsett, "I asked Earl, 'Why don't you let one man bring you down sometimes?' He said, 'I got to get them. They're talking that noise.'"

Soon after he retired, Campbell insisted all the pounding had been worth it. Born the 6th of 11 children to a working-class family, one of his early wishes as a pro football player was to earn enough money to buy his mother Ann a new house, which he did. Sadly, though, all those on-field collisions and noisemakers wreaked havoc on Campbell, not so initially, but later on in life.

Now in his late 60s, Campbell has trouble walking. Sometimes the pain is so bad he has to get around in a wheelchair. He recently underwent back surgery to remove the bone spurs from his spinal column that had prevented him from sleeping in a bed. Instead, he would sleep in a recliner to ease the discomfort. "Earl was the biggest, baddest player in the game," said Dorsett. "But no matter how big or strong you are, the game ultimately wins."

If you ever want to get a sense of what Campbell was like as a young, powerful football player, go to the southwest entrance of Darrell K. Royal-Texas Memorial

Campbell on the sideline in his career year, 1980: 1,934 yds, 13 TDs.

Stadium in Austin and look for the statue of Campbell, wearing his Longhorns jersey No. 20. The statue is made of bronze and stands 9-feet tall. Ask a lot of those 175-pound NFL defensive backs Campbell plowed through, and they'll probably tell you his statue would be easier to bring down. ■

28 ERIC DICKERSON

RUNNING BACK

THE STRAIGHT UP GOODS

Long before he totaled an astonishing 2,105 yards in a single season, before his 13,259 career yards earned him a place in the Pro Football Hall of Fame, NFL general managers and coaches looked at Eric Demetric Dickerson and wondered, "How can he run like that? He's so rigid, so straight up and down he looks like an exclamation mark. One big hit and he'll be carried off the field on two stretchers."

Dickerson's style was nothing like Jim Brown's or Earl Campbell's, which is to say he wasn't bent at the waist just waiting to lower his shoulder into an oncoming tackler. Instead, Dickerson had the perfect posture of a butler. He carried his head high, as if he were looking over downtown traffic for an empty cab.

But what seemed dangerous for Dickerson turned out to be more so for the guys trying to cut him in half. Dickerson was 6-foot-3, 220 pounds, as fast as any receiver, and could move, this way or that, in the blink of an eye.

"I believe if I stay tall and run high, I can see better," Dickerson explained. And when Dickerson saw people coming to-wards him, he could do his thing and give them the slip. "I don't give players a chance to hit me," he added.

Dickerson's NFL career began in the September of 1983, and to the delight of his we-told-you-so critics, the big exclamation mark fumbled six times in his first three games with the Rams. One fumble led to a game-winning field goal by the opposition. In his fourth game, he snapped off an 85-yard touchdown run and got himself on track. At season's end, he had rushed for 1,808 yards and 18 touchdowns and was named the league's top rookie.

What would he do in his sophomore season? Even more, it turned out.

Enabled by the Rams' superior run-blocking techniques, Dickerson went wild. He ran for more than 100 yards in 11 games breaking the previous record of 10 set by O.J. Simpson in 1973. He set his sights on Simpson's single-season record of 2,003 yards and, as he got closer, Dickerson obsessed about his pursuit and often dreamed he would finish short of his goal.

He need not have worried. He bettered Simpson's record by 102 yards. To be com-

The well-protected Dickerson hurdles a 49er on his way to a substantial gain.

pletely fair and accurate, Dickerson did it in 16 games while Simpson played in 14.

There is no doubting Dickerson was a bona fide star, a virtuoso. But in his five years with the Rams and a second five seasons with the Indianapolis Colts, Dickerson was often described as disgruntled. He got into several contract disputes. Sometimes he held out and was suspended. Sometimes he got what he wanted. Through it all, he earned a reputation for being "arrogant, inconsiderate, greedy, self-centered, a malcontent," he said. "I could go on and on."

With the Rams, Dickerson uttered a quote that finished him in L.A. Knowing head coach John Robinson's salary was slightly less than his own, Dickerson remarked, "Let him run 47 Gap," the Rams' bread-and-butter play. Less than two weeks later, Dickerson was traded to Indianapolis in a three-way deal that included

the Buffalo Bills. And for a time, things were good in Indianapolis.

Eventually, he said the game had lost its appeal for him and that he was going to retire. Then he asked for more money and began chastising the Colts in a bid to be traded. The Colts signed him to a four-year, $10.65 million deal. And again, for a time, things were good. In 1991, he missed three games for supposedly refusing to practice. He asked to be traded. The Colts happily obliged and shipped him to the Los Angeles Raiders.

One year later, he was traded to the Atlanta Falcons, where he was traded to the Green Bay Packers and retired after failing a physical.

"Some of the things I've done, I've been wrong in doing," he admitted. "I've been hasty. You lose your cool and say things you don't really mean. I think mine was

out of frustration. It's not fun losing a lot of games."

Along with his aptitude and attitude, Dickerson amused his teammates by donning every piece of protective gear he could find. He wore elbow pads, sometimes gloves, a neck collar and even goggles. There were jokes he would have strapped old tires to himself, the way they do on tugboats, if he could have gotten away with it.

No matter. Dickerson proved he could run his way and no one could slow him for long. At retirement, he owned the record for needing only 91 games to surpass 10,000 yards in his career. He picked up a telling compliment along the way, too.

"If you were blind," Robinson, his former coach, said, "he could run right by you, and you wouldn't know it unless you felt the wind. He's the smoothest runner I've ever seen." ▪

33 TONY DORSETT

RUNNING BACK

THE LITTLE BIG MAN

When Tony Dorsett was young, he dreaded the night and going to sleep. Sleeping meant dreaming, and dreaming meant going to the dark places he wanted to avoid. The worst ones were about living inside the soulless, soot-covered confines of a Pittsburgh steel mill, the kind his father endured for 30 years so he could support a wife and seven children.

Wes Dorsett was a hard-working man. Sometimes he came home so dirty his family couldn't recognize him. Always, he told his children they should concentrate on getting an education and finding a job they loved. Tony Dorsett took those words to heart. He would become a football player. Somehow, he would go to university, get his degree, then play professionally. It would be his ticket out.

From star running back to superstar running back, from college hero to NFL All-Pro, Tony Dorsett made good on his promise. He won an NCAA national championship at the University of Pittsburgh one season (1976), then a Super Bowl with the Dallas Cowboys the next. He was a Heisman Trophy-winning standout, a sought-after first-round draft pick, and the NFL's Rookie of the Year, with just over 1,000 yards rushing and 12 touchdowns. He exceeded everyone's expectations, even his own.

"Coming out of college, everyone said I would be too small to play professional football at 188 pounds," Dorsett recalled. "To be honest with you, I figured maybe I would play four or five years [in the NFL] and that would be it. I never dreamed I would play 12 seasons."

In those dozen seasons, Dorsett ran for 12,739 yards and 77 touchdowns and gave tacklers third-degree burns with his searing speed. His 99-yard scoring run against the Minnesota Vikings on January 3, 1983, is an NFL staple. He became the league's first player to surpass the 1,000-yard mark in each of his first five seasons. In 1981, he rambled for 1,646 yards, narrowly missing out on the NFL rushing title — all remarkable feats considering how things could have turned out.

Having convinced himself that football was the key to his future, Dorsett almost quit after agreeing to attend Pittsburgh. He was shy and lonely, and the school's preseason

Dorsett runs in 1983; the third consecutive year he was both a Pro-Bowler and an All-Pro.

practices were taking their toll. At one point, Dorsett called his mother, Myrtle, and talked about coming home. His mom told him to stay strong; that things would get better. Things would work out. They did.

As a 155-pound freshman, Dorsett led the NCAA in rushing with 1,586 yards and carried Pittsburgh to the 1973 Fiesta Bowl. He added 30 pounds of muscle and two more 1,000-yard seasons before his senior year, which began with a 181-yard performance in an easy win over Notre Dame.

When his college days ended, Dorsett had become the first player to rush for more than 6,000 yards in four seasons. The NFL beckoned, and that's when things once again worked in Dorsett's favor, as if fate had taken a liking to the young man with the big dreams.

Tex Schramm played the pivotal role this time. The Dallas general manager wanted Dorsett's speed and pass-catching skills in

the Cowboys' multiple-formation offense. Unfortunately for Dallas, the Seattle Seahawks had the second pick overall in the 1977 draft and were keen to select the Pittsburgh prize. So Schramm made a deal. He packaged the Cowboys' first-round pick with three second-round choices and exchanged them for Seattle's No. 2 pick, which Schramm used to take Dorsett.

Had he gone to Seattle, would Dorsett have been as prominent a player in the NFL? Not likely. The Seahawks had just completed their debut season and were very much a work in progress. Dorsett would have played behind so-so blockers in an offense that had quarterback Jim Zorn, receiver Steve Largent and little else.

Dallas was the right fit for Dorsett and Dorsett was right for Dallas. Granted, the Cowboys could have given him the ball more, but how they used Dorsett proved to be as effective as how often they used him.

"If I wanted to risk Tony, I think he could gain as many yards as [Walter] Payton and [Earl] Campbell," Dallas coach Tom Landry once explained. "But Tony is much different from Earl, who is so big. Payton is probably the strongest little man I've ever seen. Then there is Wilbert Montgomery, who did get used a lot and got hurt. I don't want that to happen to Tony."

Eventually, the injuries came and Dorsett had to retire. At his induction to the Pro Football Hall of Fame in 1994 he talked of his father and the desires forged by a working man's life.

"He taught me an awful lot about common sense, about street sense," said Dorsett. "He never forced me to do anything. He always told me, 'Son, if you're going to accomplish anything in life, do it yourself.'"

Tony Dorsett did, and he rarely had trouble sleeping again. ■

14 DAN FOUTS

QUARTERBACK

JUST THROW IT

With the San Diego Chargers of the Don "Air" Coryell years, when footballs filled the air in Jack Murphy Stadium like golf balls whizzing over a crowded driving range, one man, and one man only, was in charge. His word was sacrosanct. So was the way he threw the ball — at any time, under any circumstance, on any down.

"It was a real joy to be able to operate in that system," said Fouts years later. "I've been out of the game a long time now, but it's nice when people come up to you and say they really enjoyed the way we played the game in those years."

Daniel Francis Fouts was seemingly born to play pro. His father, Bob, called the San Francisco 49ers' games for years. Young Dan worked as a ball boy for the Bay Area team.

Fouts and the Chargers proved to be a fortuitous combination—a happy collaboration of man and moment. Selected in the third round, 84th overall, out of Oregon, he at first struggled to find his identity.

The hiring of Coryell as head coach in 1978 changed all that. Future 49ers legend Bill Walsh (an assistant with the Chargers in 1976) and Washington Redskins' architect Joe Gibbs (San Diego's offensive coordinator for 1979–80) certainly can be credited with having a hand in the nurturing of Fouts, but Coryell's master plan, and his reading of the innate qualities of his strapping young field general, were inspired and decisive.

The Chargers surrounded their strong-armed, strong-willed quarterback with a huge force field of an offensive line and a cast of exceptional pass-catching talents from the likes of Charlie Joiner and All-Pro tight end Kellen Winslow, to John Jefferson and Wes Chandler.

The results were electrifying: In 1980 and 1981, Fouts, nicknamed the Bearded Bomber, registered unheard of numbers. He threw for a combined 9,517 yards (including a then-league record 4,802 in '81) and 66 touchdowns. In the pocket, he was absolutely fearless, and ruthlessly single-minded. He simply could not be rattled. Throw an interception? He could've cared less. He knew where his strength lay. He'd be up gunning on the next series.

"He's like E.F. Fouts," Winslow said in

Fouts looks to pass in 1981; he led the NFL in every major passing category that year.

reference to the E.F. Hutton television commercials of the day. "When he talks, people listen."

As his offensive line aged and crumbled in the twilight of his career, Fouts absorbed a tremendous amount of physical punishment. His toughness was legendary.

In fact, for years in the Chargers' offices, a particular photo of Fouts held prominence. His nose, broken by a Ted Hendricks forearm, stuck out at an awkward angle, a swatch of tape holding it together. Blood spattered on the front of his white jersey. His left shoulder, dislocated by another hit, hung limply under center, forcing him to take the snap with only his right arm.

"Darn fool, that guy," muttered Fouts, when reminded of the photo.

He remained a Charger his entire career, from 1973 through 1987. Perhaps his, and the team's, greatest moment came in the 1982 AFC Divisional playoff game against the Dolphins, Jan. 2, at the Orange Bowl. *Sports Illustrated* called it "The Game No One Should Have Lost," a wild 41–38 overtime San Diego victory.

Fouts finished the afternoon that stretched into evening with 33 completions on 53 attempts for 433 yards and three touchdowns, all NFL postseason records at the time. He led the Chargers on a 74-yard drive to set up the decisive 29-yard Rolf Benirschke field goal.

But the euphoria was to be short-lived.

An Associated Press photo from San Diego's subsequent 27–7 loss to the Bengals at Riverfront Stadium — the steam of Fouts' breath in the arctic chill all but obscuring his head — remains a heart-wrenching symbol of lost opportunity to frustrated Bolts' fans of the era.

So the Fouts years never produced what many had expected — a Super Bowl triumph. An over-reliance on the pass and a middling defense are generally accused of being co-conspirators in the failure.

But neither Dan Marino nor Fran Tarkenton won a Super Bowl, which puts Fouts in pretty fine company. What he did, superlatively, was entertain a generation, set off fireworks for a decade, and leave a lasting image of a commanding presence hanging in the pocket, oblivious to the chaos around him, scanning downfield.

He exited the game as a three-time All-Pro with six Pro Bowl appearances, and as only the third man to throw for over 40,000 yards. His famous No. 14 is one of only three numbers that have been retired by the Chargers.

The only thing missing? A ring.

"I'm over it," Fouts said the day he was enshrined among the game's immortals in Canton. "You strive to win a Super Bowl and you do everything you can to get there.

"But being in the Hall of Fame, you never play for that honor. It's incredible." ■

28

DARRELL
GREEN

CORNERBACK

SPEED, SPEED AND MORE SPEED

Watching the play over and over, it's as if everyone else on the field is running in slow motion, except for Washington's Darrell Green. He is moving in an effortless, purposeful way. A shark drawn to its prey. Tony Dorsett, the prime running back for the Dallas Cowboys is in the midst of a 77-yard gain with only six yards to go for a touchdown.

No one has ever caught Dorsett from behind when he is out in front, headed for the end zone.

Most fans watching know little about Green, who is starting the game as a rookie cornerback, only because veteran Jeris White has yet to sign a contract.

But there's Green, running past two of his teammates and tackling Dorsett from behind to prevent a Dallas touchdown.

It was a "Did-you-see-that?" moment, replayed throughout the NFL in the fall of 1983 and for years beyond. Darrell Green had arrived, and Jeris White's career with the Washington Redskins was over.

For 20 years, no one played cornerback like the mercurial Green. How could they? The man was a speeding bullet. He stood only 5-foot-9 and weighed 184 pounds,

but every receiver who thought they could out-muscle, out-jump and out-run Green thought wrong. No one could out-run Green.

Once, he clocked a 40-yard dash in 4.125 seconds. In 1986, he unofficially covered 40 yards in 4.09 seconds. Four times, he won the NFL's fastest man competition. When he attended Washington's training camp in 2000, he was still the fastest player on the team — at age 40.

Green was so adept at covering and tackling, that opposition quarterbacks would avoid his side of the field and throw elsewhere. Still, he finished his career with 54 interceptions for 621 yards, six touchdowns and seven Pro Bowl selections, earning enduring accolades.

It didn't start out that way.

Green was laughed at in Grade 11 when he first tried out for his high school football team. He attended Texas A&I University (now Texas A&M-Kingsville) and was invited to try out for the NFL's scouting combine as it prepared for the 1983 draft.

"Going to the combine in my Texas A&I jersey, they didn't know me from a chicken.

Green helps lead Washington to a playoff win against Atlanta on Jan. 4, 1992.

They didn't even know our school," said Green. "[Redskins' general manager] Bobby Beathard said, 'If you're there, we're going to draft you.' In the back of my mind, I was, 'Yeah, okay. Thanks.'"

The Redskins did draft Green, in the first round, which mystified and angered some of their fans. Who was this guy, anyway? After his celebrated tackle on Dorsett, everyone took notice and Green's career was off and running.

Another of his highlights came in a 1987 NFC playoff game in Chicago against the Bears. On fourth down from deep in their own territory, the Bears punted to Green, who was an occasional punt return specialist, and a good one at that. Catching the ball at his 48-yard line, Green headed down the sideline, hurdled over a Chicago tackler and made a hard cut that tore cartilage in his ribs. He ran the last 25 yards into the end zone

clutching his right side with his left arm.

The touchdown finished the Bears and Green's afternoon, too.

A week later, Green wasn't sure he'd be ready for the NFC championship game against the Minnesota Vikings. His ribs were still sore, but as Bostic and others suggested, "You need to be out there."

Green didn't want to take a needle's worth of pain killer but eventually did. He later said that six minutes into the opening quarter the painkiller wore off. Green stayed in and made the play of the game.

The Minnesota Vikings were at the Washington six-yard line, fourth down, last play of the game. Trailing 17–10, Minnesota quarterback Wade Wilson threw a pass that looked like it was going to be caught at the goal line. Green, who was covering Anthony Carter, came off his man and hit the intended receiver Darrin Nelson so hard

the pass fell incomplete. The Redskins were off to Super Bowl XXII, where they'd defeat the Denver Broncos.

When he retired in 2002, Green was still playing corner at age 42. In 19 of his 20 years with Washington, he recorded at least one interception, an NFL record. No wonder his teammates admired his commitment and dubbed him the Ageless Wonder.

In the years following football, Green has worked at his Youth Life Foundation, which he started in 1988. His program is aimed at helping young students stay in school. Green has been involved in several charitable causes, including the NFL/NFL-PA's Sept. 11 Relief.

"I worked and I got a check," Green said of his time in the NFL. "[Working after football] is a totally different feeling because it deals with a person's life … it has no equal."

Ageless wonder, indeed. ∎

32 Franco HARRIS

RUNNING BACK

OF HUSTLE AND SHOE TOPS

The eerie life-size likeness, situated near the escalators leading to the baggage carousel at Pittsburgh International Airport, is in mighty good company.

There, leaning down to snatch the football, maybe a foot from the ground, is the spitting image of Franco Harris, the famous No. 32 in Pittsburgh Steelers black. Directly beside, stands a statue of another fairly recognizable American hero, George Washington. That's how much Franco Harris means to the city breast-fed on pig iron. That's how much one play can linger in memory, decades later — the Immaculate Reception.

Even had Harris not rushed for 12,120 yards over 13 seasons, eight times for 1,000 or better; even if he had not played in nine Pro Bowls, or piled up 14,622 all-purpose yards. Even if he had not been part of four Super Bowl championship teams, or been named MVP of Super Bowl IX, or eventually been enshrined among the immortals in Canton, even then, Franco Harris would still be a part of NFL history.

"I've played football since the second grade," marveled Steelers quarterback Terry Bradshaw in the aftermath of arguably the NFL's most famous single play. "And nothing like that ever happened. It'll never happen again."

The details are familiar to all football fans across North America: 22 seconds remaining, the hometown Steelers trailing the Oakland Raiders 7–6 in the AFC divisional playoff game, Dec. 23, 1972. Bradshaw was flushed out of the pocket on fourth and 10, then pushed back inside. His desperation throw, too far for the intended receiver, caromed off Raiders safety Jack Tatum and/or Pittsburgh wideout John "Frenchy" Fuqua. And there, to pluck the ball off his shoe tops on the ricochet was Franco Harris. Forty-five yards later, he crossed the goal line, and the entire city of Pittsburgh went absolutely nuts.

"When I see the film," Harris told ESPN years later, "that's like proof that it happened. But it still seems like a dream."

If the ball did — as the Raiders of that day insist — hit Fuqua at all, the play should've been ruled invalid as it had touched two offensive players. If it only struck Tatum, the catch and the touchdown were

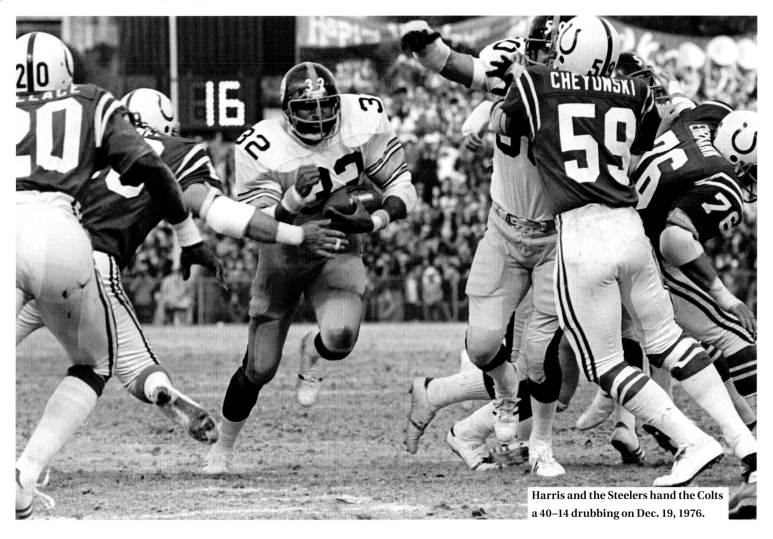

Harris and the Steelers hand the Colts a 40–14 drubbing on Dec. 19, 1976.

legitimate. The debate rages on. Replays seem inconclusive.

Steelers coach Chuck Noll praised his prize rookie's attitude in the controversial aftermath.

"Franco made that play because he never quit on the play," he said. "He kept running. He kept hustling. Good things happen to those who hustle."

To remember one of the NFL's most versatile, durable backs for that piece of drama alone would be a disservice to the man, an injustice to his legacy.

They all became a legendary lot. Bradshaw. The balletic Lynn Swann. The menacing Jack Lambert and Jack Ham at linebacker. Center Tom Webster. And, of course, the Steel Curtain defensive front of Mean Joe Greene, L.C. Greenwood, Dwight White and Ernie Holmes — the four horsemen of any quarterback's apocalypse.

"Halfway through the decade [1970s]," recalled Harris, "we realized that we had a great team and could do great things, that we could probably have something here that we believed had a chance to reach greatness."

Coach Chuck Noll's Steelers reached greatness, and then kept topping it. They had swagger. They had style. And they had Harris, the perfect complement to Bradshaw's aerial game. At 6-foot-2 and 230 pounds, he had size enough to run over people, and enough spring in his legs to slide past them.

Besides his Hall of Fame career rushing totals (he ran for 100 or more yards on 47 occasions), the 13th overall pick in the 1972 NFL draft also caught 307 passes for 2,287 yards and nine touchdowns. When he retired, his combined yardage of 14,622 was the third highest total ever. Sparking

Pittsburgh's first Super Bowl triumph in 1975, Harris rushed 34 times for 158 yards, breaking Larry Csonka's record of the year before to earn MVP honors.

He spent his final year in Seattle as a Seahawk, but never looked right in anything other than vintage Steeler black.

During his dozen seasons in the Steel City, the man who inspired Franco's Italian Army in the stands at Three Rivers, who developed into one of the most dependable backs of his era, could run away from the most punishing, the most pursuant, of NFL defenses.

What he can never run away from is that incredible, improbable play, and Franco Harris will never be able to shake that.

One play forever frozen in time, beside the escalators leading down to the baggage carousel at Pittsburgh International Airport — right beside George Washington. ▪

58 JACK LAMBERT

LINEBACKER

A STEELER TO THE END

John Elway was a rookie quarterback for the Denver Broncos when he looked across the line of scrimmage and almost wet his football pants. There, in the cold heart of the Pittsburgh Steelers defense, was the scariest man he had ever seen. Count Dracula from Pittsburgh, Transylvania. Jack Lambert.

With his pronounced bicuspids and snarling mood, Lambert played middle linebacker like a lion tearing into a fallen gazelle, and just the look of him was enough to send a trickle of fear through the young quarterback.

"He had no [front] teeth, and he was slobbering all over himself," recalled Elway. "I'm thinking, 'You can have your money back, just get me out of here. Let me go be an accountant.' I can't tell you how badly I wanted out of there."

Elway couldn't have been alone in his fear of Lambert, who would sometimes play up his evil image by saying, "I am very aggressive and very physical. On the field I guess I am just plain mean."

Lambert was a brutal hitter. He'd drive himself into the ball carrier, then sort through the pieces to find the ball. In his second season in Pittsburgh, in the Super Bowl no less, Lambert went after Dallas Cowboys defensive back Cliff Harris, who had tapped Steelers kicker Roy Gerela on the helmet after a missed 33-yard field goal and said, "Way to go." Lambert took offense, tossed Harris to the ground, and then had to talk his way out of being ejected by the officials.

Lambert also had a trio of run-ins with the Cleveland Browns after flattening their quarterback Brian Sipe. He was penalized three times for a late hit on Sipe, ejected twice and fined by the league. All three times, Lambert was mobbed by Cleveland players who took exception to his actions. A week later, Lambert told Howard Cosell on *Monday Night Football*, "Quarterbacks should wear dresses."

The Steelers drafted Lambert from Kent State, where he had played a rambunctious game at linebacker despite weighing only 204 pounds. While it was assumed Lambert lost his teeth playing football, he actually had them knocked loose by a teammate during a high school basketball practice. (Was he a good basketball player? He av-

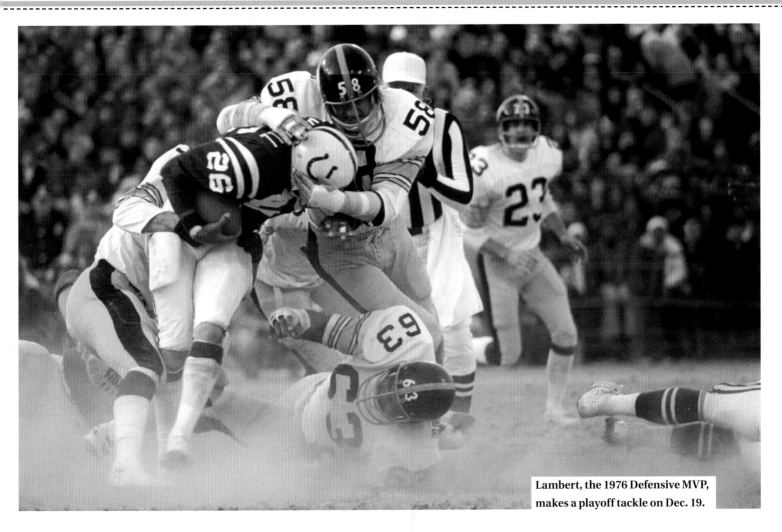

Lambert, the 1976 Defensive MVP, makes a playoff tackle on Dec. 19.

eraged 17.9 points and 13 rebounds per game.) Still, Lambert's image as a menacing predator was already well established. On the eve of training camp in 1974, Steelers' defensive line coach George Perles told one of his players, "We've got a rookie who's so mean he doesn't even like himself."

Being drafted by the Steelers afforded Lambert two early opportunities. Pittsburgh was a two-and-a-half-hour drive from where he was born in Mantua, Ohio, so Lambert was able to drive to the team's office every weekend to watch game film before training camp opened. Then, starting middle linebacker Henry Davis got hurt in the preseason. Lambert moved into the position and never stepped out. The Steelers won their first Super Bowl in 1975 in Lambert's rookie season and four in a six-year period.

The Steelers' defense of 1976 was one of the best in league history. Led by Lambert, it allowed just two touchdowns in a nine-game span, recorded five shutouts, and finished first in almost every defensive statistic kept by the NFL. Overall, the Steelers gave up just 9.9 points per game over a 14-game schedule while 8 of their 11 defensive starters were selected to the Pro Bowl. Lambert was named Defensive Player of the Year.

"Jack had the image of a wild man, but he killed opponents with his perfection," said linebacking partner Andy Russell. "His greatness has nothing to do with his popular image."

The blood-sucking, wild-man persona was awfully tough to get past, though. Lambert was as fiercely private away from the game as he was punishing during it, which simply added to his myth. He didn't like to talk much. His teammates recalled how Lambert would cringe when recognized in public. Once, when spotted by some young fans, he was asked, "What's your sign, Jack? You know, astrology."

"Feces," he said.

Lambert once joked that he was from Buzzard's Breath, Wyoming. Some people took him seriously.

In the end, the man who almost turned John Elway into an accountant finished with more than 1,400 tackles, 23.5 sacks and 28 interceptions. He was voted to the 1970s All-Decade Team as well as the 1980s All-Decade Team, and played in nine consecutive Pro Bowls.

In 1990, Lambert achieved the ultimate recognition when he was inducted into the Pro Football Hall of Fame. His acceptance speech was delivered with the passion and purpose that punctuated the way he played his position.

"If I could start my life all over again, I'd be a professional football player," he said, "and you damn well better believe I would be a Pittsburgh Steeler." ■

81

DICK
LANE

CORNERBACK

THE MIDNIGHT EXPRESS

If you pitched a movie script based on the life and professional football career of Dick "Night Train" Lane, even the most agreeable Hollywood producer would have a hard time buying it.

"Let me see if I've got this straight," the producer would say. "Our star is found in a dumpster at the age of three months by a woman who decides to raise him as one of her own. The kid loves sports but later joins the Army and serves in World War II and Korea. One day, he walks into the office of the Los Angeles Rams and asks for a contract. He never went to college, and all he has with him is a scrapbook full of clippings from his high school days. Somehow, the Rams go for it. Our hero wants to play receiver, but the Rams are loaded with receivers so they say, 'Try cornerback.' He does, and not only does he make the team, he intercepts a record 14 passes in 12 games in his first NFL season and goes on to become a Hall of Famer."

"Right," the producer would add, "and maybe we should do a movie about a palooka fighter who gets a shot at the title and call it *Rocky*."

The story of Night Train Lane is two parts improbable, one part incredible. Everything mentioned happened. Lane was left in a dumpster in Austin, Texas. His mother was a prostitute, his dad a pimp. The woman who discovered him in the dumpster, Ella Lane, was a widow, who mothered young Night Train along with her two other children.

Lane had risen to the rank of Lt. Colonel before leaving the Army. And in 1952, after duty in two wars, the 24-year-old was working at a dead-end factory job when he decided to take his high school scrapbook with him and ask the Rams for a tryout.

Head coach Joe Stydahar had two future Hall of Fame receivers in Tom Fears and Elroy (Crazy Legs) Hirsch, but he loved Lane's speed and size (6-foot-2, 200 pounds) so he made him a cornerback. Little did anyone know Lane was about to set the standard for a position he had never played before.

"Train will always be the Godfather of cornerbacks," said former Detroit Lions defensive back Lem Barney. "He was as large as some linemen of his era. He also was agile and very fast. His tackling was awesome. He did the clothesline and other tackles that just devastated the ball carrier."

Most everything about Lane was a contradiction. He played corner but kept the number he'd been assigned as a receiver, 81. He initially hated the nickname Night Train, since it was taken from a hip tune of the day. Lane changed his mind when he saw his moniker used in a headline that read, Rookie Dick "Night Train" Lane derails Charlie "Choo Choo" Justice. If it was good enough for the newspapers, it was good enough for Lane.

Cornerbacks aren't supposed to frighten their opponents but Night Train did. He had a habit of tackling receivers high around their head and neck. Back in those days it was called a horse collar. Later, it became known as a clothesline. With Lane, it was dubbed the Night Train Necktie, and it was a punishing move that injured several players.

"I've never seen a defensive back like him," said Green Bay Packers Hall of Fame cornerback Herb Adderley. "I mean, take *them* down, whether it be Jim Brown or Jim Taylor."

Lane was so effective at neck-tying ball carriers that the NFL banned its practice. In 14 seasons, Night Train also played for the Chicago Cardinals and Detroit. He was selected to seven Pro Bowls and was voted to the 1950s All-Decade Team. His final statistics included 68 interceptions for 1,207 yards, five touchdowns, 11 fumble recoveries and another touchdown. And to top things off, he added eight pass receptions for 253 yards and a touchdown.

"I was a small, very wiry kid so therefore

The veteran Night Train spent his last six seasons in Detroit Lions blue.

nobody gave me a ghost of a chance of making it," Lane said. "But I had a big heart."

Lane was such a physical presence he is credited with inventing the bump-and-run technique. The cornerback jams the receiver as he leaves the line of scrimmage, then runs with him downfield. Lane's bumps were strong enough to knock some receivers to the ground.

"My object is to stop the guy with the ball

before he gains another inch," said Lane, who revised his plan and stopped guys before they even got the ball.

In 1969, four years after he retired from the Lions, Lane was voted the best cornerback in the NFL's first 50 years. He was inducted into the Pro Football Hall of Fame in 1974. He died at age 73 after fashioning an inspirational life and a most improbable tale. ▪

80 STEVE LARGENT

WIDE RECEIVER

187 POUNDS OF PURE HEART

Four preseason games into Steve Largent's NFL dream, the bottom seemed to drop out. Largent was deemed surplus by the Houston Oilers — over before it had even had the chance to begin,

Fate, obviously a football fan, then intervened in the shape of a trade to the Seattle Seahawks. For an eighth-round draft pick, yet.

Seems absurd now, traded for an eighth-round pick, since for the next 14 years, Largent caught more footballs than anyone who had gone before him. But because of the mediocre teams he played on during his years in Seattle, Steve Largent has been largely overlooked by the casual fan when listing the greatest receivers in NFL history. But he rates. He definitely rates.

From the perspective of the defensive backs assigned to cover him, the clean-cut, religious kid out of Tulsa wasn't super-fast like a Bob Hayes. Or built as if he'd been chiseled from a block of Carrara marble like a Kellen Winslow. He was … just… : Just fast enough. Just slippery enough. Just tough enough. Just flat-out good enough to beat you just about every time he wanted to.

We're all so quick to measure things when judging an athlete — height and weight, speed in the 40, how much weight someone is able to bench press. What remains elusive, what cannot ever be measured or quantified, is heart. There has never been, will never be, an instrument capable of calibrating that.

The No. 80 in blue and silver who would go on to the Hall of Fame is further proof of that.

Seems amazing now, but pro scouts weren't all that impressed with Largent, despite the All-American status at the University of Tulsa and despite leading the nation in touchdown catches his final two seasons. He wasn't selected until the fourth round of the 1976 draft, 117th overall.

How good was Largent?

So good that Jerry Rice, who would eventually shatter all of Largent's receiving records, admitted studying the way he ran pass routes, picking up pointers to incorporate into his own game. Sort of comparable to Orson Welles running John Ford's iconic western *Stagecoach* over a hundred times in preparation for *Citizen Kane.*

Largent catches one of two touchdowns in a 1984 game against Buffalo.

So good that when he retired, the guy who wasn't big enough, strong enough or fast enough, who only missed four games due to injury in his first 13 NFL seasons, had latched onto every major receiving record available: receptions (819), yards (13,089), TD catches (100) and games with a reception (177).

He caught 50 or more passes for 10 seasons. He caught 70 or more in six seasons. A tireless worker for community and charity, he was voted the NFL's Man of the Year in 1988.

Not bad for a guy the Houston Oilers, in all their wisdom, were convinced didn't have the right stuff to be in the NFL.

He might've been only 5-foot-11 and 187 pounds, but Seahawk fans still recall with relish the afternoon he chased down Denver Bronco defensive back Mike Harden on the return of an intercepted pass thrown by Seahawk quarterback Dave Kreig. Largent not only tracked him down, but leveled his prey, knocking the ball loose and then recovering the fumble.

Sweet justice, in that Harden had almost ended Largent's career earlier in the season, hitting him with such viciousness that the Seahawks' All-Pro, as legend has it, lost two teeth and wound up with a dented helmet.

A quiet, humble person and exemplary pro, Largent wouldn't crow about his payback, a play that has now entered franchise lore. Well, not much, anyway. "It wasn't meant to be a vindictive thing," he is quoted on the Spirit of the Seahawks website as saying, "but it sure felt good."

His final two years represented a significant drop-off in production. He caught only 39 and 28 passes for five touchdowns. But nothing could diminish the glories of what had gone before.

In his post-football life, Largent entered politics, serving in the U.S. House of Representatives for Oklahoma from 1994 to 2002 as a Republican. He was once asked which press corps was tougher: beat writers who cover the NFL or the political writers who cover Capital Hill? Largent laughed and replied: "Let's put it this way. On Capital Hill, I still need a helmet."

Largent later moved to the business world, as president and CEO of the CTIA Wireless Association, after losing in a three-way dogfight for the governorship of his home state.

Perhaps his mistake was in where he decided to run. Maybe he should've just shifted over to the State of Washington. In Seattle, as one of a handful of athletes who has attained iconic status, it goes without saying, he could've gotten elected to anything he wanted. Anything at all. ■

52 RAY LEWIS

LINEBACKER

A LION IN SHEEP'S CLOTHING

Some believe Ray Lewis is not human. How else is there to explain how he played football with complete savagery, as if his whole being depended on the outcome of a single play.

Then there was the business of the torn tricep muscle he suffered in Week 6 of the 2012 NFL season. The injury required surgery; the doctors proclaimed the Baltimore Ravens' 37-year-old linebacker was done for the year, perhaps for good. Lewis didn't agree, and by December was telling everyone he'd be back. And back he came to help his team win Super Bowl XLVII, a remarkable finale to a career spiked with platitudes and controversy.

Say what you will about Lewis' ways, from his religious ramblings to how he manhandled ball carriers like a Central Park mugger. He was the NFL's most daunting interior linebacker, as tough as he was devastating. From his 1996 rookie season, right up until his Super Bowl swan song in New Orleans in 2013, Lewis was renowned for pillaging offenses, all the while convincing people he was one scary dude. Boastful, too.

"I already believe I am the best linebacker in the game," he has said. "Now I have to show one more thing: that I am the most dominating, influential person in the game and the best football player to ever put on a pair of cleats."

Even when it was suggested he was losing a step at the age of 32, Lewis managed 120 tackles, 10 pass deflections, 2 sacks, 2 interceptions and a touchdown to earn his ninth Pro Bowl selection. If that's what losing a step means there are plenty of NFL linebackers longing for a decline in speed.

"It's amazing that as long as he's been playing in this league the amount of explosion he has, the strength … with the physicality of a 25 year old," Rashard Mendenhall, the Pittsburgh Steelers running back, said of Lewis before his retirement.

Lewis was once featured on the cover of *Sports Illustrated* magazine looking skyward and praying with a headline that read, "God's Linebacker." It seemed a rather inappropriate statement considering Lewis was implicated in the murders of Jacinth Baker and Richard Lollar, who were stabbed to death outside an Atlanta nightclub on January 31, 2000.

Lewis does his customary pre-game pump-up ritual prior to kickoff between the Baltimore Ravens and Seattle Seahawks on Nov.13, 2011.

Lewis and two friends were questioned by police, who later indicted the three for murder and aggravated assault. Lewis agreed to plead guilty to a lesser charge of obstruction of justice in exchange for his testimony against his two friends. For that, Lewis was sentenced to a year's probation. His two friends were eventually acquitted of the murder charges.

While the NFL fined Lewis $250,000, it did not suspend him, which produced a second incongruous event. Almost one year after the double stabbings in Atlanta, the Ravens advanced to the Super Bowl, clobbered the New York Giants and Lewis was named the game's MVP. At his post-game news conference, he addressed the media by saying, "If the world wants to see me stumble now, I'll stumble with a [Super Bowl] ring on my finger."

Lewis was reminded of that time in the lead-up to Super Bowl XLVII against the San Francisco 49ers. His defenders pointed to the many charitable acts he's done, how he's staged celebrity auctions, bowling tournaments, food drives and youth camps in Baltimore and also in Angola and Ethiopia, where he helped war victims and championed their need for help all the way to the U.S. Congress.

Lewis was born in Lakeland, Florida, became the star of his high school football team and even a state champion in wrestling for his weight class. He went to the University of Miami and starred some more before leaving after his junior year to play in the NFL, where he was an instant success.

Between 1996 and 2000, Lewis won dozens of awards while the Baltimore de-

fense set a league record for fewest points allowed. His stature as one of the NFL's most voracious and vocal leaders grew to mythical proportions in subsequent years. He retired as the only defender in league history to record more than 40 career sacks and 30 interceptions. He was voted to the league's 2000s All-Decade team, has been a multiple Pro Bowler and All-Pro selection. He did it all — heaven and hell and the NFL — and it defied conventional thought.

"He's Ray Lewis," linebacker Jameel McClain said of his former Baltimore teammate. "Everybody knows how much that means."

Lewis has worn many hats, from hellraiser to MVP to God's linebacker, and before his story is complete he'll surely wear one more, Hall of Famer. ■

75

Howie
LONG

DEFENSIVE END

FROM BEANTOWN TO HOLLYWOOD

For the longest time, Howie Long was a massive contradiction. He played a prickly game for the NFL's nastiest team, the Oakland/Los Angeles Raiders. Yet he was funny and engaging out of uniform, a media darling who used his charm to get into acting and broadcasting.

As a kid, Long didn't care for school. Yet his high school tutor was surprised to hear Long speak with perfect grammar, a gift from his grandmother, who raised Long in one of Boston's working-class neighborhoods.

When younger, Long secretly wanted to play hockey like Bobby Orr, but he enjoyed football as well. The problem was, he hated playing it in front of big crowds with people watching and counting on him to produce. He loathed that kind of pressure. "I had no confidence," he said of himself as a teenager and rookie professional. "None."

Still, Long matured into a good high school football player, a better college player, and one of the NFL's most formidable defensive linemen, easily able to separate his football actions and transgressions from his desire to be just a regular, everyday normal guy, with good grammar.

It was that fully developed, fully secure 6-foot-5, 270-pound Long who became a Raiders' mainstay and terrorized offenses to the point where he once walked into an opposing team's huddle during a time-out and yelled at the trainer, "Give me that water. They don't need it. They're not doing anything."

Then there was the game against Chicago where Long screamed at a Bears offensive lineman, "I'm going to get you in the parking lot after the game and beat you up in front of your family!"

This guy could be prickly.

"I think the moment you're content is the moment you're heading backwards," said Long, who was never content with his level of play. "It's the proverbial quest for perfection, which is unattainable, and therein lies the dilemma."

Long's childhood was rife with hardship. He was turned over to his grandmother after his parents separated and later divorced. He was 12. His future seemed destined for thankless work in anonymous jobs, although he had to overcome some early ailments.

Long gets one of two sacks in a 19–10 victory over the Chiefs in 1985.

"I was sick a lot, and doctors told my grandmother I'd never grow up to be big and strong. Isn't that ironic?" Long recalled.

Long was shipped to an uncle who lived in the suburbs and was fortunate to meet a high school football coach who not only believed in him but had him tutored by his wife, a math and English teacher.

Long responded by becoming a Scholastic Coach All-American defensive player in his senior year, 1977. He was spotted by a coach from Villanova and offered a scholarship. In the 1980 Blue-Gray All-Star game, Long was named Defensive MVP. A year later he was drafted by the Raiders in the second round.

Not having played at a major Division 1 school, Long's inexperience became obvious when he arrived at the Raiders' training camp. In no time, he was taken to the woodshed by the Raiders veteran offensive linemen and later by rival offensive line-men, who thwarted his every rush. Aware that he had much to learn, Long convinced himself he could play in the NFL if he prepared himself better than anyone else.

He took a VCR with him on the road and watched game tape while staying in hotels. He started the last five games of the 1982 NFL season and became a regular in 1983, when he went to the Pro Bowl for the first time after recording what would be a career-high 13 quarterback sacks. There would be seven more such visits in a career that included 84 official sacks, two interceptions, 10 fumble recoveries, and a 1980s All-Decade Team nomination.

Long and the Raiders made it to Super Bowl XVIII against the Washington Redskins and won handily, 38–9. In that game, Long recorded five tackles as the Raiders forced two interceptions, a fumble, and allowed just 90 yards rushing.

Two seasons later Long turned in a distinguished campaign using his patented rip move, an uppercut-like blow that separated him from his blocker. He was voted the 1985 George Halas Trophy winner as Defensive Player of the Year. By the time he retired in 1993, Long had earned the admiration of his NFL peers and coaches, particularly Raiders defensive line coach Earl Leggett, who said, "In those 13 years, I thought that he became the most disruptive force in pro football."

Once finished as a player, Long jumped into acting. He became an action hero starring in the movies *Firestorm*, *Broken Arrow* and *3000 Miles to Graceland*. Most recently, he has been an NFL analyst for the FOX Network.

At his induction into the Pro Football Hall of Fame in 2000, Long thanked his family, friends, coaches and teammates, and then his grandmother, Ma Mullan, who "is up there somewhere saying, 'See, I told you you'd be somebody special.'"

Turned out she was right on the mark. ▪

42

RONNIE LOTT

SAFETY

TRUTH LIES IN THE DIGITS

The story of Ronnie Lott and his left pinky finger has become as mangled as the defensive back's damaged digit.

Some say the finger was so badly fractured during a game that doctors cut it off at halftime, and let Lott return to action. Others insist Lott hacked it off when doctors told him his finger was a goner.

"It's like Babe Ruth pointing to center field," Lott said of his legendary tale. "That's the kind of story it's turned out to be."

It's a telling saga, even if the facts have been mutilated over the years. What is without any doubt is Lott's deserved reputation as a fearless, ball-seeking missile who played it rough as a Pro Bowl cornerback and even rougher as a Pro Bowl safety. He was as vital to the San Francisco 49ers' four Super Bowl wins as Joe Montana and Jerry Rice. He would do anything, make any hit, intercept passes, create fumbles, and score touchdowns to ensure the 49ers' success.

Even lop off a finger? The acknowledged version of events goes like this:

In San Francisco's last game of the 1985 regular season, the baby finger on Lott's left hand was crushed in a full-bore collision with Dallas Cowboys' running back Tim Newsome. Lott's hand was caught between his chest and Newsome's helmet and "exploded," according to Lott. A piece of his finger was left on the field as Lott was taken to the dressing room, done for the day.

He refused to miss the following week's playoff game and played with his hand taped up. The 49ers lost to the New York Giants and, in the offseason, doctors gave Lott the choice of undergoing an intricate surgical procedure involving pins and skin grafts or having the tip of the finger removed.

"The doctors thought it would be better for me to [have part of the baby finger amputated] since I was continuing to play," said Lott, who was told the surgery would require months of recovery and rehabilitation. "It wasn't like I was going to have a good-looking finger, because it was pretty much destroyed."

By agreeing to have his finger pruned, Lott was ready for the start of the 1986 season, one that would see him snare a career-

Lott snags an interception in 1989; his fifth consecutive season with five or more.

high 10 interceptions, make 77 tackles, force three fumbles and record two sacks, despite missing the final two games of the regular season with a leg injury.

"That shows [Lott's] dedication to the game," said Dennis Thurman, who played for the Cowboys and was Lott's teammate at the University of Southern California. "I think it's a tremendous story about courage, determination and grit, and how important football was to Ronnie, and still is. I'm sure if he could still play, he would."

Lott arrived at USC as a potential running back. He lost out to Marcus Allen and was asked to play safety, which turned out to be a good thing for the Trojans. Lott helped his school garner enough votes to win a share of the 1978 national championship alongside Alabama. He played in two Rose Bowls, was a team captain and a unanimous All-American selection.

Drafted in the first round by the 49ers,

he stepped in as a rookie cornerback and made seven interceptions, returning three for touchdowns — tying an NFL record for a rookie defender. In 1985, he switched to safety and was able to punish receivers and running backs from his new vantage point.

One of his best mood-altering hits took place Jan. 27, 1989, in Super Bowl XXIII. Cincinnati Bengals runner Ickey Woods was gaining significant yardage early in the game when Lott promised his teammates that was about to stop. The tackle he put on Woods was so nasty it should have come with a warning, "Viewer discretion is advised."

"It just knocked Ickey's spark right out of him," said 49ers defensive coordinator Ray Rhodes. "The game turned right then because Ickey just didn't run with the same authority after that."

Lott did the same thing to a number of other players over the years, but was also

quick and heady enough to intercept 63 passes in his career. He was even better in big games, notching 89 tackles, nine interceptions, a fumble recovery and two touchdowns in 20 playoff games.

"He's like a middle linebacker playing safety," Dallas head coach Tom Landry once said. "He's devastating. He may dominate the secondary better than anyone I've seen."

Lott was showered with awards and honors. He was voted to both the 1980s and 1990s All-Decade Teams and elected to the Pro Football Hall of Fame in 2000.

Asked if he had made the right decision about his left pinky being shortened, Lott replied, "All in all, yes. I don't have any regrets. You do that because you just love playing the game of football … That's the ultimate compliment to pay to your teammates, to play hurt."

With nine-and-a-half fingers, no less. ∎

88 John MACKEY

TIGHT END

LEAD BY EXAMPLE

He was the proverbial bull in a china shop. The man they couldn't bring down with ropes or a tranquilizer gun. He did more than reinvent the tight end position — he made football fans forget anyone had ever played it before he came along.

Watching John Mackey catch a pass and shrug off tacklers was like watching a rhinoceros shake off a batch of pestering egrets. You marveled at the ease, the power, the way he raced downfield — and he could run.

In 1966, his fourth season with the Baltimore Colts, Mackey caught nine touchdown passes, six of which were 50 yards or more in length. That was unheard of at the time. Tight ends were supposed to be accomplished run blockers, extra offensive tackles that could occasionally slip out of their yokes to catch a pass or two. Never for 50 yards, though. That was the wide receiver's job.

But there was no controlling Mackey. In college at Syracuse, he had been a 220-pound fullback and had learned how to challenge tacklers. When he got to the Colts, head coach Don Shula wasn't sure

where to play the 6-foot-2 Mackey. Shula watched him overpower smaller defensive backs and out-maneuver linebackers in practice and decided, "Tight end it will be."

Mackey started every game in his rookie year (he also ran back kickoffs for a 30.7-yard average) and became a Pro Bowl fixture in the 1960s, being named three years in a row. Twice, he averaged more than 20 yards per catch in a season. His career average after 10 years was 15.8 yards. When the NFL voted on its All-1960s team, Mackey was picked at tight end, by a landslide.

He played in two Super Bowls. The first was the Colts stunningly wretched 1969 loss to the New York Jets in Super Bowl III. In that game, the Colts were supposed to leave their hoofprints all over the Jets. They didn't. Two years later, the Colts beat the Dallas Cowboys in Super Bowl V on Jim O'Brien's late field goal. The game was a Marx Brothers movie of goofs, gaffes and comedic blunders except for one play. Quarterback Johnny Unitas threw a pass for Eddie Hinton that was off the mark. The ball deflected off Hinton's hands, off the

Mackey avoids a tackle to score after taking a pass from quarterback Johnny Unitas.

hands of Dallas defensive back Mel Renfro and into the hands of Mackey, who ran untouched for a 75-yard touchdown. The Cowboys complained, noting that a ball can't be tipped from one receiver to another. Replays showed Renfro had touched the ball in between the two Colts and the touchdown stood.

Mackey left the Colts in 1972 and signed with the San Diego Chargers, where he was bothered by a knee injury and retired. His career statistics were 331 catches for 5,236 yards and 38 touchdowns. As soon as he was out of the game, Mackey was back in the thick of things. He had been named president of the NFL Players Association and sued the NFL for its restrictive policies regarding free agency.

"They gave us what they wanted to give us," Mackey said of the NFL owners, "made us smile and say 'thank you.' But from that day forward we decided to build a legitimate union."

Mackey saw to it the NFLPA hired its first executive director, attorney Ed Garvey. Mackey fought the NFL's free agency policy and today's players, who can move at will when their contracts expire, owe a debt of gratitude to Mackey's tenacity.

"John revolutionized the tight end position," said Shula. "[But] as much as he made an impact on the field, he did the same off the field. He was a leader of men of all colors at a time when that was not an easy thing to do."

Mackey wasn't the first true tight end to be inducted into the Pro Football Hall of Fame. Mike Ditka was and even he asked, "Why wasn't John in first?" Eventually, the petty politics that branded Mackey a militant union man were put aside and he joined the Hall in 1992. Eight years later,

the NCAA commissioned the John Mackey Award to be presented to the best tight end in college football. That same year, Mackey received something else, something unwanted. He was told he was suffering from frontotemporal dementia.

Ultimately, his conditioned worsened to the point where he required fulltime care. His plight prompted the 88 Plan, named in honor of his jersey number. It guaranteed $88,000 annually in nursing home care for afflicted former NFL players.

On July 6, 2011, Mackey died at the age of 69. Researchers at Boston University determined he had chronic traumatic encephalopathy (CTE), brain damage symptomatic of dementia believed to be caused by repeated hits to the head. Mackey's case added more fuel to the debate over player safety in the NFL. Even in death, the former Colt couldn't help but lead the way. ▪

18

PEYTON
MANNING

QUARTERBACK

LIKE
FATHER
LIKE SON

It was almost as if he were a rookie again at the age of 36, starting at quarterback for a new team, facing new obstacles, with critics lining up in blitz formation. And just like that, Peyton Manning went back to doing what he's always done — completing passes and winning games.

Whether an Indianapolis Colt or a Denver Bronco, the Manning approach has never altered. "Pressure is something you feel when you don't know what the hell you're doing," he has said.

With a football in his hands, Manning has always known what needs to be done. It's been that way since he was old enough to watch his dad play quarterback in the NFL, since he started at the University of Tennessee as an 18-year-old freshman, and since he joined Indianapolis as the first pick overall in the 1998 NFL draft.

And when the Colts released him in March 2012 after he spent a year on the shelf recovering from neck surgery, it didn't take long for Manning to show his new Denver teammates there was still plenty of game left in a right arm that was supposedly spent, and a body that some feared might no longer hold up to the rigors of NFL football. In the Broncos' 2012 season opener, Manning passed for two touchdowns in a 31–19 win over the Pittsburgh Steelers. His first scoring toss was the 400th of his career, putting him in an elite group with Dan Marino and Brett Favre.

From there, Manning guided the Broncos to a 13–3 record only to lose in the 2012 divisional playoffs to the Baltimore Ravens in overtime. The following campaign, he threw for the single-season NFL record of 55 touchdowns and earned his fifth MVP award; early in 2014 he tossed his 509th career touchdown pass to put him in sole possession of first place for career TD passes.

Through every stage of his career, Manning has known how to win a lot of games. But being impervious to pressure didn't come easily. Imagine what it must have been like always being Archie Manning's son, the one with the blood lines and newspaper headlines. Some people are born great, the expression goes. Some have greatness thrust upon them. Peyton Manning had both.

Because his father was a Pro Football

Manning about to pass for the Denver Broncos in his first season with the club.

Hall of Fame quarterback, Peyton was supposed to be something special. When he played well, it was because of his lineage. When he played poorly, it was because he couldn't handle the stress.

Manning was expected to step into the Colts' offense in 1998 and perform spontaneous miracles. He did amazingly well, passing for 3,739 yards and 26 touchdowns while setting five NFL rookie records. The problem was the Colts' inexperience coupled with a hole-in-the-wall defense. At season's end Indianapolis had won just 3 of 16 games.

In 1999, Manning lifted the Colts to a 13–3 record. But when the team lost 19–16 to the Tennessee Titans in the playoffs, Manning drew criticism for not living up to his promise. People began to openly wonder if the prodigy could win the big ones.

Manning never saw his heritage as a burden. He grew up not just with a celebrity dad, but also with two brothers who competed at everything. Their most infamous battles were on the basketball court. The loser had to drag the family garbage cans from the house, down a long bumpy dirt path to the road, often having to stop to pick up the smelly droppings that fell out.

Manning's older brother Connor went on to play at Archie's alma mater, the University of Mississippi, as a receiver. Unfortunately for Connor, he needed surgery to correct a spinal problem and had to quit football. Younger brother Eli Manning played quarterback at Ole Miss and was the first pick overall in the 2004 NFL draft. He would continue to progress all the way to being a two-time Super Bowl champion and two-time Super Bowl MVP.

As for Peyton, his playoff critics will never abate. The Broncos were drubbed 43–8 by the Seattle Seahawks in Super Bowl XLVIII and Peyton is now 1–2 in Super Bowl appearances. It's been a long time since he marched the Colts to victory in Super Bowl LXI against the Chicago Bears in 2006, where he was also named MVP. But that memory and the losses of 2009 and 2014 are what stoke Manning's inner fire.

Just as he was written off for good in 2011 only to bounce back from the injury that cost him the entire season, it would be silly to count him out now. ∎

74 BRUCE MATTHEWS

OFFENSIVE GUARD

IRON MAN ON THE OIL FIELD

Someone once wrote of Bruce Matthews, he "is so old school he's log cabin." It's a wonderful line and positively true.

Matthews played a working man's position and worked it hard. For 19 years, he was the offensive line of the Houston Oilers (later the Tennessee Titans). He started a full season at every position, from tackle to guard to center. He played in 296 career games, the fourth most by a non-kicker. He appeared in 14 consecutive Pro Bowls, tying him with Los Angeles Rams defensive lineman Merlin Olsen for the most appearances. The difference between Matthews and Olsen was that Matthews made the Pro Bowl at two positions — nine times at guard, five at center — and thought nothing of it. No big deal. Just doing his job.

"I have seen Bruce injure a [medial collateral knee ligament] on Sunday," said former Oilers general manager Floyd Reese, "walk on crutches Monday through Wednesday, participate in limited practices on Thursday and Friday and play at an All-Pro level on Sunday."

Rarely missing a game and giving his all was a point of honor for Matthews, a matter of family pride.

Clay Matthews Sr. (Bruce's father) was an All-American at Georgia Tech, playing two positions: offensive tackle and defensive end. He went on to become a defensive lineman with the San Francisco 49ers in the 1950s. Clay Matthews Jr. (Bruce's brother) spent 19 years (and 278 games) in the NFL as a linebacker with the Cleveland Browns and Atlanta Falcons. When Matthews Jr. retired in 1996, the father and the two brothers stood on the 50-yard line at the Georgia Dome and soaked up the adulation of the crowd. "I had a set of rules I could use on all of my kids," Matthews Sr. told ESPN.com. "I told them all, 'You can do whatever you want to. You can go and play any sport you want to … But there are two rules you can't ignore. One of them is, 'I don't care if you're on the last string and sitting on the bench all of the time and are the worst guy out there, you can't quit.' And No. 2 is, 'If I ever see you play or practice and you're not giving 120 percent, I'll yank you out of there myself.' I think they all pretty much got the message."

Matthews at center in Pittsburgh, 1994: his seventh of 14 consecutive years with 16 starts.

Bruce Matthews settled on football and enrolled at the University of Southern California, where he played every position along the offensive line and made All-American in his senior year. He was drafted by Houston in the first round in 1983 and was soon blocking for Earl Campbell, the bone-crushing running back who laid waste to tacklers.

Those early seasons in Houston were wretched for Matthews, who experienced just 13 wins in his first three years. But by 1987, the Oilers would begin a string of seven consecutive trips to the postseason. The team's offense was changed to more of a passing game with the emergence of quarterback Warren Moon, the former CFL star who would establish himself as one of the NFL's top passers. The Oilers, with Moon, would challenge, but never make it to the Super Bowl. One of their most inexplicable

playoff losses came against the Buffalo Bills when they blew a 35–3 lead and lost 41–38 in overtime. "The 35–3, that was such a freak thing," said Matthews, who would suffer additional tough losses in the years ahead.

One such loss was in Super Bowl XXXIV in 2000, when the Oilers (who, by this time, had been transformed into the Tennessee Titans) lost to the St. Louis Rams. Receiver Kevin Dyson was stopped one-yard short of a game-tying touchdown. The other came the year after the Super Bowl, when the Titans lost to the Baltimore Ravens in the AFC championship game.

"I was so tired," Matthews said of his only Super Bowl showing. "I saw [Dyson] was tackled and said, 'It's over.' I walked straight into the dressing room … Next year, we lost to the Ravens. Losing that game was the most difficult playoff loss I ever endured."

His spirit may have been sapped, but it always recovered when the next game or season rolled around. That's how Matthews was taught and that's what he did until he retired after the 2001 season. He was voted onto the NFL's 1990s All-Decade Team and he had his No. 74 retired by the Titans. He was also inducted into the Pro Football Hall of Fame. He recalled how, in his third NFL season when the Oilers played the New York Giants in a preseason game at Canton, Ohio, he watched the inductees arrive at the shrine by motorcade. "I shook Joe Namath's hand. That was a huge thrill," Matthews said. "I've always appreciated the history of the game … I never contemplated that's where I belonged. It seemed too big to me."

But him there, among the greats of the NFL, seems just right, for the old-school lineman. ■

143

78 ANTHONY MUNOZ

OFFENSIVE TACKLE

FROM THE WRONG SIDE OF THE TRACKS

A split-second after Anthony Munoz had knocked NFL Hall of Famer Forrest Gregg to the ground, he thought, "Oh no. I'm in trouble now."

Gregg was the head coach of the Cincinnati Bengals and a gridiron immortal, who had played for the Green Bay Packers and Vince Lombardi. Munoz had just finished his university career at Southern California, playing in only one game at offensive tackle. His knees had been operated on three times in four years and the book on him was "talented but a medical risk."

Gregg had come to Los Angeles to workout Munoz and see if he was really damaged goods. Here's how Munoz remembered the session: "He put me through some drills and I moved along and all of sudden he decided to pass rush me. I wasn't sure how to react but I reacted like any offensive lineman would react. He made a move inside, made a move outside. Just as he made them, I stuck both hands right into his chest and jammed him to the ground.

"You better believe I was scared," Munoz said. "I extended a hand, I apologized, and he said, 'No problem.' He smiled, he goes, 'That's okay.'"

It was better than okay. On that day, Munoz proved he had the footwork and strength to be a good player, perhaps a great one in the NFL. With Gregg's recommendation, the Bengals selected Munoz with their first-round choice in the 1980 draft, making him the third pick overall, behind Billy Sims of the Detroit Lions and Johnny (Lam) Jones of the New York Jets.

With the 6-foot-6, 278-pound Munoz manning the all-important left tackle position — for right-handed quarterbacks, at least — the Bengals experienced instant results. In 1979, the offensive line had been an off-ramp to the quarterback, giving up 63 sacks. In Munoz's rookie season, that number dropped to 37. A year later, it dropped to 35, and Munoz won his first of three NFL Offensive Lineman of the Year awards.

Like many star NFL players, Munoz's childhood was not an easy one. He never knew his father, who bolted and left Esther Munoz to raise five children by herself. Munoz's neighborhood in Ontario, California, was poor and laced with gangs, drugs and hostility. The Munoz family had no car.

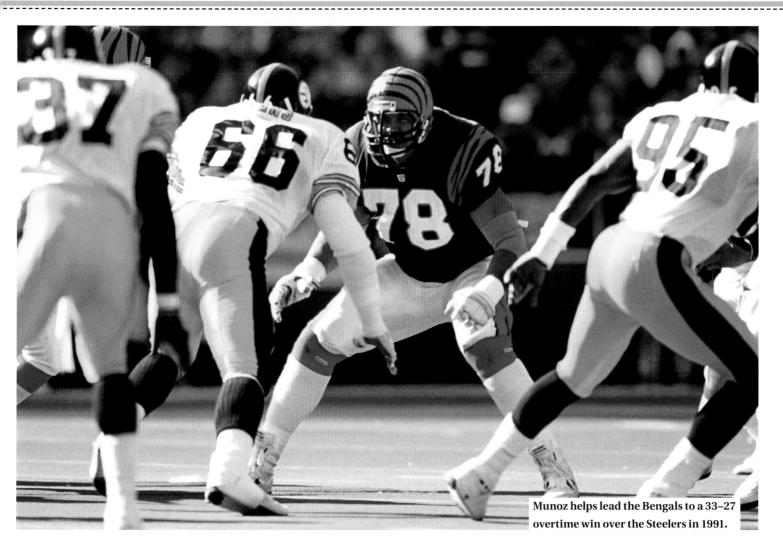

Munoz helps lead the Bengals to a 33–27 overtime win over the Steelers in 1991.

Anthony went everywhere on his bicycle.

Munoz played flag football because he grew to be too big for Pop Warner's kids' football program. He played a lot of baseball and liked to pitch. When he earned a scholarship to USC, Munoz pitched for the Trojans' 1978 national championship baseball team before settling on football. That same year he was named All-American at tackle.

In his final season at USC, Munoz vowed to recover from his third knee operation and play in the 1980 Rose Bowl against Ohio State. He made that pledge while still wearing a cast. He told his coach, John Robinson, he'd be back for the Rose Bowl. Robinson said sure, he'd put Munoz in for a play or two at wide receiver, just to reward his senior lineman.

Munoz wanted no such pity. He wanted to play and he did, helping USC to a 17–16 win for the national championship, while winning the Lombardi Trophy as college football's best lineman.

"[Munoz] is one of the greatest players at any position I ever saw," Robinson said later. Cincinnati head coach Sam Wyche would say the same after coaching Munoz in the NFL.

For 11 straight years, Munoz was voted to the Pro Bowl. During that time, the Bengals won three AFC Central Division titles and two AFC championships. The first came in 1992 when they hosted the San Diego Chargers in what became known as the Freezer Bowl. The temperature at Riverfront Stadium was minus 13 Fahrenheit, but with the wind chill it was a lung-shattering minus 59.

"You've never seen anything until you've seen Anthony Munoz and our offensive line trying to get into Hanes queen-sized panty hose," former Bengals receiver Cris Collinsworth said of his teammates' desire to wear anything to stay warm.

The Bengals won the game 27–7 to earn their first trip to the Super Bowl. There would be another such trip in Munoz's career, in 1989, but Cincinnati would lose to the San Francisco 49ers (both times) by a total of just nine points.

Nowadays, Munoz does his best to knock down poverty and intolerance. He has his own foundation that sponsors student athletes and teaches leadership. In addition, he runs a football camp that teams inner-city kids with those from the suburbs.

"As someone who comes from a diverse environment in Southern California, I grew up that way," said Munoz. "Having played athletics for as long as I have, the primary goal was to win games. It didn't matter where you were from. You did it as a unit. I think it works that way in life." ■

12 JOE NAMATH

QUARTERBACK

SASS, SWAGGER, SAVIOR

At some time or other, every male in North America of a certain generation would've sold his soul to spend a week as Broadway Joe.

The guy who'd called his shot before Super Bowl III — "We'll win. I guarantee it" — just like the Babe. He owned Manhattan's trendiest club, Bachelors III, and could be spotted on the bench wearing a full-length mink coat.

"I like my Johnnie Walker red and my women blonde," he said, and everyone lapped it up.

Joe Willie Namath, the slope-shoulder kid with the lopsided grin from Beaver Falls, Pennsylvania, did more over the years than become a great quarterback, although arguably the finest pure passer in history. He came to symbolize a moment in time, the way author F. Scott Fitzgerald had.

He threw more interceptions than touchdowns over his career, finishing with a 50 percent completion rating. And yet, to this day, remains one of the game's most famous quarterbacks.

Why, this guy could pitch pantyhose and get away with it. He didn't look ridiculous in a Fu Manchu moustache (which he later shaved in a Remington commercial for a fee of $10,000). He wore white shoes. If he wasn't autopsying defenses with chilling precision, he was off starring in a chopper flick, cozying up to sex kitten Ann Margaret.

Those knees may have been held in place by ruinous ligaments. But that pass release? Ohhhh, heaven-sent.

"He was like a cause," former teammate John Dockery told ESPN Classic. "It was like traveling with a rock star. He just was a magnet. Talk about energy and excitement. Wow!"

The time was ripe for an anti-hero, a rebel, and Joe Namath fit the bill brilliantly. The '60s were a decade of musical and political upheaval. The young believed in dissent, thumbed their noses at the status quo and sought their heroes through the classic anti-hero. The Johnny Unitas crew-cut and Bart Starr's bible studies didn't wash anymore. But Joe Willie did.

Namath broke rules and ruffled the establishment. His hedonistic lifestyle drove the old guard crazy. In hospital, battling the cancer that would claim his life, the ultimate rules/establishment coach, Vince Lombardi, vented his displeasure. His widow, Marie, would later recall "He talked once in his sleep about Namath. I just heard his end of the conversation. He was shouting at Namath, telling him to sit down and yelling about how he was a disgrace to football."

Lombardi might've hotly disagreed with the methods and the style. But no one could dispute Joe Namath's gift.

Lost in the fact that Namath was a state of mind, as much as a quarterback, are the accomplishments. He is, never forget, the only man to throw for 4,000 yards in a 14-game season — his third year in the league, first as starter, in 1967. Three times he led the league in passing.

In addition to that sublime right arm and a great football intellect, he possessed a tremendous will to win. When Joe Namath talked, people around him listened, and believed.

"To be a leader, you have to make people want to follow you," he said. "And nobody wants to follow someone who doesn't know where he's going."

Where Joe Willie planned on going was right to the top against Don Shula's seemingly unbeatable Baltimore Colts in the 1969 Super Bowl III.

His signing by the AFL Jets for a reported $400,000 a season in 1965 was a huge coup for the fledgling league, determined to rival the clout and star-wattage of the established NFL. Namath had been selected 12th overall by the NFL's St. Louis Cardinals, first by the Jets. Typically, Joe made the risky choice. Now the moment had arrived to back up the hype.

The lead-in surrounding "the guarantee" of victory is a bit hazy. He made his bold — some would claim insane — promise in response to a heckler at the Miami Touchdown Club dinner three days before the Jets were predicted to be wiped out by the NFL's monster truck from Baltimore. It made for headline-grabbing fodder.

Broadway Joe in his twilight years in New York, where he played 12 seasons.

Then Namath went out and backed up the talk, completing 17 of 26 passes for 206 yards to snare MVP honors, as the upstart AFL cemented its legitimacy in the neon glow of a 16–7 New York victory. It may not be the most memorable Super Bowl ever, but it remains the most famous.

"When we won the league championship," quipped Namath, "all the married guys on the club had to thank their wives for putting up with all the stress and strain all season. I had to thank all the single broads in New York."

100-proof Joe.

The knee injuries that compromised his brilliance and cut short his career dated back to his senior year at Alabama. We are only left to ponder what he would've been like on two healthy pins. What we saw, however, was more than enough. For his swagger and sass, boldness and daring, Broadway Joe remains timeless. ▪

66 N RAY ITSCHKE

LINEBACKER

THE GRIDIRON IMMORTAL

Born in Elmwood Park, Illinois, in 1936, Ray Nitschke lost his father at age three, was orphaned when his mother died at 13 and was raised by an older brother.

Add to that growing up in a rough-and-tumble Chicago neighborhood, and it's a small wonder he turned out to be as tough as his last name. Nitschke. Just the sound of it, the hardness of the syllables, the spit-in-your-eye indomitable ethnicity of it, provided an understanding into the man. For the rest, you simply had to watch him at work. Balding, wild-eyed, missing his four front teeth and apparently some of his mind, Nitschke became the beating heart, the obstinate backbone, of Green Bay's underappreciated defense during the glory decade of the '60s.

Legend has it that a metal tower on the Packers' practice field fell over on top of Ray Nitschke. Coach Vince Lombardi ran over to see what was going on. Informed that it was Nitschke underneath the structure, Lombardi barked, "He'll be fine. Get back to work." Nitschke's biography states that the tower actually drove a stake into his helmet, but he went unharmed. The helmet (complete with hole) is on display in the Packer Hall of Fame in Green Bay.

A caring man with a hard shell, Nitschke went from being a notorious hell-raiser to happy family man, working the off-season in a bank. His is one of the great success stories of football. Perhaps not as famous today as his linebacking contemporary, Dick Butkus of the Chicago Bears, he was nonetheless every bit as visceral, as violent, and as uncompromising between the lines on a football field.

Drafted by the Packers instead of his beloved Bears, Nitschke took $300 of his $500 signing bonus, bought a used Pontiac and drove to Green Bay. He spent the next 15 seasons in Packer green and gold. "Oh, that Nitschke was crazy as hell," said defensive back Emlen Tunnell of the early years. "He had the locker right next to mine. Tom Bettis was the middle linebacker then, so Nitschke didn't play much. And Ray used to get on Vinnie [Lombardi] about it. He'd say, real loud in the locker room, 'Just call me the judge. Just call me the judge. 'Cause I'm always on the bench.' Oooh, that would make Vinnie mad."

Nitschke on the sideline in 1965; his fourth of seven Pro Bowl seasons.

Under Lombardi's tough-love guidance, though, Nitschke channeled his rage and energy into football. The coach knew what he had in the raw, untamed beast prowling the middle of the field: one of the most competitive people ever to grace that highly competitive business.

Paul Hornung gleefully recounted a memorable nutcracker drill during practice one day. Future Hall of Fame fullback Jim Taylor was the ball carrier. "There was very little running room," said Hornung, "because the [blocking] dummies were up there tight and the blocker — some rookie — just screened Nitschke while Taylor slid by." Lombardi stopped the drill, walked over to Nitschke and said, "Mr. Nitschke, I have read that you are the best linebacker in the NFL, but after watching you

just then I find it hard to believe. Now, do it again!" This time, continued Hornung, "Ray grabbed the rookie by the shoulder pads, literally lifted him up and threw him into Jimmy. All Vince said was, 'Next group.' It took them two minutes to get the rookie to come to."

Nitschke the indomitable met his match in his wife-to-be, Jackie. She provided balance and meaning to his life. "Getting married, settling down, getting responsibility for someone beside myself, having someone to love and later adopting the children — all those things were enough motivation for me to quit making a fool of myself," he wrote in his autobiography, *Mean On Sunday.*

Of all the great Packer players of that era, arguably the most loved in Green Bay was, and is, Nitschke. When he died

unexpectedly at 61 in 1998 — the heart, of all things, giving out — the whole of Wisconsin mourned.

The brawler who used to pitch people through windows of bars when the mood struck him would doubtless be astounded to learn that a six-inch NFL Legends action figure, No. 66, has been modeled in his image, and that both a bridge in Green Bay and the luncheon prior to induction at the Pro Football Hall of Fame are named in his honor. In 1999, *Sports Illustrated* named him the third greatest linebacker in history, behind only Dick Butkus and Lawrence Taylor. But people in Titletown, U.S.A., know better.

Ray Nitschke didn't just leave his imprint on anyone daft enough to dare to run between the tackles. He left it on the game. ▪

32 O.J. SIMPSON

RUNNING BACK

THE GLORY YEARS

Long before the lurid headlines and the courtrooms and the late-night talk show punch lines and the police mug shots and the posted bail and the almost cartoonish-buffoonish persona, Orenthal James Simpson was known far and wide as a running back.

A running back different from any seen before — The Juice. No. 32 of the Buffalo Bills: a sublime concoction of speed, power and misdirection that ran through NFL defenses as easily as he dashed through airports in Hertz Rent a Car commercials.

Simpson was the first rusher ever to top 2,000 yards in a season. And in only 14 games, at that. He was a man who established records for yards along the ground in a game (273), and touchdowns during a season (23); a three-time UPI Player of the Year, four-time leading rusher, All-AFC and All-Pro for five consecutive years, he participated in six Pro Bowls and was the NFL's MVP in 1973.

Here was an athlete so extraordinary, so unique, that legendary University of Southern California coach John McKay declared, "Simpson was not only the greatest player I ever had — he was the greatest player *anyone* ever had."

Watching videos of Simpson now still has the power to amaze and delight. He provides viewers with the same sort of goose bumps that Gale Sayers had before him: the dramatic, seemingly impossible changes in direction, that rare inexplicable ability to make opponents miss, as if he alone were enacting a dance of joy.

"The fear of losing is what makes competitors so great," he said of the game he came to dominate. "Show me a gracious loser and I'll show you a permanent loser."

For the length of his stay there, O.J. Simpson turned frigid Buffalo into Broadway on Sunday afternoons or Monday nights, providing the greatest theater in the state outside of the Great White Way.

Because of the benevolent, charming façade Simpson studiously built during his decade as a superstar with the Bills, people forgot, or never knew, that he grew up in the rough Potrero Hill section of San Francisco, and was raised by his mother Eunice after his dad walked out on the family. Early on, Simpson hardly seemed a candidate

Simpson runs on Oct. 7, 1973. He posted 171 yards in the game and 2,003 on the year.

for football immortality. At just two years old, he developed rickets, leaving his legs skinny and bowed. He joined his first gang at 13, and at 15, Simpson landed in a Youth Guidance Center for a week after one of many fights. There had always been a dark side to O.J. Simpson — the kid-from-the-shabby-side-of-the-tracks side.

But football ability, the great equalizer, was his ticket out of the squalor and into the limelight of mainstream American culture. He only ever wanted to play collegiately, for the Trojans, at USC. And it was there his legend began to take shape. During his phenomenal Heisman Trophy-winning senior season, Simpson set NCAA records for most rushing yards in a season (1,709) and most carries (355). USC won the Rose Bowl that year. In 17 of his 21 career games for the Trojans, he ran for over 100 yards, in five of them, for over 200.

Chosen first in the 1969 college draft, Simpson languished for three seasons in Buffalo, unhappy with how he was being used. When Lou Saban took over as head coach in 1972, though, he built his offense around the workhorse back and was rewarded with 1,251 yards, the NFL high that year.

In 1973, Simpson exploded into the national consciousness. He had 1,000 yards by the midway point of the season, and people began to speak openly about his chances of hitting 2,000. In Buffalo's next-to-last start, he rambled for 219 yards, leaving him 197 short of the mythical mark. On a bitter, snowy, windswept New York day at Shea Stadium, The Juice bulled, slalomed and slashed for 200, giving him 2,003 on the season. He was carried off the field on the shoulders of his teammates.

During his 11 NFL seasons, Simpson ran for over 11,000 yards and, while he never brought the Super Bowl title to Buffalo, his accomplishments were many and lauded. He was inducted into the Pro Football Hall of Fame in 1985, and he remained an amiable and familiar presence on TV and in film. Until, that is, June 12, 1994, when his wife Nicole Brown Simpson and friend Ron Goldman were found dead outside her condominium.

O.J. Simpson, football icon, was charged with the double murder. Following a year-long trial that gripped a nation and divided public opinion, he was acquitted. Later, Simpson was found financially liable in a civil trial for damages to the grieving parties, and in 2008, he was sentenced to 33 years in prison for kidnapping and armed robbery in Las Vegas.

His legacy as one of the game's great running backs, however, remains wistfully uncompromised. ▪

50 MIKE SINGLETARY

LINEBACKER

A CRAZY-EYED WONDER

The eyes of Mike Singletary were indeed the windows to his soul. They looked as if they were going to pop right out of his head. Right out of his helmet, too. They burned with intensity. One look from Singletary and wild animals would have run for cover.

Singletary's soul was no less passionate. He wanted to be the best middle linebacker in the game. The best teammate. The best husband. The best father. Everything worth doing was worth doing to its fullest; that was Singletary's guiding principle. "If you want to be the best, if you want to be the best at something, you will not be denied," he said. "You're not going to quit. You're not going to stop. You're going to keep fighting."

Singletary was a never-quit fighter who overcame his lack of size (6-foot, 230 pounds) with a crackling disposition. His tackles bordered on assault and battery. One of his all-time favorite targets was Los Angeles Rams running back Eric Dickerson. In a 1985 playoff showdown in Chicago, Dickerson took a handoff on third and one and looked to have room running through the right side of the Bears' defense. Singletary charged in, stopped Dickerson dead in his tracks, then threw him for a loss. To celebrate, Singletary began barking like a dog.

A bemused linebacker, Wilbur Marshall, said after Chicago's 24–0 win, "Dickerson didn't know where he was at."

Chicago head coach Mike Ditka had a better story about that playoff game. The day before, he was talking to the offense while Singletary was addressing the defense in a room next door. As Ditka tells it, what started out as a calm and rational speech quickly turned into a Knute Rockne rant, complete with Singletary screaming and his defensive mates turning over tables and trashing chairs.

With his determination and his smarts, Singletary was the defensive catalyst of the Bears' 1985 season, which saw them go 15–1. In the ensuing playoffs, Chicago dominated from start to finish, ravaging the New England Patriots in Super Bowl XX. That season, Singletary recorded 109 solo tackles, three sacks, one interception, three fumble recoveries and knocked down 10 passes. He was named the NFL's Defensive Player of the Year.

A rookie Singletary in 1981 displays the ferocity for which he became famous.

Singletary's need to be the best was forged in childhood. He was born the last of 10 children in Houston, Texas. When he was five years old, his brother Dale died. When he was 12, his parents divorced and his dad, a Pentecostal pastor, left. That same year, another brother, Brady, was killed in a car crash.

Singletary was lost, with "no confidence … no self-esteem," he said. His mother sat him down and told him he could accomplish anything he wanted because there was greatness in him. She told Singletary to trust in his faith and believe in its values. Singletary said as soon as his mom finished her talk he went to his room and wrote down his goals: "Find a way to get a scholarship to go to college; become an All-American in college; get my degree; go to the NFL; and buy my mom a house and take care of her for the rest of my life."

Singletary went to Baylor University and was a two-time All-American. The Bears drafted him in the second round in 1981 and, by the seventh game of his rookie season, Singletary was giving opponents fits with his crazy-eyed look and Samurai warrior attacks.

In 12 seasons in Chicago, the voracious defender appeared in 10 Pro Bowls, made 1,488 tackles and was voted to both the Pro Football and College Football Halls of Fame.

It was his wife, Kim, who met Singletary while they were attending Baylor in the late 1970s, who was the presenter that introduced him as a Pro Football Hall of Fame inductee. He called her his best friend.

"A lot of people think I'm corny," Singletary told the Chicago Tribune. "I want it that way, and I like it that way. You watch me as close as you can, and I'll do my best to teach you something."

Corny, keen, a natural leader; those qualities have served Singletary well in his post-playing career where he has coached in different capacities and tutored stars such as Ray Lewis and Patrick Willis. In his new position as senior advisor to Troy Vincent, the NFL's executive vice president of football operations, Singletary will get the opportunity to impart his wisdom on young players coming into the league.

Offensive stars of tomorrow, be warned. ◼

78

BRUCE SMITH

DEFENSIVE END

THE ALL-TIME HUNTER

Tommy Kramer was the first to go down in 1985. Jesse Palmer became the record-breaker in 2003. In between, the list of victims included John Elway, Joe Montana, Phil Simms, Dan Marino, Steve Young and 70 others, including Ken O'Brien, who was hunted down and bagged more than a dozen times by Bruce Smith.

It's a wonder that O'Brien, a Pro Bowl quarterback for the New York Jets, didn't jump like a startled cat at the mention of Smith's name. The Buffalo Bills defensive end had that effect on quarterbacks.

He had the same effect on his teammates.

With the Bills trailing the Kansas City Chiefs in a key AFC match-up, Smith stomped into the offensive meeting at half-time and yelled at his teammates, "Gosh darn it, stop turning over the football." (Okay, he didn't say gosh darn it.) Aware Smith would be even angrier if the game ended the same way it began, the Buffalo offense held onto the ball, scored 17 points and easily defeated Kansas City.

"I'm not a very outspoken person until the time comes," Smith said afterward. "If I step on somebody's toes, I'm not sorry about it because it's the truth and it hurts."

Smith stepped on toes, rammed helmets and did whatever he could to make quarterbacks worry and wince. He chased lesser-knowns such as Browning Nagle and Dave Brown as unremittingly as he hounded Drew Bledsoe and Donovan McNabb. As a harasser of quarterbacks, Smith was an equal opportunist.

"I watched my first NFL game in Detroit in 1934 when I was a kid," Bills owner Ralph Wilson once said, "and I think Bruce Smith is the best defensive lineman I have ever seen. I'm not saying that because he's a Buffalo Bill. I'm saying that because I have seen all the great ones and I don't think anyone was ever better."

Statistically, Smith holds the overall sack record with 200. It took him 19 seasons, including four with the Washington Redskins, to put up that number, which may stand for some time. But Smith's pursuit of the record was not well received in all corners.

Several sports columnists and NFL commentators criticized him for staying in the game longer than he should have and for taking a roster spot that should have gone to a younger player. He was called selfish and record hungry. And when he was benched by Washington coach Steve Spurrier, Smith spoke out, saying he was still the team's best pass rusher, even at age 40.

One newspaper quoted an unnamed NFL scout as saying, "Bruce Smith is just limping toward that sack record. The first four games [of his final season] he seemed to be pumped up, but the last two weeks he looks bad."

No one ever thought Smith looked bad when he played for the Bills. Buffalo's first-round selection in the 1985 draft, he was the team's all-time sack leader by 1989 (with 52) and one of the Bills' undisputed leaders. With Jim Kelly, Andre Reed and Thurman Thomas holding onto the ball on offense, Smith inspired a defense that back-stopped Buffalo to a record four consecutive Super Bowl appearances.

In 13 of his 19 seasons, Smith recorded 10 or more sacks. His best showing came in 1990, when he got to the quarterback 19 times and earned his first of two NFL Defensive Player of the Year awards. The same year, he was voted to the Pro Bowl, an honor he would receive 11 times. Virtually each time the ball was snapped, he was double-teamed by offensive linemen and blocking backs.

"There are five players in this league who can take a team on their shoulders and make a difference," Jets quarterback Boomer Esiason said. "Barry Sanders, Jerry Rice, Emmitt Smith, Thurman Thomas and Bruce Smith."

Buffalo fans wanted Smith to retire as a Bill but it was not to be. In 1999, he was released to free up salary-cap room for the Bills and, two days later, he signed with

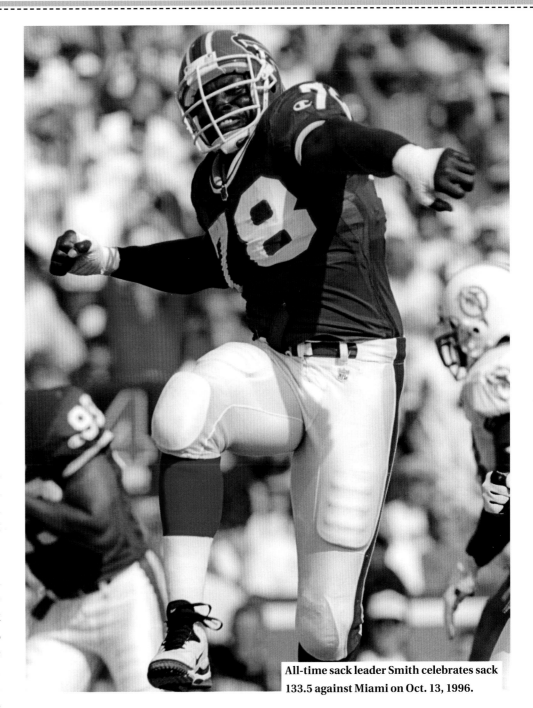

All-time sack leader Smith celebrates sack 133.5 against Miami on Oct. 13, 1996.

Washington, which was close to his hometown of Virginia Beach.

With the Redskins, Smith was not the player he once was. And yet, he managed 29 sacks in four seasons, including the 199th of his career, the sack that lifted him ahead of Reggie White and his record count of 198.

It happened Dec. 7, 2003, at Giants Stadium. Smith had knocked New York's starting quarterback Kerry Collins out of the game and, in the fourth quarter, was able to

tackle Collins' replacement, the Canadian-born Jesse Palmer, for a seven-yard loss.

The Redskins players rushed onto the field to congratulate Smith, who was given the game ball. Later in the Washington dressing room, he opened a gift that had been given to him by his tailor. It was a burgundy-colored robe with the Redskins' logo on the back and "All Time" written across the front.

He wore it with pride; the all-time hunter content at last. ▪

15

BART STARR

QUARTERBACK

FROM SIDELINES TO HEADLINES

Controlled. Precise. Economical. Humble. Cerebral. Efficient.

Bryan Bartlett Starr came to embody the perfect Vince Lombardi quarterback: the ultimate game-manager. He was the brain center of those legendary Packers' teams of the 1960s that had folks in tiny Green Bay answering their telephones with "Hello, Titletown U.S.A.!"

Ironically, at the beginning, Lombardi was far from convinced. Largely lost in the mists of the time and the almost mythic reverence in which that Packer era is held by football fans of two generations is the moment during the 1960 title game, which the emerging Pack lost 17–13 to the Philadelphia Eagles: Starr failed to spot a wide-open Max McGee at a critical point in the game. The missed opportunity gnawed away at Lombardi long after Eagles linebacker Chuck Bednarik stuffed running back Jim Taylor at the Philadelphia nine-yard-line to end Green Bay's bid.

"Yeah, some guys see them and some guys don't," Lombardi groused to NFL executive director Jim Kensil during dinner early in 1961. "Then," recalled Kensil, "he told me 'I'd really like to get that guy [Don] Meredith.' He told me he'd offered the Cowboys, who had just played their first season, any two players on the Packers' roster. I said 'Any two?' He said, 'Any two.' He really didn't think that Bart Starr was what he wanted in a quarterback. I thought that was very interesting when Starr started seeing *every* receiver. I always meant to ask Vinnie what happened to that two-for-one deal."

Over the course of a 15-year career, Bart Starr threw for more than 24,000 yards, won the 1966 NFL MVP, played in four Pro Bowls, and, here is the most telling testament to the man and his capabilities, captured five championships, including the first two Super Bowls. No one else — not Joe Montana, not Terry Bradshaw, not nobody — can make that claim.

He arrived in Green Bay a 17th-round draft choice, chosen 200th overall. He signed for $6,500. It's no wonder Lombardi didn't know whether he wanted Bart Starr or not — pretty much no one did. He languished on the bench his first season, shared playing time the next. In 1958, he started. The Packers went 1–10–1. During his first five seasons, Starr threw 41 interceptions and only 23 touchdowns. Then Lombardi arrived from the New York Giants, and so began the good times.

"Earlier in my career, many fans misinterpreted my calm demeanor for lack of imagination," Starr wrote in his autobiography.

No imagination?

The most famous single play of Starr's career, arguably in all of Packer lore, can be put down to his imagination: the famous third-down sneak at Lambeau Field in the "Ice Bowl" on Dec. 31, 1967. In almost inhuman conditions — a minus 45 Fahrenheit with wind chill that prompted Cowboys owner Clint Murchison to quip, "If I owned Green Bay, I'd dome the whole town." — with 13 seconds left, and the Pack down by three points with zero timeouts remaining, positioned two feet from the Cowboy end zone, Bart Starr dove into history. Cowboys coach Tom Landry felt certain the Packers would throw the ball. Halfback Donny Anderson had slipped on the two previous plays and an incomplete pass would at least give Starr time to run a final play.

Instead, Starr pitched the idea of a quarterback keeper to his coach on the sidelines, a simple dive right over offensive tackle Jerry Kramer (the basis of which would become Kramer's 1968 best-selling book *Instant Replay*). "I told Coach Lombardi there was nothing wrong with the plays we had run," Starr recalled afterwards. "It's just that the backs couldn't keep their footing. I said, 'Why don't I just keep it?' All he said was 'let's run it and get the hell out of here.' That's all he said."

They ran it and got the hell out of there. All the way to Miami two weeks later where the Packers paddled the Oakland Raiders to claim their second straight Super Bowl.

In retirement, the success he enjoyed as a player proved elusive. Starr's nine years as head coach in Green Bay netted only

The ever-calm Starr coolly fakes a handoff, eluding defenders to set up a pass.

one playoff game, and he was fired after an 8–8 season in 1983. Off the field, he suffered tragedy. In 1988, his oldest son, Bret, battling cocaine addiction, died of a heart attack that doctors felt was brought on by drug use.

Often, life leaves us no control. On the field, though, with Taylor and Hornung in the backfield, with Boyd Dowler and the madcap McGee split wide, and with Forrest Gregg, Jerry Kramer and Jim Ringo providing protection, Starr was in complete control.

"Bart Starr," said Lombardi once in tribute, "stands for what the game of football stands for: courage, stamina and co-ordinated efficiency. You instill desire by creating a superlative example. The noblest form of leadership is by example and that is what Bart Starr is all about."

All talk of Dandy Don Meredith had by then been long forgotten. The best two-for-one deal Vince Lombardi never made. ∎

34 THURMAN THOMAS

RUNNING BACK

THE TRIPLE THREAT

Few players smoldered the way Thurman Thomas did. He could bristle during practices. He glowed red hot during games. His intensity was a three-alarm blaze waiting for a strong wind to make it uncontrollable.

It didn't matter if you were friend or foe, teammate or media type, if you got near Thomas's blast furnace you got scorched. Even Jim Kelly, the Buffalo Bills star quarterback, felt the sting of Thomas's ire if he didn't play up to his potential.

"He brings an edge to the team because he's not afraid to get in anybody's face," Buffalo linebacker Darryl Talley once said of Thomas, "In my opinion, he was the best back I've ever seen at being able to catch the ball out of the backfield and being able to run the ball at the same time."

He could run, he could catch and he bubbled with a desire that matched his versatility. Thomas is the only player in NFL history to lead the league in total yards from scrimmage for four consecutive seasons, and also the only player to have scored a touchdown in four consecutive Super Bowls.

He is one of six running backs to date to have rushed for more than 1,000 yards in eight consecutive seasons. And he was one of a breed of rare backs known for their hands as well as their feet; Thomas and only eight other backs have managed to rush for more than 12,000 career yards while pulling in more than 400 career receptions.

"I don't believe there has ever been a more complete player at his position than Thurman," Bills coach Marv Levy said when he delivered Thomas's induction speech at the Pro Football Hall of Fame in 2007.

Branded the "Thurminator," Thomas was such a complete competitor that his teammates marveled at everything he did on a football field, including the way he blocked.

"I swear to God, I watched film of it at times to remind myself of the proper way to do things," said Buffalo center Kent Hull. "If Thurman had been bigger, he would have made a heck of an offensive lineman."

Thomas was such an outstanding running back at Oklahoma State University he kept Barry Sanders glued to the bench,

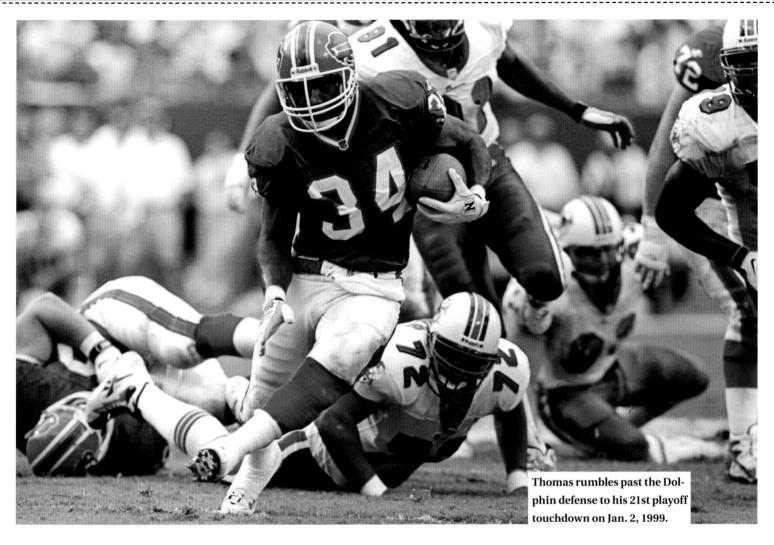

Thomas rumbles past the Dolphin defense to his 21st playoff touchdown on Jan. 2, 1999.

a pretty neat trick considering how good Sanders was.

In four seasons at OSU, Thomas ran for 4,595 yards and 43 touchdowns. He had 21 100-yard games but caught just two passes for 15 yards. By the time he left for the NFL, Thomas was his school's all-time leading rusher and a likely first-round draft pick in 1988. But a knee injury sent Thomas's stock plummeting. He was taken in the second round, 40th overall, by a Buffalo team that was eager to add a skilled running back to its budding offensive arsenal.

With Thomas locked in, the Bills revamped their attack to take advantage of his skills. They became the masters of the hurry-up offense and used it, not just as time was winding down late in the second and fourth quarter, but as a change-of-pace tactic that caught opponents flat-footed.

"One [game] that really started the no-huddle was when he caught a playoff record against the Cleveland Browns, like 13 catches or something," recalled Kelly. "Defensive coordinators really didn't know how to guard against what we had."

Not being able to stop Buffalo's multi-faceted offense was a common problem in the AFC. The Bills won four conference titles in a row to earn four consecutive trips to the Super Bowl, a feat no team has managed since.

Unfortunately for the Bills, their first Super Bowl appearance in 1991 was their best, and it was still a loss. Thomas totaled 190 yards rushing and receiving, and scored a touchdown, but the Bills were left heartbroken when kicker Scott Norwood's 47-yard field goal sailed wide right, sealing their 20–19 loss to the New York Giants.

A year later in Super Bowl XXVI, everything went wrong for the Bills. At the start of the game, Thomas couldn't find his helmet and had to miss two plays. He didn't touch the ball until 12 minutes had been played. That set the tone for the game, as the Bills lost to the Washington Redskins, 37–24. In their next two Super Bowl appearances in 1993 and 1994, the Bills would be drubbed by the Dallas Cowboys by a combined score of 82–30. It was a bitter experience for Thomas, who would, years later, joke about the case of the missing helmet:

"You always sent me out well-equipped," Thomas told Levy at the Hall of Fame ceremony, "except for that one time when you played tricks on me with my helmet."

When it came to giving his best in a number of ways, from performing to keeping his teammates honest, few players in NFL history were better equipped than Thomas. He gave the Bills their spark.

And he burned brightly doing it. ■

8 STEVE YOUNG

QUARTERBACK

IN THE FOOTSTEPS OF THE GODS

Someone has to follow in the footsteps of the gods. Someone had to be the heavyweight boxing champ after Muhammad Ali was stripped of the title. Someone had to be the Chicago Bulls shooting guard after Michael Jordan retired. Someone had to coach in Green Bay after Vince Lombardi moved on.

And someone had to play quarterback after Joe Montana was traded away by the San Francisco 49ers. Steve Young was that someone. He was the follower who bore the brunt of comparative greatness. Montana was king — a four-time Super Bowl champion of mythical proportions. Young came after: a good player who never seemed to measure up when it counted.

It stayed that way until 1995 when Young finally won a Super Bowl, won Super Bowl MVP honors, and set a Super Bowl record by throwing six touchdowns (nosing out the previous record holder, the unparalleled Montana, who had tossed five touchdown passes). In that glorious moment in Young's career, the comparisons ended, and the true appreciation commenced. Theoretically, it should have started sooner.

Young was jaw-droppingly good with the 49ers before his win in Super Bowl XXIX. He could run like a fullback and deke like a halfback. He could throw off the run or from deep in the pocket. Either way, he was utterly proficient, always completing a high percentage of his passes.

"Steve is doing things no other quarterback has ever done," 49ers tight end Brent Jones said. "But there are still people who think they can only like Joe. Steve can't please all the people in the world. There's never going to be another Joe, and Steve knows that. What more can he do? … People have to realize that if they want to follow us, then their favorite quarterback ought to be Steve Young."

Young certainly waited for his chance to succeed Montana. After spending two seasons in the USFL, then another two with the Tampa Bay Buccaneers, Young was traded to the 49ers where he waited another four years before becoming a starter. He got his chance when Montana was sidelined with an elbow injury. Unfortunately, Young suffered a knee injury that limited his playing time.

Young in the 1992 playoffs; he led the regular season with 25 touchdown passes.

Still, there were signs that Young was the one to eventually replace Montana. In 1992, despite a serious concussion, Young passed for 3,456 yards and 25 touchdowns and won the NFL's MVP award. The King was dead. Long live the King.

Montana was traded to the Kansas City Chiefs in 1993, clearing the way for Young, who overcame a sluggish start to finish the year with 4,023 passing yards and 29 touchdowns. Losing to the Dallas Cowboys in the playoffs for the second year in a row revved up the critics who thought of Young as a flawed substitute to you-know-who. It didn't help that when Montana's Chiefs played Young's 49ers in September 1994, the Chiefs won 24–17, while Young was sacked and harried all afternoon.

"I really feel like, in being after Joe, I've learned how to be a great quarterback and now I have a chance to go prove it," Young said of his situation. "I think a lot of people feel they have untapped potential in their bodies and don't get a chance to bring it out. In San Francisco, with the pressure, I have a chance to see how good I really can get."

The Chiefs game was the last tough loss San Francisco endured that season. Young threw for 35 touchdowns, led his team past Dallas in the playoffs and would need just one minute and 24 seconds to begin his Super Bowl rout of the San Diego Chargers. He hit receiver Jerry Rice for a 44-yard touchdown, and then found running back Ricky Watters for a 51-yard touchdown on the 49ers' second possession. The game's final stats showed San Francisco with 28 first downs and 455 yards in offense with Young as the game's leading passer and rusher.

"All along, I felt I was playing against the past," Young said afterward. "Honestly, I have distanced myself from all [the Montana comparisons]. I did so a couple of years ago. I want my performance to stand for myself and my teammates."

That it did. Although several more concussions forced Young into early retirement, his numbers stood tall, throwing for more than 3,000 yards in a season six times and for 20 or more touchdowns five times. He holds the NFL record among retired quarterbacks for the highest career passer rating (96.8), and the record for most rushing touchdowns by a quarterback (43).

In 2005, Young was inducted into the Pro Football Hall of Fame — the first left-handed quarterback to be so honored. Arguably, the reward that was just as meaningful was the 49ers decision to retire his No. 8 jersey.

Like the man before him, Young left behind some mighty good footsteps for the next guy to follow. ■

FUTURE GREATS

Drew Brees
Antonio Brown
Larry Fitzgerald
Antonio Gates
Rob Gronkowski
Justin Houston
Andre Johnson
Calvin Johnson
Luke Kuechly
Andrew Luck
Marshawn Lynch
DeMarco Murray
Darrelle Revis
Aaron Rodgers
Richard Sherman
Terrell Suggs
Joe Thomas
DeMarcus Ware
J.J. Watt
Russell Wilson

9 Drew BREES

QUARTERBACK

PASSING PERFECTION

The Big Easy, as everyone knows, has wrapped its arms around Drew Brees and welcomed him into the family as its adopted son.

The Texas-born graduate is now as much a part of Bayou lore as Louis Armstrong, the French Quarter or those delectable powdered-sugar doughnuts locals call "beignets."

Frustrated by a predominately incentive-laden contract offer from the San Diego Chargers, Brees went searching for other opportunities. But when the surefire first-ballot future Hall of Famer first signed on in New Orleans, more than a smattering of fans and media pundits were skeptical, to put it mildly.

Brees' signing came only six months after the devastation wrought by Hurricane Katrina and the Saints were a 3–13 mess. What many thought the team needed was a can't-miss pivot, but Brees — however dynamic and already accomplished — was a quarterback endeavoring to rebound from surgery to repair a torn rotator cuff and damaged right labrum to his throwing wing.

One particular opinion holder, however, had an immediate inkling of how the Saints had made out like bandits. Lorean Tomlinson, mother of Chargers superstar tailback LaDainian Tomlinson, said: "The San Diego Chargers have lost their mind" about how badly her son's employers had misread the situation.

With all due respect to current Chargers QB Philip Rivers, time has proven LaDainian's mom an astute judge of sanity because since the Chargers decided to let Brees go, the once damaged quarterback has not only won a championship, but he's taken a shredder to the NFL record book, leaving legends like Dan Marino and Dan Fouts in his wake.

For his air and for his care, the Who Dat Nation has bestowed on him divinity status. "Breesus," they call him reverentially.

"For me," Brees said at the time, "I looked at [going to New Orleans] as an opportunity. An opportunity to be part of a rebuilding process. How many people in their life get to be a part of something like that? They had as much confidence in me returning from my shoulder injury that year as I had

Brees looks to throw against the Vikings in 2014; he threw for a league-high 456 passes that season.

in myself. And that meant a lot to me."

The Saints' 31–17 Super Bowl victory over Peyton Manning and the Indianapolis Colts in 2009 continues to resonate among the most emotional championships ever claimed, symbolizing as it did a shattered city's indomitable spirit and brave resurgence in the wake of profound natural devastation.

Leading the charge, Brees went 32 of 39 passes — tying an NFL completion record set by the iconic Tom Brady — for 288 yards and 2 touchdowns that day at Sun Life Stadium in Miami. For his part, Brees took home MVP honors, and the victory touched off a celebration that thrust the fabled bacchanalia of Mardi Gras into the shade.

"He is," said Saints GM Mickey Loomis at the time, "the perfect person for an imperfect situation."

And really for any situation as it turns out. Among the records Brees already holds are most yards in a season (5,476) and most 300-plus yard passing games in a season

(13). He's reached 40,000 career-passing yards faster than any other player and is tops in career passing yards per game, too. In the 2014 season, New Orleans failed to make the playoffs, despite Brees playing up to his usual standards and leading the league with 4,952 yards passing.

"At 211 degrees," Saints coach Sean Payton once famously said, "water is just scalding hot. But at 212, it boils. It's the significance of one degree. Everything about Drew Brees' preparation is about that one extra degree."

That one degree, and what he could wring from it, has become the stuff of greatness. And the kid from Dallas has continued to shine, even if that second Super Bowl championship has proven elusive for the Saints.

In Week 5 of a troubled beginning to the 2012 season — one which included the fallout from the infamous bounty hunting sanctions — there was more Brees history to lift tattered spirits. In the first quar-

ter, Brees delivered a 40-yard touchdown pass to Devery Henderson against his old team, the Chargers. This pushed Brees to a 48 consecutive game touchdown streak, which surpassed Johnny Unitas, the slope-shouldered, crew-cut deity.

That record had stood for over half a century. To put the feat into perspective, 10 different men have occupied the White House since Unitas set it.

"You watch guys like Johnny U on some of the highlight film, and watching the way he threw the ball in that era was pretty unbelievable," Brees said, savoring the moment. "He really revolutionized the game and the quarterback position… Certainly, his accomplishments speak for themselves. His Baltimore Colts teams, I think that was the heyday and paved the way for what we have now."

Just as the heyday of Drew Brees is paving the way for the next generation of rocket-armed QBs who might someday eclipse his records. ■

84 ANTONIO BROWN

WIDE RECEIVER

TRUTH IN NUMBERS

The NFL has seen its share of streaks — some good, some bad, many of them beyond explanation.

And then there's Antonio Brown's streak. It's an extended show unto itself.

For 22 consecutive games, the pride of the Pittsburgh Steelers' receiving corps caught at least five passes for 50 yards. That's far more impressive than making a single catch a game for any number of games, which has long been an NFL benchmark. What Brown has done is magnify a whole new category, the 5/50 Club. Others may have tried it, but they have never owned it the way Brown does.

From late in the 2013 season through the entire 2014 season, Brown has been the constant in the Steelers' offense. Whenever he's been pushed to be better, he has responded with big plays and big numbers. His receiving statistics for 2014 were 129 catches for 1,698 yards and 13 touchdowns, all of those numbers being franchise records.

By December 2014, Brown had made 122 catches through 15 games, the fourth-highest number of catches in NFL history. (Former Indianapolis Colt Marvin Harri-

son holds the league record of 143 catches in a single season.)

Brown was so good for so many games that people who had never really followed him before became his biggest fans. Former San Francisco 49ers Hall of Fame receiver Jerry Rice said Brown was "killing it right now." Rice was also impressed with how Brown wanted to glean every detail he could from Rice's football habits.

"He wanted to know my workout regimen and how [I sustained a high level of play] for so many years," Rice said after meeting with Brown. "I just told him it was all about work ethic and never getting complacent and never getting to a point where you can [let yourself relax]."

Brown has made a lifestyle out of pushing himself to be better. Born in Miami, Brown described his childhood as "a little rough." That's a colossal understatement. When Brown turned 16, his mother and stepfather kicked him out of the house. He would spend his nights staying with his high school teammates at their homes. Occasionally, when he had the money, he would pay $20 to sleep in a sleazy hotel that

Brown makes his first of two touchdown receptions in a game against the Colts on Oct. 26, 2014.

operated on a maximum stay of two hours.

"It taught me never to take anything for granted," Brown told ESPN of his teenage years. "At that point, it was time to become a man."

He parlayed his high school heroics in track and field and football into a scholarship at Central Michigan University. He played receiver and returned punts. At the 2010 NFL Draft, Pittsburgh went with the speedy Brown. He was the 195th selection in the sixth round.

Having earned a spot on the Steelers' roster, Brown burned the Tennessee Titans in his NFL debut with a reverse kickoff return that covered 89 yards for a touchdown. It was a sign of good things to come. By the end of the 2011 season, he was the first player in NFL history to record 1,000 yards in both kick returns and receiving in the same season.

"He's a great runner after the catch," said former NFL coach turned TV analyst Herman Edwards. "He's got great hand/eye coordination, body control, and he's fast. He runs a fast 40 time [4.48 seconds]. Some guys, when they play football, they don't play to that time. He plays to that time."

Brown, as he is quick to admit, has benefited from Pittsburgh's pass-it-first offense built around the strength of quarterback Ben Roethlisberger's right arm. The Steelers can, and do, run the ball, but when it comes to crunch time, the call usually goes out to Brown. It's a call that some teams have had a hard time handling.

Such was the case in a 2014 game between the Steelers and Jacksonville Jaguars. Pittsburgh was ahead 17–9 coming out of the fourth quarter's two-minute warning. The Steelers had the ball at the Jacksonville 33-yard line, the game essentially over. Rather than run out the game with a couple of kneel downs, Roethlisberger called a swing pass to Brown, who needed one more reception to maintain his consecutive 5/50 record.

Roethlisberger threw; Brown made the catch then tacked on some yards. After the game, Pittsburgh head coach Mike Tomlin had to defend the throw to Brown.

"He's got a significant record that exemplifies what he's doing in his career," Tomlin explained. "We want to support that."

Tomlin added that if the swing pass was botched, his team would not have thrown another. "If he doesn't get it on that play, it's a wrap," he said.

With Brown on the receiving end, one take was all that was needed. ▪

11 LARRY FITZGERALD

WIDE RECEIVER

SLEIGHT OF HAND

What makes Larry Fitzgerald so special are his hands. Fitzgerald has never been the biggest or fastest receiver in the NFL, but his hands are surely the best. He has the kind of hands you want when someone is packing your fine china for a move. And that degree of steady-handedness is why he's so deft at catching footballs.

"Larry Fitzgerald could catch a bee with chopsticks," a television announcer once gushed. Okay, so that's a stretch, but the Arizona Cardinals wide receiver does have a knack for making every kind of catch — short, deep, improbable and "Did you see that?" If a pass is anywhere near him, he's all over it with a butterfly net. Defenders can be waving their arms, trying to position themselves in front of Fitzgerald, and he'll reach over or around them and snag the ball. Makes it look easy, too. Like the time he juggled a pass in the air against the San Francisco 49ers, only to corral it at the last moment and run for the touchdown. Or the time he out-fought and out-jumped two Carolina Panther defensive backs for a spectacular long gainer downfield.

Fitzgerald's NFL peers have routinely voted him one of the top players in the league. In 2012, he topped the 10,000-yard mark for his career, making him, at the time, only the second NFL receiver to gain 10,000 yards before his 30th birthday. Calvin Johnson has since joined Fitzgerald and Randy Moss on the elite list.

In 2013 Fitzgerald topped Moss as the youngest player in NFL history to reach 11,000 yards receiving.

"Just throw the ball up. I'm going to catch it," says Fitzgerald.

It worked that way at the University of Pittsburgh, where the Minneapolis-born Fitzgerald racked up yardage and set an NCAA record by catching a touchdown pass in 18 consecutive games. It helped make him a Heisman Trophy runner-up and the third pick overall in the 2004 NFL draft. And it didn't take him long to show the Cardinals he could be just as valuable in the pros.

In his first season, at age 21, he became the youngest player in NFL history to catch two touchdown passes in the same game. He finished the year with 58 receptions for

780 yards and 8 touchdowns. The following season he was stunningly better — 103 catches, 1,409 yards and 10 touchdowns. He and teammate Anquan Boldin became only the third pair of NFL receivers to surpass 1,400 yards in the same season.

But the best was yet to come.

In the 2008 NFL playoffs, Fitzgerald went from local star to national icon. His catapult to fame began in the NFC Championship Game against the Philadelphia Eagles. By halftime, he had scored three times, setting an NFC Championship Game record for touchdown catches. It helped lift the Cardinals into a Super Bowl XLIII showdown with the Pittsburgh Steelers. Pittsburgh ended up winning the title, 27–23, despite Fitzgerald catching two touchdowns, one in the final half of the fourth quarter. Overall, Fitzgerald set a post-season record with 30 catches, 546 yards and 7 touchdowns, knocking Jerry Rice out of top spot.

A week after his Super Bowl loss, Fitzgerald competed in the Pro Bowl, where he caught two more touchdown passes and was named the game's Most Valuable Player. He eventually fessed up and said he had played the entire postseason with a broken left thumb and torn cartilage in the same hand, a revelation that made his receiving numbers shine even brighter.

The Cardinals struggled for a time following their Super Bowl appearance. Boldin was traded to the Baltimore Ravens, and quarterback Kurt Warner, the elder statesman of the club, retired. For two years, 2010 and 2011, the Cardinals posted a combined 13–19 record and failed to make the playoffs. Yet through it all, Fitzgerald worked on his timing with a carousel of quarterbacks. His 2014 season (63 catches, 784 yards, 2 touchdowns) was modest due to a lingering knee injury that forced him out of two games and parts of others. Carson Palmer, behind center since 2013, figures to be Fitzgerald's part-

Fitzgerald catches the ball in a 17–10 Cardinals victory over the Seahawks.

ner in crime again after coming off a similarly injury-shortened 2014 campaign. For the Cardinals, the hope is the pair will pick up where they left off in 2013, when the duo hooked up for 10 touchdown passes.

As for his off-field ambitions, Fitzgerald is a self-proclaimed "student of life." He's involved in a series of charitable works, including distributing hearing aids to the needy in Uganda. He's also taken a liking to photography, with some of his photos from Africa, Vietnam, Japan and Easter Island being shown on *Sports Illustrated*'s website.

Fitzgerald has a good eye for detail. It has been said he's exceptionally good behind a camera. When it comes to catching a football, he's the best in the business, hands down. ■

85

ANTONIO GATES

TIGHT END

HOOP DREAMS TO GRIDIRON SENSATION

Antonio Gates never set out to make the good people of San Diego forget Kellen Winslow. But to be held in the same regard as the Hall of Fame tight end has certainly been special.

By doing it his way, by making plays and gaining the trust of his teammates, Gates has put himself in an elite category. What he's been through and where he came from have provided his career with depth and resonance.

If Winslow is revered in San Diego for those seasons spent playing pitch-and-catch with the pass-happy Dan Fouts in the "Air" Coryell era, where coach Don Coryell wanted the ball in the air as often as possible, Gates has emerged from the shadow of Winslow to conjure up an even more pyrotechnic partnership with Philip Rivers.

The fact that he made it at all is quite remarkable.

Antonio Gates grew up in inner-city Detroit, in a neighborhood teeming with drugs and other dangers. He credits his parents with steering him out of trouble, channeling his energies toward sports,

which led him to star for Central High School in both football and basketball.

"You have to affiliate yourself [with] people that want to become something, that want to do something in life," Gates said in a documentary on his life, *Forging a New Path*.

"I was trying a different path than a lot of my friends. You always want to hold onto that friendship and you still can, you just have to understand that your path is so different you can't do the same things. The first thing, for me, was that I had to surround myself with better people. Not that the people I was hanging with, my friends, were bad people, but I wanted to go to college, I wanted to become a professional athlete. If you didn't want to go to college, how much [did] we really have in common?"

Gates yearned to become a pro basketball star, to line up on coast-to-coast TV against LeBron James or Kobe Bryant. He never figured his path would put him opposite J.J. Watt or Richard Sherman.

Truth be told, the hardwood was always Gates' first love. In his senior year at Kent

State, he became the Golden Flashes' top scorer (20.6 PPG) and rebounder (7.7 RPG), and was selected an Associated Press Honorable Mention All-American. His great play propelled his school into the Elite Eight of the NCAA's March Madness tournament in 2002.

But, at 6-foot-4, NBA scouts weren't convinced. And so Gates dropped his hoop dreams and decided to see where football could take him. He arranged a tryout for NFL bird-dogs. He hadn't played football in four years. Not a down in college. It didn't matter. The Chargers took a look at his 255-pound frame, his competitiveness and quickness, and signed him to a contract in 2003. A little faith can sometimes pay huge dividends.

"In basketball, I always had a first step. A separation step. That works now, too," Gates has said of his transition to football.

Since a rookie season that saw him rise from third on the depth chart to a starting spot, Gates has found himself at the forefront of an NFL-wide re-emergence of the tight-end position. With size, speed and hands as soft as a roll of Charmin, he's the prototype of a new era. With fellow tight end Tony Gonzalez, the two have inspired a whole crop of tight ends, from Vernon Davis to Jimmy Graham and Rob Gronkowski. "The best," said the Chargers All-Pro safety Eric Weddle to ESPN of Gates' ability. "You can't guard him."

Gates signed a hefty six-year, $38 million deal in the fall of 2010, but since then

Gates gains yards after catching the ball in a 2013 game against the Bengals.

has been slowed by nagging foot injuries. Still, Gates, an eight-time Pro Bowler and five-time All-Pro, remains a force of nature when healthy. His 2014 season proved that. Not only did he become the Chargers' franchise leader in receiving yards, surpassing Lance Alworth, but Gates also became the fourth tight end in NFL history to gain more than 10,000 yards. Additionally, he finished the year with 12 touchdowns.

No longer merely the heir apparent to a long-ago legend, Gates is casting a rather large shadow of his own.

"I believe potential is a dangerous word; it can be used for anybody," Gates said early on in his career. "I don't want people to always say, 'He has the potential to be good.' Or, 'He has a couple of years to go.' I want somebody to say, 'Damn, that's a good tight end.' Period."

One of the best. Ever. ■

87 ROB GRONKOWSKI

TIGHT END

THE HUMAN BATTERING RAM

"The Gronk." Could there be a better nickname for a football player of Rob Gronkowski's man-crushing abilities?

He is, after all, a demolition looking for a place to happen. He drags players, sometimes multiple players, who try to tackle him and knocks them flat. Sometimes he "Gronkowskis" them — leaving them looking like a pile of strewn rubble. It's his full-on approach to football.

While John Mackey reinvented the tight end position in the 1960s, the 6-foot-6, 265-pound Gronkowski has taken it to the stratosphere. He scored 10 touchdowns his rookie season in the NFL. He scored 17 his second year and caught passes for 1,327 yards, both single-season records for tight ends. He caught 11 touchdown passes in his third year, becoming the third tight end to post three 10-TD seasons, and the first to do it consecutively. Gronk also signed a six-year, $54 million contract extension with the New England Patriots, the richest deal ever for a tight end. And he even got to work on a book entitled *Growing Up Gronk*.

He did all that by the age of 23, making The Gronk the NFL's most uniquely outra-geous athlete both in and out of uniform. In and out of clothes, too. Posing nude for *ESPN The Magazine*'s body issue was one thing; posing shirtless with an adult film actress who just happened to be wearing his New England jersey was another. So was his shirtless dancing at a nightclub hours after the Patriots' loss to the New York Giants in Super Bowl XLVI. That act was caught on video and had some people wondering, "Wasn't this the guy who was hobbled the entire game by a bad left ankle? And now he's bouncing around like a 265-pound jackrabbit?"

Gronkowski shrugged off the criticism and reveled in his new-found status.

"He never ceases to amaze me," said Patriots quarterback Tom Brady.

The Gronk's amazing adventure began in Williamsville, New York, where he grew up the second-youngest of five sports-mad brothers. Did the brothers fight? Always. Did Gronkowski get the worst of it? More often than not; but it did toughen him up and feed his anything-goes nature. In high school, he played on both sides of the ball, a receiver on offense, a pass rusher on de-

Gronkowski takes flight for a touchdown in a 42–20 romp over the Colts on Nov. 16, 2014.

fense. He chose the University of Arizona for the next stage of his development and evolved into an All-Pac-10 tight end. He was twice named the John Mackey Tight End of the Week. Back surgery affected his 2010 NFL draft ranking and it wasn't until the second round that the Patriots chose him with the 42nd pick overall. A delighted Gronkowski mugged for the television crew. It was a sign of things to come.

Right from the start, most everything Gronkowski did with the Patriots was larger than life. He carried defenders who jumped on his back before shaking them off and rumbling into the end zone. He scored three touchdowns in one game as a rookie. His second season dwarfed his first and it carried on through the 2011 playoffs. Against the Denver Broncos, Gronkowski scored three touchdowns on 10 catches. A

week later against the Baltimore Ravens, he suffered what was dubbed a high-ankle sprain as the Patriots advanced to the Super Bowl. (Gronkowski played in the 21–17 loss to the Giants, went dancing afterward, then had surgery to repair ligament damage.)

For the start of the 2012 season, Gronkowski insisted there was still a lot for him to work on as a tight end, even though many were declaring him the best in the business.

"If I'm going out there and doing my job, doing what I'm being asked to do blocking-wise, pass-blocking, run blocking, doing what I'm asked to do in the passing game, I believe that we'll be fine," he told reporters. "We'll be successful out there as a whole. And if as an offense we're successful, I believe my role is being completed, too."

He had to alter his role after team-

mate Aaron Hernandez was arrested and charged with the first-degree murder of Odin Lloyd. In 2011, Gronkowski and Hernandez had combined for 169 catches for 2,237 yards and 24 touchdowns, the highest totals ever recorded by two tight ends on the same team. Without Hernandez in 2013, Gronkowski ended up going it alone and suffered a slew of injuries, from a broken arm to a back injury that required surgery.

He managed to pull himself back together in 2014 and became the first tight end in NFL history to catch at least 10 touchdowns in four separate seasons. Gronkowski also scored a touchdown in the Patriots' Super Bowl XLIX win.

So, how did he celebrate during the off-season? He played a cop in a movie project called *You Can't Have It*. Apparently, when you're the Gronk, you can. ∎

173

50 JUSTIN HOUSTON

LINEBACKER

SACK MACHINE

Every NFL quarterback who plays against the Kansas City Chiefs' defense knows the deal: that guy over there, wearing No. 50, anticipating the snap count so he can explode off the line, he's coming for you. It is in his DNA.

Show Justin Houston a quarterback then stand back and watch him hunt. It is what Houston does better than any outside linebacker in the league; it is why he has totaled 43 sacks in his last three seasons. He chases, he catches, he sacks. His opponents know he's coming for their quarterback and still they can't find a way to stop him.

"He's coming off the edge with a bad attitude on every play," Oakland Raiders' running back Darren McFadden said of Houston.

"He's a guy, on any given down, who can change a game with one quarterback sack," added Kansas City receiver Jeremy Maclin.

Houston eluded blockers and punished quarterbacks from the beginning to the end of the 2014 season. He finished with 22 sacks, good enough to break the previous franchise record of 20 set by the legendary Derrick Thomas. Houston's 22 also came within a whisker of equaling Michael Strahan's NFL single-season record of 22.5 sacks. Assuredly, it stamped Houston's reputation as a genuine A-list defender.

"My goal is to get as many sacks as I can," he said unashamedly. "That's my job."

Houston has been doing his job well enough to transform from local star to ascending NFL great. While he has been clear about his role in the Chiefs' defense, he has been careful not to put his needs above the team's, an act of leadership that wasn't lost on his coach or observers around the league.

"At no point did you feel like he was going for the [sack] record. You felt like everybody around him was pulling for him, but it wasn't from him," Chiefs coach Andy Reid told KCChiefs.com. "He was all about winning."

"He's good with his hands," assessed Cincinnati Bengals defensive lineman Geno Atkins. "He's got a good first step off the ball … He's a tremendous player."

Houston was a remarkable player as far back as his high school days. He helped his teammates advance to three consecutive state championship games and winning one in 2005. He enrolled at the University of Georgia and proved to be a quick study. He had seven sacks his sophomore year and 10 as a junior. He was later voted All-South Eastern Conference and a first team All-American.

That carried Houston to the 2011 NFL Combine, where all the top collegiate players were put through drills while scouts looked on and took notes. They took a lot of notes after watching Houston, who was then listed as 6-foot-3, 270 pounds and could cover 40 yards in 4.62 seconds. That should have made him a first-round pick. Instead, he was chosen by Kansas City in the third round with the 70th pick overall. There were reports Houston had tested positive for marijuana and that had scared several teams away.

In his first season with the Chiefs, Houston had 5.5 sacks and 49 tackles. By 2013, he was listed as one of the NFL's top 100 players and a first team All-Pro. Chiefs' defensive coordinator Bob Sutton has been quoted as saying opposing offenses have to pay extra attention to blocking Houston, which allows his teammates more room to attack.

"He's not just a pass-rusher," Sutton said. "He's involved in multiple roles in coverage. We move him around to both cover and to pressure … The nature of the beast would say sack, sack, sack, but this guy played really good football in a lot of areas for us."

It hasn't hurt Houston to have another dangerous pass rusher on the Chiefs' defense. Veteran Tamba Hali has worked the other outside linebacker position and been a five-time Pro Bowl player who led the AFC in sacks in 2010. Together, the Hali-Houston combo has made Kansas City's defense one of the stingiest in the NFL.

And there's one more defensive gem Houston brings to the Chiefs — the strip sack. That's when Houston not only wraps

Houston stops Ben Roethlisberger in 2014, one of a league-leading 22 sacks.

up the quarterback; he strips the football away on a forced fumble. Houston had three of those in 2014 to rekindle the memories of Derrick Thomas, arguably the greatest player in the history of the franchise.

Thomas posted 126.5 sacks in 11 seasons with Kansas City and added 41 forced fumbles. His career ended when he was left paralyzed from the chest down after a

horrific car crash on Jan. 23, 2000. Sixteen days later, he died when a blood clot traveled into his lungs.

Thomas once had seven sacks in a single game and was elected to the Pro Football Hall of Fame. Houston hopes to get there one day, but only when he has finished hunting — and that's not about to happen any time soon. ∎

80 ANDRE JOHNSON

WIDE RECEIVER

QUIETLY DOMINANT

Teammates say Andre Johnson doesn't fool around with words. His actions are so much more emphatic. In a league loaded with good receivers, Johnson has flown higher and leaped further than most. His numbers shout "Pro Football Hall of Fame, here I come!" In his 12 seasons with the Houston Texans, he caught 1,012 passes for 13,597 yards receiving and 64 touchdowns. He is the only player in league history to record 60-plus pass receptions each season for his first eight years in the NFL. His three 1,500-yard seasons are one shy of the NFL record held by Jerry Rice, and in 2013, he was less than 100 yards shy of matching that.

Simply put, throw a football in Johnson's vicinity, chances are he'll locate it and catch it. Just don't expect him to say much about it.

Johnson is the prototypical strong and silent sort. At 6-foot-3 and 230 pounds, he is big enough to swat aside defensive backs and fast enough to run away from them. He makes it look so easy that the folks in Houston called him "The Natural."

That he would excel as a pro was never in doubt. At the University of Miami, he scored 20 touchdowns and was named MVP of the 2002 Rose Bowl along with his quarterback Ken Dorsey. The Texans selected him third overall in the 2003 NFL draft, and he responded with a respectable rookie season. His sophomore year was off the charts — 79 receptions, 1,142 yards and 6 touchdowns. Since then, Johnson has supplanted himself among the league's best receivers, earning extra nods for his overpowering strength and his ability to go after and "attack the football," as his peers have duly noted.

Yet Johnson found himself under attack in 2012 for not being as dominant as he had in years past. Through six weeks of the season, he had just 25 catches for 358 yards. Fans and media began to wonder if Johnson was showing his age, if all the physical wear and tear had begun to take its toll. He had missed the majority of the 2011 season with a hamstring injury, and although he made it back for the playoffs where he caught a 40-yard TD pass against the Cincinnati Bengals for a Houston victory in the franchise's first playoff game, the talented receiver struggled in the early going of 2012.

Gary Kubiak, the Texans' head coach at the time, stood up for his man, noting how defenses were continuously double covering Johnson and how the lack of a consistent running game was bogging down Houston's passing game. Johnson, who was bothered by a sore groin, remained stoic. When he got healthy, he went to work ripping the Jacksonville Jaguars for 273 yards, including a 48-yard, game-winning touchdown in overtime, and setting an NFL record with a combined 461 yards in back-to-back games.

"The life span in this league is four years. I've been fortunate to be here for 10 seasons," he said. "I don't feel old at all. I missed a lot of time [in 2011] and I feel like I have a lot to prove. I want to show people that I can still play at a high level."

Johnson ended up setting a career-high in yards caught in 2012, with 1,598. He followed that up with 1,407 yards in 2013. Then, he slumped. The 2014 season saw the Texans go with a new quarterback in Ryan Fitzpatrick who spent more time targeting second-year receiver DeAndre Hopkins than Johnson. Coupled with a concussion Johnson suffered toward the end of the season, the star wide receiver collected less than 1,000 yards for only the second time in seven seasons (the previous time being his 2011 injury-shortened campaign).

Instead of playing second fiddle, Johnson requested out of Houston, the only team he's ever known. The Indianapolis Colts were more than happy to sign the All-Star receiver, and they gave him what he wanted, a three-year contract worth $21 million.

That gives Johnson a new chance to show his dominance. He won't be talking up his game in Indy; he'll be delivering it for a Colts franchise that is on the rise with superstar quarterback Andrew Luck.

In fact, there might not be a better place for Johnson to quietly make a difference. ■

Johnson jumps for a reception against the Jaguars on Dec. 28, 2014.

81 CALVIN JOHNSON

WIDE RECEIVER

THE MOTOR CITY MARVEL

It wasn't merely history Calvin Johnson found himself chasing. No, he was in hot pursuit of one of football's most cherished records: Jerry Rice's single-season standard of 1,848 yards receiving.

Rice wrote his name in the record book nearly two decades ago, and when Johnson surpassed him on December 23, 2012, the accolades came pouring in.

"I've been an NFL fan my whole life, dating back to watching Johnny Unitas and Raymond Berry as a kid, and I've coached in this league for 19 years," marveled Johnson's Detroit coach, Jim Schwartz. "I've seen a lot of Hall of Famers, but I've never seen a better player than Calvin Johnson. He just broke a record set by Jerry Rice, who is arguably the best player in the history of this league."

They call Johnson "Megatron." It's a nickname former Lions wide-out Roy Williams stuck on him years ago for his out-of-this-world ability to catch footballs. No, Johnson may not be able to shape shift like his fictional namesake from *Transformers*, but in the eyes of many, the skills of the Detroit Lions receiver sure seem larger than life.

Johnson is 6-foot-5 and 240 pounds with a 47-inch vertical, and he can run the 40 in 4.3 seconds. Add that to his extremely large hands, deft instincts and willingness to sacrifice his body to make the grab, and you have one All-World receiving threat who, after eight NFL seasons, has cemented himself as football's best receiver. And maybe, just maybe, he's football's best player; be that at any position or in any city. Full stop.

It was after his fifth year that he signed an eight-year, $132 million contract extension to make him the NFL's highest paid player at the position. The signing came on the heels of his 96-catch, 1,681-yard, 16-touchdown 2011 season — the seventh-most yards compiled in a single season to that point. Some may have argued that many franchise players see a dip in production after a big-money extension. So, was Johnson worth it?

"Some guys are big," said Schwartz. "Some guys are fast. Some guys are strong. Calvin is all of that … whatever they pay him is not enough."

As he approached the Rice standard

midway through the 2012 season, talk began circulating about Johnson perhaps going one better and shattering the once unthinkable 2,000-yard barrier. Although he finished just shy of the record with 1,964 yards, Johnson set new marks for consecutive 100-yard games (8) and consecutive games with 10 or more receptions (4). He also tied Michael Irvin's record of eleven 100-yard games in a single season.

"I didn't know where I stood until people started telling me about it," Johnson admitted to the *Detroit News*. "My thing is [to] just continue grinding like I have been."

His mind-bending feats continued in 2014, when he heightened his reputation by reaching 10,000 yards receiving in just 115 games; no other player had caught so much in so few games.

"I mean, how many teams done stopped him?" former Indianapolis Colts cornerback, and now Lions teammate, Cassius Vaughn lamented at the time. "None."

It may sound trite, but this kind of success always seemed in the cards. The prodigy out of Newnan, Georgia, more than lived up to his potential in college. After two years of solid play, he exploded in 2006, his junior year, for 15 touchdowns and 1,202 yards. For his stellar play, Johnson was named a Consensus All-American and won the Fred Biletnikoff award as the nation's top receiver; *Sports Illustrated* even named him as their midseason consensus No. 1 pick for the 2007 NFL draft. When the Lions selected the prize catch out of Georgia Tech second overall, Johnson, who would have been a welcome addition to any of the NFL's 32 franchises, was reportedly almost flipped to the Tampa Bay Bucca-

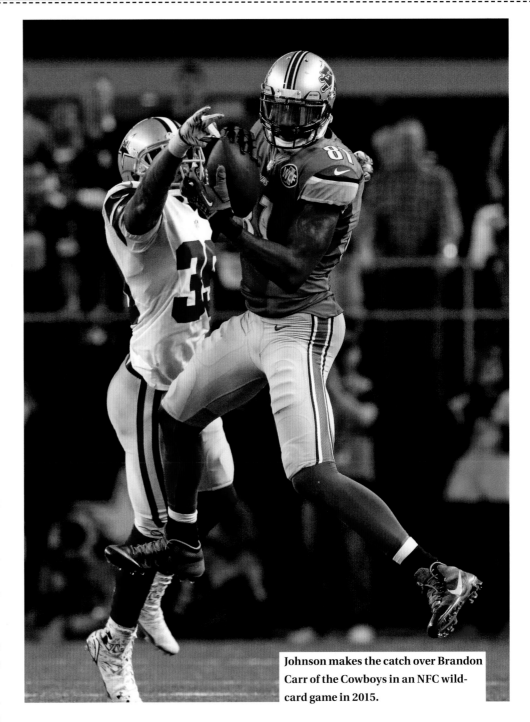

Johnson makes the catch over Brandon Carr of the Cowboys in an NFC wild-card game in 2015.

neers. The Lions were a desperate franchise that needed more than one good player to fill the holes in its very thin roster.

Often the smartest decisions come from the impulses you decide not to act upon; for while the Lions continue to seek roster depth and on-field consistency, Johnson and quarterback Matthew Stafford continue testing the boundaries of NFL secondaries. They've made the Lions a legitimate playoff threat, something the franchise

has rarely been in the last decade.

"He brings everything," lauded Indianapolis cornerback Darius Butler of Johnson's attributes. "If you want to go create a receiver on Madden [the NFL video game], that [receiver] is going to look like Calvin Johnson. He brings everything to the table."

There are many good receivers in football today. There are a handful of truly great receivers. But there's only one real-life Megatron. ▮

59 LUKE KUECHLY

LINEBACKER

THE HUMBLE HITTING MACHINE

There was little doubt Luke Kuechly was going to be a pro football star. Coming out of Boston College, he won: the Vince Lombardi Award as the best lineman/linebacker in U.S. college football; the Lott IMPACT Trophy as defensive player of the year; the Bronko Nagurski Trophy as the best defensive player in the NCAA; and the Dick Butkus Award as the top linebacker at the collegiate level.

Think about that roll call: from the legendary Lombardi to Ronnie Lott to football icons Nagurski and Butkus, all those men stood for greatness, and all their awards ended up on Kuechly's mantel. Right next to his declaration as a two-time consensus First-Team All-American.

Destined for stardom, Kuechly has made good on all those awards and honors. He is the focal point of the Carolina Panthers' defense; the middle linebacker who has redefined the word "relentless." As Atlanta Falcons receiver Roddy White put it, "Luke Kuechly is a tackling machine." The Exterminator.

In 2014 Kuechly topped the NFL with 153 tackles and added 11 pass deflections, three sacks, a forced fumble and an interception. He was voted to the NFL All-Pro First Team for the second year in a row, a sure sign he's going to need a bigger mantel.

"If I had to do a quarter of what he does [on the field] I'd need an oxygen tank," Carolina center Ryan Kalil said of Kuechly. "You'd have to bring me out in a golf cart."

Kuechly has done so much, earned such extravagant praise, that it is easy to forget he's only been in the NFL since 2012. For three consecutive seasons, he has never missed a game and rarely missed a tackle. He is as reliable as he is dogged. They were the traits that drew national attention when he took to the field for the Boston College Eagles.

In 2009, Kuechly started for the Eagles and led the NCAA in tackles as a freshman. By the time he left Boston College, scouts were keen to see him at the NFL Combine training sessions, where he would be compared to the other top linebacker prospects. It didn't take long for scouts and onlookers to realize there were no holes in Kuechly's game.

"I call him Clark Kent," said NFL Net-

Kuechly tries to take the ball from the Falcons' Roddy White on Nov. 16, 2014.

work announcer Mike Mayock, "and he can turn into Superman on Saturdays and Sundays. He's one of the cleanest players in this [2012] draft. His instincts and his pass-coverage ability might be the best of any linebacker I've seen come out of the draft."

Carolina agreed, taking Kuechly with the ninth pick overall. By the 2012 season opener, he was a starting outside linebacker, with Jon Beason in the middle. When Beason tore an Achilles tendon, Kuechly was moved into the middle spot. Three games into the 2013 season, Beason was traded to the New York Giants.

Former Dallas Cowboys personnel director Gil Brandt was so impressed with Kuechly's development he described the young Panther as "someone under the age of 25 who has a chance to become one of the best of his era." Brandt noted that with

Kuechly in the middle, Carolina gave up 66 fewer points than in 2011.

NFL head coach Rex Ryan went a step further calling Kuechly "a young Urlacher." It was a direct and complimentary comparison to former Chicago Bears middle linebacker Brian Urlacher. Kuechly later showed why such praise was warranted. In a 2013 game against the New Orleans Saints, he was credited with 24 tackles. That tied the NFL record for most tackles in a single game. The Panthers reviewed the video of that game and found two more tackles by Kuechly, giving him the solo record with 26.

Asked what it felt like to make that many tackles in one game, Kuechly kept to his Clark Kent alter-ego: "I was running around a lot. Our defensive line was awesome. When they play great it allows us to run around and make some plays."

Being so unassuming is not an act for Kuechly. When told that Pro Football Focus had called him one of the NFL's most overrated players, Kuechly replied, "Everyone's entitled to their own opinions … Some people say you're not doing your job if you don't have certain stats, but you ignore that. It's all about whether you're helping your team win."

On that count, Kuechly's presence invigorates the Panthers even when they're practising. Quarterback Cam Newton said he and Kuechly have a one-on-one contest every time they run plays against each other.

"It's an unspoken challenge not to throw [an interception] to him," Newton explained. "We have our own way of challenging each other … He's an unbelievable person. He knows he's good but he's extremely humble." ▉

12 ANDREW LUCK

QUARTERBACK

MOLDING THE FUTURE

After watching Andrew Luck prepare for the 2015 Pro Bowl, New Orleans Saints quarterback Drew Brees offered some lavish praise for his Indianapolis Colts' counterpart.

Brees said Luck might be the shape of things to come.

"If you say there's a mold, he fits the mold," Brees told Colts.com. "He might be the mold."

As Luck will have it, he is fast becoming the measure of NFL quarterbacks. He is powerful in size (6-foot-4, 240 pounds) and proficient in delivery. In the 2014 regular season, he passed for a league-leading 40 touchdowns along with 4,761 yards. Only Brees threw for more yards.

In Week 9, Luck unleashed four touchdown passes against the New York Giants. In Week 13, he bettered that by throwing for five touchdowns against the Washington Redskins. In Week 15, he led the Colts to a victory over the Houston Texans that put Indianapolis in the AFC playoffs for the third straight year, an accomplishment not lost on his peers.

"From everything I've seen, he's got all the physical tools. He's got all the mental tools," said Brees. "He seems like a great leader."

Luck is the quarterback the Colts hoped he would be when they drafted him first overall in 2012. Leading up to that, the Colts were at a crossroads with incumbent quarterback Peyton Manning. The Super Bowl–winning pivot had two neck surgeries in 2011 and missed the entire season. At one point doctors told him that he might never play again.

Indianapolis fans assessed the situation and decided the team should "suck for Luck," meaning they should lose all their games and thus earn the No. 1 pick in the 2012 NFL Draft. The Colts did precisely as advised, winning only two of 16 games during the 2011 season to secure the first overall pick. On March 7, the Colts released Manning, who signed with the Denver Broncos 13 days later. That cleared the way for Luck, and he didn't disappoint.

The former Stanford University standout, who many believed was the best quarterback from his school since John Elway, settled into the Colts' offense in

Luck makes a play during a victorious AFC wild-card game against the Bengals.

2012 and impressed his new teammates with his dedication on the field and in the weight room. That helped Luck set NFL records for the most passing yards in a single game by a rookie quarterback [433], most passing yards in a season [4,374] and most fourth-quarter comebacks [seven]. In the playoffs, though, the Colts went to Baltimore and were beaten convincingly by the Ravens, 24–9.

The following postseason, the Colts hosted a playoff game and defeated the Kansas City Chiefs in a 45–44 thriller. Luck engineered a 28-point comeback by throwing for 433 yards and four touchdowns. Indianapolis then faced the New England Patriots and lost by three touchdowns.

The 2014 postseason saw Luck and the Colts take another step forward. After beating the Cincinnati Bengals in a Wild Card matchup, Luck and his teammates flew to Denver to take on Manning and the Broncos. It was the first time Manning and the man who replaced him in Indianapolis played opposite one another in such a meaningful game. Luck wasn't always at his best against Denver, but he did enough to help his side to a 24–13 win and another date with the New England Patriots.

Asked about beating Manning and what effect that had on him, Luck said that was never the point.

"I never felt, from day one, that I had to [fill] someone's shoes," Luck answered. "We have a lot of great leaders and they made me feel welcome from day one, which I'm very thankful for."

Prior to the 2015 AFC Championship game against New England, even the Patriots were talking about how much they respected Luck and his emergence as an elite quarterback. Defensive end Chandler Jones called Luck "a phenomenal player."

New England head coach Bill Belichick noted, "He's already done a lot in the time that he's been in the league, and I'm sure by the time he gets done, he'll pass a lot of guys by."

The Patriots, however, breezed past Luck by a score of 45–7 on their way to the Super Bowl. It was more than a humbling experience for Luck; it was embarrassing. "I think every loss in the playoffs leaves a really, really terrible taste in your mouth," Luck told the Indianapolis Star. "But this one has been worse than the other two because we did get so close [to the Finals this time]. And the way we lost, it was just embarrassing."

And yet, common sense tells us it will happen one day — Luck will lift his team and carry it into the Super Bowl. He is, after all, the quarterback of the present and the future. The guy who sets — and perhaps breaks — the mold. ■

24 Marshawn LYNCH

RUNNING BACK

BEAST MODE

"I'm here so I won't get fined." The seven words you can say during Super Bowl media day so that you won't get fined. Marshawn Lynch could say more, but what would be the point? If he talked, really talked to the media, they'd ask him to do it all over again, Monday through Sunday. So why bother?

He's just here so he won't get fined.

It is not often the NFL has a star running back that wants nothing to do with fame and glory. Jim Brown and Duane Thomas were the same way. Lynch, however, has taken his silence to a whole other place. On a Seattle Seahawks team that has won a Super Bowl and includes such relentless talkers as Jeremy Lane and Richard Sherman, Lynch is the Sphinx. The NFL, which wants its players talking up games for promotional value, has fined him repeatedly for refusing to say anything to the media.

It happened during the regular season and it would have happened at Super Bowl's XLVIII and XLIX had he not been warned in advance that silence is not golden, it's expensive. So, Lynch attended media day and said only what he had to.

On the field, though, his running style not only defines Lynch, it comes with its own nickname: Beast Mode. When Lynch is at full Beast, it is next to impossible to tame him. The New Orleans Saints can attest to that.

In a 2011 playoff game, his first in the NFL, Lynch ripped through the heart of the New Orleans defense and easily shook off four tacklers. Saints defensive back Tracy Porter tried to close in only to be sent flying by what Lynch called his "little baby stiff arm." After that, it was Lynch hurtling himself into the end zone to cap a 67-yard run that highlighted all his talents — power, speed, strength, determination. Total Beast Mode.

The same thing occurred against the Arizona Cardinals. In a December 2014 game, Lynch took the hand-off and began flicking tacklers out of his way before tiptoeing down the sidelines and completing a 79-yard touchdown with another end-zone hurtle.

"If you love football, it has got to be one of the greatest runs of all time," said Seattle quarterback Russell Wilson. "He's had one before … so to watch that one [against Arizona] was pretty cool."

The Buffalo Bills used the 12th pick overall to select Lynch in the 2007 NFL Draft. He racked up a pair of 1,000-yard seasons but managed less than half that in 2009. That was the year Lynch drew a three-game suspension for violating the league's personal conduct policy. (He had been arrested in California for having a gun in his backpack, which was found in the trunk of a car he was occupying.)

Buffalo decided it was time for Lynch to move on. He was traded to Seattle for a fourth-round draft pick in 2011 and a fifth-round draft pick in 2012. It turned out to be a steal. Lynch topped the 1,000-yard mark from 2010 to 2014. In 2012, he posted a career best 1,590 yards. In 2014, he carried the ball 280 times for 1,306 yards and 13 touchdowns. He added another four touchdowns as a receiver. His combined count of 17 led the entire NFL.

But to talk about his accomplishments is something Lynch has never been comfortable doing. Baltimore Ravens receiver Steve Smith told *Sports Illustrated* that some people think Lynch's silent stance is an act.

"People think he's hiding something because he doesn't want to talk," said Smith, one of Lynch's friends. "He does his job and does it well, and he's not interested in other

Lynch battles Leon McFadden of the 49ers when the teams met on Dec. 14, 2014.

things. There are people who use the media to give false perceptions of who they are. He's not interested in any of that. He just wants to [play] ball."

Lynch should have been given the ball in Super Bowl XLIX. With Seattle down by four points and at the New England Patriots one-yard line in the waning seconds of the game, the Seahawks decided to go for the win with a touchdown pass. The ball was intercepted; New England won the game. Lynch said little at the time but later

acknowledged, "I would be lying if I didn't tell you I was expecting the ball. But in life these things happen. I mean, you know it cost us the Super Bowl. But the game is over, and I am in Turkey."

Yes, Lynch was in Turkey, where he participated in an American Football Without Borders camp. When he returned to the U.S., he signed a two-year contract extension with the Seahawks worth $24 million. Chances are he's not going to say much about it. ▪

29 DeMarco MURRAY

RUNNING BACK

RUNNING WITH THE ENEMY

It wasn't the nicest break-up, not by a long snap. In Dallas, where he was once showered with love and attention, disgruntled Cowboys fans took to burning his No. 29 jersey. Dallas quarterback Tony Romo added fuel to the fire by saying he would have taken a pay cut to keep the team's star running back in Big D.

But Dallas never asked Romo to renegotiate his contract, never budged off its contract pitch for its free-agent-bound running back. And so, just like that, DeMarco Murray left the Lone Star State to sign with a heated rival, the Philadelphia Eagles.

Of all the player moves made for the start of the 2015 NFL season, Murray's departure from Dallas was the one that stirred the most resentment. This wasn't just any player who left the Cowboys; this was the NFL's leading rusher in 2014. A man who ran for 1,845 yards — a total neither Emmitt Smith nor Tony Dorsett reached in their eminent careers.

Every time Murray took to the field, he had tacklers missing their marks and records falling. He broke the NFL record for most consecutive 100-yard rushing games

to open a season. The legendary Jim Brown had six such prolific games in 1958; Murray set the record at seven and did it on a bad ankle.

"I think we did this as a group," Murray said after his record performance carried Dallas to a win against the New York Giants. "I definitely give a lot of credit to those guys [his offensive teammates], and I'm blessed to be mentioned with that, but there's a lot of hard work that needs to be done. It's a long season."

Weeks later, Murray learned the hard way just how long and arduous an NFL season can be. In Week 15 against Philadelphia, Murray suffered a broken ring finger on his left hand and had surgery done the next day. When Dallas head coach Jason Garrett was asked if he expected Murray back on the field for the next game, he replied: "He's as strong-willed and determined an individual as I've ever been around … And if anybody has a chance to come back, he does."

And he did. Although well shy of his typically high standards, Murray carried the ball 22 times for 58 yards to help inspire

Murray escapes a tackle from the Redskins when the teams met in 2014; he rushed for a league-high 13 touchdowns that season.

the Cowboys in a 42–7 humbling of the Indianapolis Colts. A week later against the Washington Redskins, Murray's 32-yard gain in the first quarter surpassed Smith's single-season franchise record of 1,773 yards.

Looking back at the 2011 NFL Draft, there was no great affection for Murray. He may have set a bucket full of records at the University of Oklahoma, but the NFL Combine said Murray "didn't have the vision to consistently find open lanes … lacks power to get the difficult yards between the tackles." Murray ended up being selected in the third round, 71st overall, by Dallas.

In Murray's rookie year with the Cowboys, he was listed third on the depth chart behind Felix Jones and Tashard Choice. When Jones was injured in October 2011,

Murray stepped in and gained 34 yards on 11 carries against the New England Patriots in Week 6. In Week 7, Choice was given the start for a game against the St. Louis Rams, but it was Murray who exploded. He ran for 253 yards, breaking Smith's single-game franchise record of 237 yards. Murray even had a 91-yard touchdown romp to establish himself as the Cowboys' prime runner.

They were so convinced of that they released Choice after the game.

Murray's 2012 sophomore season offered flashes of brilliance until a foot injury cost him two games. He finished with just 663 yards. But in 2013, he was back on track, posting 1,121 yards and nine touchdowns. It was a set up for everything he accomplished in 2014, the year he was named AP

NFL Offensive Player of the Year.

Knowing Murray was closing in on free agency, the Cowboys offered him a four-year, $24 million contract. Dallas was too close to the salary cap and had Romo's contract to restructure. It meant the offer to Murray was the best the Cowboys could manage and that was firm.

The Eagles then swooped in and inked Murray to a five-year deal worth $42 million, including a guaranteed $18 million. News of the Murray loss irked Cowboys' fans and drove them to burning a batch of his jerseys. Romo told a Dallas radio show he would have taken $5 million less to keep Murray in the fold.

Instead, he got away. It will make for long days in Dallas if he gets away on the field, too. ∎

24 Darrelle REVIS

CORNERBACK

COME STAY A WHILE

It's called Revis Island, and it's a frustrating, hostile place to visit. NFL receivers who enter might not be seen again for the rest of the game. They just … disappear.

The man who rules Revis Island — cornerback Darrelle Revis, back for a second time with the New York Jets — is so dominating that his former coach often remarked, "When he's on the field, he's the best player on the field."

Revis does to opposing offenses what the Bermuda Triangle did to Flight 19: When receivers enter his side of the field, he takes them off course.

It's been that way for some of the best pass catchers in the game. Andre Johnson, Randy Moss, Terrell Owens, Chad Johnson, Reggie Wayne — they've all ventured onto Revis Island and looked lost. As an assistant coach with the New York Jets once commented about Revis' performance against the Houston Texans: "Did Andre Johnson even play today?"

Being an NFL cornerback means learning how to handle vulnerability. As a defender, he is often isolated in man-to-man coverage and asked to cover a top-flight re-

ceiver. The two conduct their private confrontation in full view, usually with television cameras trained to their every move. Win the battle and you're a hero. Lose and it can be the longest three hours of your life.

Revis wins far more skirmishes than he loses. Since the Jets took him in the first round of the 2007 draft, he has been selected to the Pro Bowl four times, named the AFC's Defensive Player of the Year and in 2011, he led the conference in interception return yards. He is, in equal parts, skilled, smart and competitive — a wicked combination that he demonstrated early in his athletic career.

In high school, while growing up in Aliquippa, Pennsylvania, Revis once scored five touchdowns in one game: three rushing touchdowns, a touchdown on a punt return and a touchdown on a blocked field goal attempt. Add to that a pass reception, a pass completion and an interception, and you have one out-of-this-world game sheet. He was also his school's leading scorer in basketball for two years. All that success carried over to the University of Pittsburgh, where Revis was named to the

All-American team his freshman season.

At Pitt, Revis developed into a shutdown specialist who could stop players in their tracks with a sure tackle. The Jets took him in the first round of the 2007 NFL draft and despite missing 20 days of training camp over a contract dispute, Revis was a member of the Jets' starting defensive unit at the beginning of the regular season. By the end of the year, the rookie corner had made three interceptions and allowed just three touchdowns. It was the start of something big.

By 2009, Revis had established his side of the field as the place where receivers are reduced to empty jerseys. He made seven interceptions and held Chad Johnson (then Ochocinco) without a catch; he added a key interception in a playoff win over the San Diego Chargers. Two years later, he ran back an interception 100 yards for a touchdown and was selected for the Pro Bowl a fourth time.

Then came the moment no one had anticipated.

Timing, wise people say, is everything. Revis had informed the Jets he wanted a new contract even though the current agreement had two years remaining. The plan was for the Jets to see how Revis performed in 2012 before engaging in meaningful negotiations. In the opening week of the season, Revis had an interception against the Buffalo Bills but was taken out of the game after suffering a concussion.

Revis defends for the New York Jets in 2011. He'll do it again for them in 2015.

He returned in Week 3, recovered a fumble but left the game with a leg injury. The next day tests revealed the 27-year-old veteran had torn the anterior cruciate ligament (ACL) in his left knee. He underwent surgery and missed the balance of the season.

"I'm sure it might raise people's eyebrows with how I'm going to look when I come back," Revis said. "I wouldn't expect anything else. I just know I work hard, and I'm going to treat it like any other offseason."

In the end, the Jets restructured financially and traded Revis to Tampa Bay. He spent one season with the Buccaneers before signing with the New England Patriots and helping them win Super Bowl XLIX. A month later, the Jets offered the free-agent defender a five-year, $70 million contract, which he gladly accepted.

Once again, Revis Island, New York–style, is open for business. All receivers are welcome to drop by for a quiet afternoon. ■

12 Aaron RODGERS

QUARTERBACK

FROM UNDERSTUDY TO STAR

It's easy now to label him a luminary among stars. The man has won a Super Bowl, and been named the Super Bowl MVP and NFL player of the year. To just say the name "Aaron Rodgers" immediately conjures up images of greatness in the minds of almost all sports fans. He is the Green Bay Packers quarterback who throws with GPS accuracy and leads his team with unsinkable confidence.

Not that long ago, though, Rodgers had a different reputation: he was the kid in waiting; the project player; a quarterback coming out of high school who was passed over by every single NCAA Division I program except one, the University of Illinois. He was offered a walk-on tryout there, no scholarship. He declined the offer.

Yet here he is today, the undisputed franchise focal point of the Packers who took over from the legendary Brett Favre, and who silenced his skeptics by proving he could win as an NFL quarterback. It's been quite the ride for Rodgers, one he's described as "an underdog's story."

It's a tale that began in the California Community College Athletic Association at Butte College, where Rodgers was asked to play quarterback by the only program that would have him. He did well enough in a single season to lead his school to a No. 2 national ranking. University of California, Berkeley head coach Jeff Tedford came to Butte to scout a prospect at tight end. He watched tape of the Butte offense and noticed Rodgers. Tedford, a former CFL quarterback, liked Rodgers' mechanics and offered him a Division I scholarship.

At Cal, Rodgers became the starting quarterback for the Golden Bears midway through his first season and he never looked back. In 2004, he took Cal to a 10–1 record and a No. 4 national ranking. His last university game was a loss in the Holiday Bowl against Texas (45–31), despite a desperate fourth quarter that saw him throw for one touchdown and run for another. He decided to skip his senior year to enter the 2005 NFL draft. His favorite team, the San Francisco 49ers, had the first pick overall, but decided not to select Rodgers. Twenty-two other teams did the same, as Rodgers sat in attendance looking sheepish, yet hopeful.

Rodgers gets ready to throw the ball against the Ravens on Oct. 13, 2013. The Packers won, 19–17.

Finally, with the 24th pick overall, Green Bay tagged Rodgers, and it was both a blessing and a curse. The blessing was the Packers had Favre and didn't have to rush their rookie quarterback. The curse was the Packers had Favre, which meant Rodgers wasn't going to see a lot of playing time, if any. And so began the three "lost" years of Rodgers' Green Bay saga. At least lost to the fans and the media, but for Rodgers it was an unbelievable apprenticeship. He went to practice every day to study and learn. He watched Favre in action. But playing meaningful minutes? That wasn't on the agenda, not yet.

Rodgers' patience was supremely tested in 2008 when it looked as if he was about to take over as the No. 1 quarterback. Favre, having retired the previous March, chose to un-retire in July. Many Packer fans wanted their veteran hero back. Rodgers could wait. But team officials defused the situation by trading Favre to the New York Jets. Rodgers emerged from the shadows and took his first steps slowly as the Packers missed the playoffs. That would be the last time that happened under Rodgers' leadership.

In 2009, the Packers won 11 games before losing to the Arizona Cardinals in the postseason. In 2010, Green Bay won 10 games and entered the NFC playoffs as the sixth seed, meaning they'd have to play all their games on the road. They beat the Eagles in Philadelphia, the Falcons in Atlanta and the Bears in Chicago to reach Super Bowl XLV in Dallas against the Pittsburgh Steelers.

Rodgers, the career underdog, commanded the spotlight and held it. He completed 24 of 39 passes for 304 yards and 3 touchdowns as Green Bay won its fourth Super Bowl championship in franchise history. And that's when everyone saw the true measure of Rodgers as a quarterback. He was named Super Bowl MVP and followed that up by being named the league MVP for 2011.

Today, Rodgers is revered for his high completion percentage, few interceptions, many touchdowns, and for being every bit the emotional leader as Favre was before him. Early in the 2012 season, Rodgers lambasted himself for a poor showing and vowed to do better. He followed up by throwing six touchdown passes in a drubbing of the previously unbeaten Houston Texans. In Week 10, he threw for six touchdowns against Chicago — in the first half.

In 2014, he received his second NFL MVP award after leading Green Bay to the league's most points as the NFL's No. 1 offense.

"The award is about consistency," he said, "and I feel confident in the way the preparation played out. The guys count on me to bring it every week."

The expectation now, for a star of his magnitude, is to bring another Super Bowl title to Green Bay. ▪

25 RICHARD SHERMAN

CORNERBACK

TALENT, TENACITY AND LOTS OF TALKING

Richard Sherman loathes silence. Put the man on a football field and soon enough he'll have the opposition trying to fill its ears with quick-drying cement. Put him at a podium with a crowd to work and he'll talk day and night. Give him an extended audience of people actively looking for bombastic personalities on social media and he'll make sure to give them something juicy to talk about.

Just like he did after Game 6 of the 2012 season, a one-point Seahawks win over the New England Patriots. After that game, during which there was some verbal sparing between Patriots quarterback Tom Brady and Sherman, the Seahawks cornerback Tweeted a photo of himself admonishing Brady with the caption, "U mad bro?" It blew up the Twittersphere.

In 2012, Sherman didn't just slide into the picture gracefully. He grabbed the national spotlight and aimed it squarely at himself. He craved attention, thrived under the pressure. The best receivers in the NFL took their runs at Sherman and most finished the game with his voice still ringing inside their helmets.

Two weeks after the Brady incident, Seattle visited the Detroit Lions. All-Star receiver Calvin Johnson, whose nickname is Megatron (in homage to the Transformers), was looking to crush Sherman and the Seahawks. In the days leading up to the game, Sherman said he was a Transformer, too — Optimus Prime — and he vowed to mega-whip the all-powerful Johnson. The final result? Johnson had three catches for 46 yards and no touchdowns. The only downside was that Detroit's other receivers not covered by Sherman had a pretty good day and the Seahawks lost.

From that point on, however, Sherman was known for living up to his own hype. He made interceptions, recovered fumbles and even collected a couple of touchdowns off turnovers. Seattle, though, lost in the playoffs.

A year later, Seattle finished first in the NFC West and stormed through the postseason. In the NFC Championship game against the San Francisco 49ers, Sherman tipped a pass to one of his defensive teammates to seal the win. The ball had been intended for 49ers receiver Michael Crabtree. After the game, Sherman approached Crabtree to shake his hand; Crabtree shoved Sherman in the facemask producing a diatribe from the triumphant defender.

"When you try me with a sorry receiver like Crabtree, that's the result you gonna get! Don't you ever talk about me," Sherman told a national television audience. "Don't you open your mouth about the best, or you know, I'm gonna shut it for you real quick."

Sherman followed that act two weeks later with a solid showing in the Super Bowl, as Seattle absolutely dismanteled the highly touted offense from Denver. It seemed the Broncos had heard Sherman and heeded his advice; they barely threw in his direction, and Denver only mustered eight total points.

The irony of Sherman's rise to the top is that he began his university football career at Stanford as a receiver. The Compton, CA, native was named a Freshman All-American but was forced to play defense after suffering a knee injury. The injury and position switch scared away 31 teams on NFL Draft day. By the time Seattle called Sherman's name, it was in the fifth round and he was already vowing to make teams pay for what he felt was a snub.

In his rookie season, Sherman made 55 tackles and four interceptions and was named to the 2011 Pro Football Writers' All-Rookie team. From then to now, his grandstanding and game-breaking plays have made him a household name, and now that he's established, his wit and playfulness are coming to the forefront.

His media sessions are must-attend events. In 2014 he brought a cardboard cutout of teammate Doug Baldwin to the podium as a silent prop in protest for the fine the NFL gave teammate Marshawn Lynch for not talking to the media. He also tore a strip off the league and what he views as its hypocritical policies.

"The league doesn't let me say anything about [Beats By Dre, the audio equipment

Sherman tackles the Cowboys' Dez Bryant in 2014; he had 52 solo tackles that season.

maker]. Why is that?" asked Sherman. "That seems a little hypocritical. It seems like we're in a league where they say, 'Players, you don't endorse any alcohol. Please don't endorse alcohol, please no DUIs.' But a beer sponsor is their biggest sponsor."

As fate would have it, Seattle and New England met in Super Bowl XLIX at the conclusion of the 2014 season. Sherman continued his verbal baiting of Brady and, after the Seahawks intercepted a Brady pass in the third quarter, sideline microphones picked up Sherman boldly informing his teammates, "He's scared. His heart's gone. It's almost gone."

Teams leading by 10 points heading into the fourth quarter, like Seattle was, had a perfect 29–0 record in the Super Bowl, until Brady showed just how much heart he had left. The veteran quarterback threw for a pair of touchdowns as the Patriots won, 28–24.

That's when TV cameras found Sherman and Brady at the end of the game. Sherman extended his hand and Brady, who had been kneeling in contemplation, got up and offered his. He told Sherman, "You're a great player." Sherman, who had gone the distance with a bad shoulder injury, tapped Brady on the facemask and walked away.

There is every reason to believe these two will see each other on the big stage again. ∎

55

TERRELL SUGGS

LINEBACKER

BIG AND BOLD IN BALTIMORE

Whether he was actually working out, as he claims, when he felt the tear in his right foot, or, as a number of witnesses have corroborated, playing some hoops in an Arizona gymnasium with pals, the reverberations went far beyond some nondescript 260-pound Shaq-wannabe hitting the hardwood.

Indeed, it was the NFL's reigning Defensive Player of the Year, Terrell Suggs, lying in a heap, and the city of Baltimore, population 2.7 million, came to a screeching halt.

Suggs, though, vowed to get back up in a hurry.

On October 21, 2012, against the Houston Texans, Suggs returned — to the amazement of many — taking his place in the Baltimore Ravens defensive unit. Not only did he return, he contributed four tackles and a sack. That he needed a mere five-and-a-half months to recover from having his Achilles tendon surgically repaired made him both a man of his word and a medical marvel.

"I wasn't surprised for the simple fact that everybody in the building knew I could do it, I could come back," Suggs told

the *Baltimore Sun*. "It was just all a matter of when. I just really wanted to get back."

Here's a football player Dick Butkus and Lawrence Taylor could love. Tough as tungsten, a voracious appetite for the hunt, superb athleticism (in a 1999 game in high school, he set an Arizona Class 5A record with 367 yards rushing), not to mention an old-school, survival-of-the-fittest mentality. Suggs has shown all those traits since being the 10th pick overall in 2003 out of Arizona State, one of the youngest players (at age 20) ever drafted on the defensive side of the ball. The Ravens chose the Arizona Sun Devils star to team with their monster marauder, Ray Lewis, who was on the verge of becoming one of the greatest linebackers of all time.

Ironically, along with a few other 2003 blue-chippers expected to be high picks in that draft, Suggs had appeared in commercials for Madden NFL 2004, with all the soon-to-be rookies seen doing menial chores for Lewis. In his bit, Suggs was seen lugging the Ravens linebacker's bags.

"The first thing I thought about [after being drafted by Baltimore] was me and Ray

Lewis doing that commercial, and how he made me do his laundry," Suggs said at the time. "And now it's actually going to be a reality."

Over the intervening seasons, Suggs became more than just a Lewis sidekick. In each of his first four pro games Suggs set an NFL record by recording a sack. In 2011, he was at his zenith, especially when Lewis was sidelined with a toe injury. In the four games Lewis missed, the Ravens won every outing, with Suggs recording seven sacks. Baltimore finished 12–4 and won the AFC North title, with Suggs taking AFC Defensive Player of the Year laurels.

That set the stage for an even more memorable 2012.

After damaging his Achilles, and then reclaiming his spot on the defense, Suggs aided Baltimore's run through the playoffs. Even with a second injury — a torn biceps muscle picked up late in the regular season, Suggs had 2 sacks, 10 tackles and a forced fumble against the Denver Broncos in the divisional playoffs. He continued to help lead the push to the Super Bowl when the Baltimore defense held the New England Patriots scoreless in the second half of the AFC Championship game. Afterward, Suggs dialed down his frequent criticisms of Patriots superstar quarterback Tom Brady: "You gotta play perfect to beat him, and we played perfect."

Suggs wasn't as domineering weeks later in Super Bowl XLVII, but his teammates did their part in a 34–31 victory over the San Francisco 49ers that gave Suggs his first NFL title. It was a long wait for a guy who was once the youngest player in the NFL.

"I don't feel the window is closing," Suggs told interviewer Bob Costas, "but I'm starting to feel a little itch, a little draft. For the

Suggs salutes the fans after recording 2.5 sacks and winning 20–12 against the Jaguars.

first two years I was *the* youngest guy in the NFL."

Still, as the elder statesman of the Raven's defense, Suggs has kept harassing quarterbacks. In Week 12 of the 2014 season, he dropped New Orleans' Saints quarterback Drew Brees to become the 31st player in league history to record 100 sacks. For that,

he was named to the Pro Bowl a sixth time and inked to a four-year contract extension. He's got plenty of game left in him, and the new contract ensures that he'll be around to mentor the next era of Ravens defenders — just as Lewis did for him.

Hopefully one of them will be hauling *his* bags and doing *his* laundry. ■

73 JOE THOMAS

OFFENSIVE TACKLE

FAR FROM AVERAGE

Joe Thomas is an offensive lineman and, in the NFL, that's about as unglamorous a position as there is. But Thomas, so efficient in his blue-collar role, holds a rare gridiron distinction, one he shares with a star whose position was much more noteworthy. Both Joe and legendary Cleveland Browns running back Jim Brown are the only Cleveland players to be named to the Pro Bowl for the first six seasons of their professional careers. Brown earned his Pro Bowl ticket for nine consecutive seasons before retiring as arguably the greatest football player of all time. Thomas has gone to the Pro Bowl seven times and likely has a few more trips ahead of him.

Being mentioned in the same sentence as Jim Brown is heady company for any football player, which speaks to Thomas' ability to play his left tackle position like few have ever played it. Thomas isn't just big (6-foot-6, 312 pounds); he's big with mobility. He can shut down some of the AFC's best pass rushers while opening holes for Cleveland's running game. Plus, he's as reliable as a hammer. You need the job done, you go with Joe Thomas.

"Cleveland's a football town," said former Browns head coach Pat Shurmur. "Cleveland's a gritty town. Cleveland's a town that appreciates good physical play. And so our fans have rallied around Joe. Through the years, what he's done is play good football at a high level."

Thomas is a fan favorite for being the regular Joe he is. As a highly touted senior from the University of Wisconsin, Thomas was invited to New York for the 2007 NFL Draft. All the top prospects were there — quarterback JaMarcus Russell, receiver Calvin Johnson, running back Adrian Peterson — and so were the television cameras, fans and media.

But Thomas wasn't there. Instead, he spent the day on Lake Michigan fishing with his dad Eric and some friends. It was on his rental boat's satellite radio that he heard he was taken third overall by Cleveland. A camera crew tagged along to film Thomas' reaction. He was thrilled. He also caught a fish.

"I didn't want to involve myself in all the craziness that goes on [with the draft]," Thomas explained. "I knew it was going to be an exciting enough time."

Once he arrived in Cleveland, the left tackle spot was his to fill, and Thomas slid in like a veteran. He quickly displayed his athleticism, having played other positions in football (defensive end, fullback, punter) as well as other sports. At Wisconsin, he was a member of the Badgers' track team and threw the shot put. Those traits underscored Thomas' text-book skills at moving his opponents out of the way, if not overpowering them.

"The fundamentals in his drop [back] technique are, bar none, one of the best," former Cleveland receiver Josh Cribbs told the NFL Network. "He has good posture; he's not being pushed back to the point where, if a guy bull rushes him, he'll get run over. What he can do with his hands, you'd think he was an MMA [mixed martial arts] fighter. That's all they do in the trenches — battling guys with their hands, getting hands off … moving them around, controlling bodies. And the way he controls guys is [like watching a] clinic tape."

With Thomas leading the push, the Browns were able to squeeze 1,000-yard rushing seasons from Jamal Lewis and Peyton Hillis — good running backs during their time in Cleveland, but neither were elite.

Unfortunately for Cleveland fans, 2014 started well then fizzled out with a 7–9 finish. Rookie quarterback Johnny "Football" Manziel, a first-round draft pick, offered

Thomas waits for a play against the Buffalo Bills on Nov. 30, 2014.

hope but was being jeered by season's end.

"Playing for a team that is not winning is awful. It's like running on a treadmill," said Thomas. "You are expending energy and working hard, but it's not fun and you are going nowhere."

Thomas, though, kept pushing ahead. His peers voted him onto the NFL Network's list of top 100 players. His placing was 18th overall.

With Manziel's first season under his belt, the hope is that the second-year quarterback and the rest of the Browns will dig down, put the distractions behind them and follow Thomas' lead to just keep pushing. ■

94

DeMarcus WARE

LINEBACKER

D-WARE MEANS BEWARE

Washington Redskins tight end Chris Cooley spoke on behalf of the terrorized offensive masses when, during a radio interview, he recalled that indelible first encounter with DeMarcus Ware.

"The only thing that surprised you," Cooley marveled, "is that as soon as you get on him you're like, 'Oh my God, this dude is a beast!'"

For nine seasons with the Dallas Cowboys, D-Ware meant Beware. The "tweener" rush linebacker/defensive end out of Troy University — the player Dallas owner Jerry Jones famously campaigned for with the Cowboys' first pick of the 2005 draft — had seven straight seasons with 10 or more sacks. And in 2014, after leaving Dallas and signing with the Denver Broncos as a free agent, Ware kept the numbers rolling with another 10-sack posting.

His feat has him keeping company with a couple of legends: Lawrence Taylor and Bruce Smith. Only the Minister of Defense, Reggie White, with nine seasons, and former Minnesota-Seattle ace John Randle at eight seasons, have strung together longer sack-happy annual streaks.

These four gentlemen just happen to be enshrined in the Pro Football Hall of Fame. Ware has his GPS programmed for Canton, Ohio, too.

When he registered career sack No. 100 in the 2012 season opener against the New York Giants' Eli Manning, in only his 113th game, he became the second fastest, behind White (96 games) to reach the milestone. Consider: Only 28 men have ever hit that magical figure.

"I always talk about consistency since my rookie season," Ware said after joining the elite century club. "Being able to try and do the same things every year and get pressure on the quarterback and being in the midst of being named with a guy like Reggie White ... Just to have that opportunity is a great honor."

At 6-foot-4 and 254 pounds, Ware isn't a Godzilla by NFL standards. But coaches are always talking about players having great "motors." And, well, DeMarcus Ware arrived equipped with the equivalent of a Wartsila-Sulzer turbocharged two-stroke diesel engine. What he may lack in sheer physical size, he makes up for in quickness and agility.

Ware didn't start playing football seriously until his junior year at Auburn High in Alabama. Future Atlanta Falcons defensive end Osi Umenyiora was there at the time and the two became fast friends.

Already a baseball, basketball and track star, Ware instantly took to the defensive end position. But upon graduation, no big schools seemed interested. Only Troy University, about an hour's drive from his hometown, offered a scholarship at the prompting of a highly regarded recruit, one Osi Umenyiora.

"I really wasn't thinking much about football," Ware admitted later. "Just making sure I was good enough to stay on the team, to keep the education going." The learning curve on the field posed no problems. He propelled Troy into its first ever Bowl appearance in 2004 and did his work in the other classroom, too, graduating with a business systems degree.

"DeMarcus … he was about 6-4, 196 when he got here," Troy coach Larry Blakeney recalled. "When he left my office to go to Dallas he was 6-5, 255. And he could really run. I don't think he ever lost a challenge race here. All those corners and wide receivers who thought they were fast, he normally dusted them."

Projected as a second rounder in the 2005 draft, America's Team seemed intent on selecting Marcus Spears or Shawne Merriman with the 11th overall pick.

Until the flamboyant Dallas owner Jerry Jones, never one to shy away from an opinion, stepped in. Give the man his due:

Ware, an eight-time Pro Bowler, gets ready to play against the Bills on Dec. 7, 2014.

When he's right, he's right.

With the Cowboys, Ware was a seven-time Pro Bowler, a four-time All-Pro, and the all-time franchise leader in multi-sack games and forced fumbles. In 2013, he was bothered by injuries to both elbows, a tear in his right quadriceps muscle and a herniated disk in his back. It limited him to 13 games. The Cowboys wanted him to take a pay cut to free up salary cap space. Ware wanted to see what he was worth on the open market. Signing with Denver has been a good fit.

"I feel like my body is being whole again," he said. "Being able to play all out and not being hurt and injured, has been the key."

And most assuredly, that doesn't sit well with those terrorized offensive masses. ∎

99

J.J. WATT

DEFENSIVE END

MAXIMUM IMPACT

Watch the man at work. See how he tosses blockers aside to get to the football. See how he does it over and over and you realize there really are no words to do him justice.

View it and remember it because Houston Texans defensive lineman Justin James "J.J." Watt won't be doing it for long. That's his plan and he's sticking to it; he wants to emulate former Detroit running back Barry Sanders, who hung up his helmet and retired with plenty of game still left in him.

"I don't want to play forever. I want to give everything I can now and then walk away knowing I gave everything," Watt said in a bleacherreport.com article. "[Sanders] was such a great player, and he left when he was still on top. I want that to be me."

When it comes to talking about the NFL's top quarterback hunter, Watt's name is mentioned in a hurry. In 2014, his statistics read: 78 tackles, 20.5 sacks, 4 forced fumbles and an interception. At 6-foot-5, 289-pounds, he has the body type and speed to throw down a running back or chase him up field — not many players can do both.

Some of Watt's actions have already taken on a legendary feel. In the 2012 season, the Wisconsin native was named to the Pro Bowl and virtually every all-star team out there, from USA Football Fundamentals to the Professional Football Writers' First-Team All-Pro to Associated Press Defensive Player of the Year.

By 2014, "Mega-Watt," as the nickname goes, was so well established that opponents were running out of ways to praise him, let alone block him. Hue Jackson, the Cincinnati Bengals' offensive coordinator, offered up three words when asked about facing Watt: "Lord. Have. Mercy."

At that point in the season, Watt had already been credited with 29 quarterback hits and four touchdowns. He finished with five touchdowns: three on pass plays where he lined up at tight end; one on an interception he returned for 80 yards; and another on a fumble recovery he returned for 45 yards. In doing that, Watt became the first defensive lineman to have scored at least five touchdowns in a season since 1944.

Lord have mercy indeed.

"People are always like, 'Does it amaze you what he does?'" said former Texans receiver Andre Johnson. "I always tell them no because [I get to] see some of the stuff he does in practice."

Watt's prowess wasn't so obvious when he accepted a scholarship at Central Michigan University. He played sparingly at tight end and was asked to switch to offensive tackle. Instead, he applied to the University of Wisconsin and played at defensive end.

There, he found his niche and was showered with accolades and awards, including his selection to the academic All-Big Ten first-team. After wowing the scouts at the 2011 NFL Combine, Watt was drafted by Houston in the first round with the 11th choice overall.

With his quarterback-squashing escapades, and his appreciation for what he's achieved, Watt has built a connection with Houston and the fans. He has lent his name and celebrity to help children's charities and visits with U.S. troops who have come home after serving their country.

Watt's teammates tease him about how they can't go anywhere in Houston, or even watch television, without seeing his face. That's a good thing for the NFL since its reputation was sullied in 2014 by the incidents of Ray Rice and Adrian Peterson. League officials and football fans are only too happy to bask in Watt's shining examples. He has told his friends and teammates that he is fully aware how one bad decision can unravel all the good.

The only off-field debate involving Watt

Watt looks to tackle some Jaguars in 2014; he was honored for his skills with the Associated Press Defensive Player of the Year.

had to do with his Wisconsin cabin, which he described as "really minimalistic. The only thing I have to focus on is training and that's the way I like it. No frills …"

It wasn't long before TMZ and Busted Coverage found the 4,500 square foot cabin. It cost $800,000, has three kitchens and even an elevator in it. Watt tweeted the whole minimalistic thing was a "miscommunication" and that he is very fortunate to live in his cabin.

It will be waiting for him when his brilliant career comes to an end, with lots of game still in him. ■

3 RUSSELL WILSON

QUARTERBACK

MEASURED SUCCESS

The measure of an outstanding quarterback isn't always about how tall he stands, which is a good thing for Russell Wilson.

From the moment he finished his university football career with the Wisconsin Badgers, Wilson has been chided, measured, dismissed and re-measured, all because he stands 5-foot-11 at a position where many of his peers are 6-foot-4 and weigh 235 to 240 pounds.

But use a different set of parameters to quantify Wilson's worth and he stands above a vast majority of NFL quarterbacks. Through his first three seasons, Wilson has never missed a start for the Seattle Seahawks. In 2012, he threw for 26 touchdowns to tie Peyton Manning's record for most touchdowns tossed by a rookie quarterback. Wilson also set a record for most wins at home by a rookie pivot, going 8–0 on the season.

More importantly, when it comes to postseason accountability, Wilson has taken his team to back-to-back Super Bowl appearances, winning the Vince Lombardi Trophy in 2014, then losing it in 2015 on a last-second pass play that never should have been called.

The latter happened in Super Bowl XLIX against the New England Patriots. With Seattle at the Patriots' one-yard line, the clock ticking down late in the fourth quarter, the Seahawks were poised to score the winning touchdown. The obvious decision was to hand the ball to running back Marshawn Lynch then step back to watch the victory celebrations.

Instead, Wilson threw a pass that was intercepted by New England's Malcolm Butler and that was it, game over.

In his post-game address, Seattle coach Pete Carroll said the play calling was his fault. Not about to let his coach or anyone else shoulder the blame, Wilson did what he felt was right, saying he accepted "full responsibility" for what happened.

"I'm the one that threw the pass, but I know I'll throw another one," he said. "And hopefully I'll be remembered for something different."

Wilson's career has been on a steady rise since he joined the Seahawks in 2012. Despite his glowing performances with Wisconsin — he led the Badgers to a Big Ten championship and an appearance in the 2012 Rose Bowl — NFL scouts couldn't get past Wilson's height. In a *Seattle Times* story, Daniel Jeremiah, a scout for the Philadelphia Eagles, recalled how Wilson asked for his number then sent a text saying, "I know I can help the Eagles win."

Jeremiah later admitted, "I hate the fact that because he came in under 5-foot-11, I dropped my personal grade [of Wilson] to the third round."

The third round of the 2012 NFL Draft was precisely where Wilson was claimed by Seattle, well back of the first two picks overall, quarterbacks Andrew Luck and Robert Griffin III. After a strong training camp showing led to some promising efforts in the pre-season, Wilson started his first NFL game and lost, 20–16, to the Arizona Cardinals. Yet in December, he led the Seahawks to a 5–0 record, which put them in the NFC playoffs. There, Wilson engineered a comeback win over the Washington Redskins before losing, 30–28, to the Atlanta Falcons.

Those experiences would work to the Seahawks' advantage in 2013.

With a 13–3 regular season record, Seattle defeated the San Francisco 49ers to secure a Super Bowl showdown against Peyton Manning and the Denver Broncos. By halftime, Seattle had a 22–0 lead. At game's end, the score was 43–8 for the Seahawks. It was quickly noted that Wilson, at 5-foot-11, was the shortest quarterback in NFL history to have won a Super Bowl.

Some of Wilson's biggest supporters are his opponents, the very people who study his game looking for faults to exploit. Before facing him in Super Bowl XLIX, New England coach Bill Belichick spoke highly of Wilson and compared him to Dallas Cowboys' Hall of Fame quarterback Roger Staubach.

Wilson in action against the Chargers in 2014; he threw a career-high 285 completed passes that season.

"I remember a lot of Staubach's spectacular running plays where it looked like he was about to get tackled by three or four guys, and he would Houdini it out of there somehow," said Belichick. "You see Wilson doing some of the same things."

You can also expect to see a determined Wilson eager to overcome that Super Bowl loss to New England. Within weeks of it, he was talking about how the future would play out by stating some lofty ambitions.

"You know, the mindset doesn't change, the focus doesn't change, the belief that I'm gonna get there again and we're gonna do it better than it's ever [been] done. That's never gonna change for me, no matter what the circumstances are," he said. "I believe my mindset is gonna take me further than anybody else has ever gone."

Now that's the measure of an outstanding quarterback, a winner. ■

THE FRANCHISES

AFC EAST
Buffalo Bills
Miami Dolphins
New England Patriots
New York Jets

AFC NORTH
Baltimore Ravens
Cincinnati Bengals
Cleveland Browns
Pittsburgh Steelers

AFC SOUTH
Houston Texans
Indianapolis Colts
Jacksonville Jaguars
Tennessee Titans

AFC WEST
Denver Broncos
Kansas City Chiefs
Oakland Raiders
San Diego Chargers

NFC EAST
Dallas Cowboys
New York Giants
Philadelphia Eagles
Washington Redskins

NFC NORTH
Chicago Bears
Detroit Lions
Green Bay Packers
Minnesota Vikings

NFC SOUTH
Atlanta Falcons
Carolina Panthers
New Orleans Saints
Tampa Bay Buccaneers

NFC WEST
Arizona Cardinals
San Francisco 49ers
Seattle Seahawks
St. Louis Rams

BUFFALO
BILLS

TEAM ORIGINS: The Buffalo Bills franchise got its start in Buffalo, New York, in the All American Football Conference (AAFC) in the 1940s. Known as the Buffalo Bisons until 1947, the team held a contest to rename the club and the winning moniker was "the Bills" in honor of western frontiersman, Buffalo Bill Cody. When the Bills joined the AFL in 1960, the same name was adopted and continues to this day. On Sept. 11, 1960, led by coach Buster Ramsey, the Buffalo Bills played their first AFL game against the New York Titans, and lost 27–3. The first win in modern Buffalo Bills history came against the Boston Patriots on Sept. 23, 1960, a 13–0 triumph.

THE GLORY YEARS: The Buffalo Bills found success in the AFL in the mid 1960s. In 1964, under the guidance of coach Lou Saban and led by quarterback Jack Kemp, the Bills won their first AFL Championship, defeating the San Diego Chargers 20–7 in front of a sold-out crowd at Buffalo's War Memorial Stadium. They defended their championship successfully the next year, again defeating the Chargers for the title. Following the victory, Lou Saban left the Bills to take a job at the University of Maryland.

Led by Hall of Fame coach Marv Levy and quarterback Jim Kelly, the Bills would find success and bring glory back to the Buffalo football scene in the early 1990s. Using the no-huddle offense, and led by power back Thurman Thomas, the Bills would win the AFC championship four consecutive times (1990–1993). However, the club was never able to convert in the Super Bowl, making them the only team in NFL history to win four consecutive conference titles, and lose four consecutive Super Bowls.

ESSENTIALS (THROUGH 2014)

Founded: **1960**
Stadium: **Ralph Wilson Stadium**
Regular Season (all-time): **385-443-8**
Playoffs (all-time): **14-15**
Super Bowl Championships: **0**
Passing (all-time): **Jim Kelly – 35,467 yards**
Rushing (all-time): **Thurman Thomas – 11,938 yards**
Receiving (all-time): **Andre Reed – 13,095 yards**

Bruce Smith

DRAFT IMPACT

Jim Kelly (quarterback)
• drafted 14th overall from the University of Miami in 1983
• owns every major Buffalo Bills' passing record
• elected to the Pro Football Hall of Fame in 2002

Bruce Smith (defensive end)
• drafted first overall from Virginia Tech University in 1985
• current holder of the NFL career sack record
• defensive MVP in 1990

RETIRED NUMBERS

JIM KELLY
12

Larry Csonka

MIAMI
DOLPHINS

TEAM ORIGINS: In August of 1965, the AFL awarded its first expansion franchise to the city of Miami and lawyer Joseph Robbie and actor Danny Thomas for $7.5 million. The nickname "Dolphins" was chosen by a local media screening committee.

The Dolphins played their first game on Sept. 2, 1966. Although they got off to a quick start by returning the opening kickoff 95 yards for a touchdown, they eventually lost the game 23–14. Miami finished the season 3–13, their first of four consecutive losing seasons.

THE GLORY YEARS: Don Shula was hired as head coach and vice president of football operations in 1970, and the move paid immediate dividends. In his first year, the Dolphins recorded their first winning season, going 10–4 and making the playoffs for the first time. Although they would lose their first playoff game, 21–14 against the Oakland Raiders, the success of the 1970 season helped build the momentum for a successful franchise through the 1970s and 1980s.

In 1972, that momentum peaked when the Dolphins, undefeated through the regular season, went on to win the Super Bowl. They are the only team in NFL history to post a perfect season and win the Super Bowl. The next year, under the leadership of Bob Griese and the rugged play of running back Larry Csonka, the team won Super Bowl VIII 24–7 over the Minnesota Vikings. Csonka was named the Super Bowl MVP, rushing for 145 yards and two touchdowns.

In 1984, Dan Marino led the Dolphins back to the Super Bowl, but lost to the San Francisco 49ers. Marino was the face of the franchise through the 1980s and 1990s and led the Dolphins to multiple playoff appearances, shattering NFL records along the way.

DRAFT IMPACT

Bob Griese (quarterback)
- drafted fourth overall from Purdue in 1967
- named to eight Pro Bowls
- named All-Pro five times throughout his career

Larry Csonka (running back)
- drafted with the 8th overall pick from Syracuse University in 1968
- Super Bowl MVP and Hall of Famer
- helped lead the Dolphins to their perfect season in 1972

RETIRED NUMBERS

BOB GRIESE **12** DAN MARINO **13** LARRY CSONKA **39**

ESSENTIALS (THROUGH 2014)

Founded: **1966**
Stadium: **Sun Life Stadium**
Regular Season (all-time): **423-325-4**
Playoffs (all-time): **20-20**
Super Bowl Championships: **2**
Passing (all-time): **Dan Marino – 61,361 yards**
Rushing (all-time): **Larry Csonka – 6,737 yards**
Receiving (all-time): **Mark Duper – 8,869 yards**

NEW ENGLAND
PATRIOTS

TEAM ORIGINS: The New England Patriots were established in 1960, when public relations executive William "Billy" Sullivan Jr. was awarded the eighth and final franchise for the inaugural season of the American Football League. Lou Saban was hired as the Boston Patriots first head coach and on Sept. 9, 1960, coach Saban led his team against the Denver Broncos in their first regular-season home game, where they were defeated 13–10. After playing at four different sites during the 1960s, the Patriots decided to settle in Foxborough, Massachusetts, in 1970. In 1971, the team was renamed the New England Patriots to honor all of the New England states.

THE GLORY YEARS: In 1996, led by former number one overall pick Drew Bledsoe, the New England Patriots made their second ever trip to the Super Bowl. The appearance, however, would end much like their first — a loss, this time to Brett Favre and the Green Bay Packers, 35–21.

In 2001, an improbable run by then back-up quarterback Tom Brady propelled the New England Patriots into Super Bowl XXXVI, where they upset the heavily favored St. Louis Rams, 20–17. The winning score was a last second, 48-yard field goal by Adam Vinatieri. This was the first of three Super Bowl victories in the next four years for the Patriots, who went on to defeat the Carolina Panthers, 32–29, in Super Bowl XXXVIII (2003), and the Philadelphia Eagles, 24–21, in Super Bowl XXXIX (2004).

After a decade of strong regular seasons followed by playoff disappointments, the Patriots made their way to Super Bowl XLIX in 2015 to face the defending champion Seattle Seahawks. Up by four points with 26 seconds left in the game and the Seahawks on second down in the New England red zone, the Patriots looked to be in trouble. But cornerback Malcolm Butler made his first NFL interception when he snagged a Russell Wilson pass at the goal line that was intended for Ricardo Lockette. It clinched the 28–24 win for the Patriots and Brady earned his third Super Bowl MVP award.

ESSENTIALS (THROUGH 2014)

Founded: **1960**

Stadium: **Gillette Stadium**

Regular Season (all-time): **450-377-9**

Playoffs (all-time): **28-18**

Super Bowl Championships: **4**

Passing (all-time): **Tom Brady – 53,258 yards**

Rushing (all-time): **Sam Cunningham – 5,453 yards**

Receiving (all-time): **Stanley Morgan – 10,352 yards**

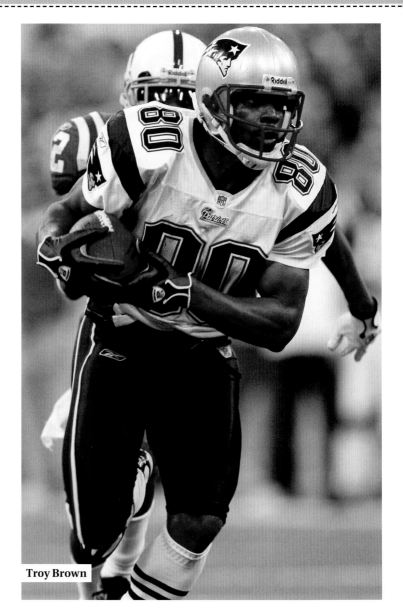

Troy Brown

DRAFT IMPACT

Troy Brown (wide receiver)
- drafted 198th overall from Marshall University in 1993
- Named to the Pro Bowl in 2001
- led the NFL with a punt return average of 14.2 yards in 2001

Willie McGinest (outside linebacker)
- drafted 4th overall from USC in 1994
- anchored the defense for three Super Bowl wins
- played 171 games for the Patriots over 12 years

RETIRED NUMBERS

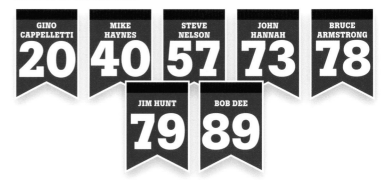

GINO CAPPELLETTI **20**   MIKE HAYNES **40**   STEVE NELSON **57**   JOHN HANNAH **73**   BRUCE ARMSTRONG **78**

JIM HUNT **79**   BOB DEE **89**

Mark Gastineau

NEW YORK
JETS

TEAM ORIGINS: In 1959, Lamar Hunt established the American Football League (AFL) to rival the NFL. The New York Titans were one of the eight charter franchises. In 1963, after several years of financial turmoil, five New York businessmen bought the New York Titans for one million dollars and renamed the team the New York Jets.

THE GLORY YEARS: The early sixties were a mediocre decade for the Jets, but in 1966 the team drafted the most recognizable face the franchise has ever seen: Joe Namath. He was drafted in the first round, first overall, out of the University of Alabama. "Broadway Joe" was known for his charisma and playboy personality. The next year, in 1967, the Jets had a solid winning season, going 8–5–1, with Namath becoming the first player in NFL history to throw for over 4,000 yards in a season. In 1968, the Jets' success continued, finishing with an 11–3 record in the regular season and beating their AFL rivals the Oakland Raiders 27–23 in the AFL Championship game.

The Jets' victory over the Oakland Raiders set up a matchup for the newly named "Super Bowl" — the final game of the year between the AFL champion and the NFL champion. Although the Jets were heavy underdogs going into the game, Joe Namath had guaranteed a victory over the Baltimore Colts. True to his word, Namath delivered a win for the Jets and was also named Super Bowl MVP. It was one of the greatest upsets in professional football history.

The club flirted with success in the 1980s and 1990s, and most recently dropped two consecutive conference finals in 2009 and 2010 under the guidance of coach Rex Ryan. Still, 1968 marks the lone Super Bowl appearance for the Jets.

DRAFT IMPACT

Joe Namath (quarterback)
- drafted first overall from the University of Alabama in 1966
- led the Jets to a win in Super Bowl III
- elected to the Pro Football Hall of Fame in 1985

Mark Gastineau (defensive end)
- drafted 41st overall from Arizona State in 1979
- held the single season sack record with 22 sacks until 2005
- five-time Pro Bowler and three-time First-Team All-Pro

ESSENTIALS (THROUGH 2014)

Founded: **1960**
Stadium: **MetLife Stadium**
Regular Season (all-time): **377-451-8**
Playoffs (all-time): **12-13**
Super Bowl Championships: **1**
Passing (all-time): **Joe Namath – 27,057 yards**
Rushing (all-time): **Curtis Martin – 10,302 yards**
Receiving (all-time): **Don Maynard – 11,732 yards**

RETIRED NUMBERS

JOE NAMATH	DON MAYNARD	CURTIS MARTIN	JOE KLECKO	DENNIS BYRD
12	**13**	**28**	**73**	**90**

BALTIMORE
RAVENS

TEAM ORIGINS: The Baltimore Colts, a proud NFL franchise, left for Indianapolis in 1984. It would be 12 years before the NFL returned, when Art Modell, in a highly controversial move (akin to the Baltimore move of 1984) relocated the Cleveland Browns to Baltimore in 1996.

The team was named in honor of Baltimore native Edgar Allen Poe's poem "The Raven." On Feb. 15, 1996, former Baltimore Colts head coach Ted Marchibroda was hired to coach the Ravens. His signing was 20 years and 1 day removed from when he was originally first named a head coach in Baltimore. The Baltimore Ravens took the field for the first time in front of 64,124 fans on Sept. 1, 1996, and defeated the Oakland Raiders 19–14.

THE GLORY YEARS: In 2000, the Ravens made an improbable run to the playoffs using the simple formula of solid defense and a powerful running game, backed by young stars Ray Lewis and Jamal Lewis. In Super Bowl XXXV, the Ravens stuck to their formula, holding the New York Giants to seven points while Jamal Lewis ran for 102 yards and one touchdown; the Ravens won the game 34–7. Ray Lewis, the heart of the defense and the team's spiritual leader, was named the Super Bowl MVP. The Ravens' Super Bowl victory was followed with two division championships and four playoff appearances in the early 2000s. At the conclusion of the 2012 season, a revamped Ravens roster — featuring quarterback Joe Flacco, running back Ray Rice, and defenders Haloti Ngata, Terrell Suggs and the soon-to-retire Ray Lewis — marched all the way to claim Super Bowl XLVII 34–31 over the San Francisco 49ers.

ESSENTIALS (THROUGH 2014)

Founded: **1996**
Stadium: **M&T Bank Stadium**
Regular Season (all-time): **168-135-1**
Playoffs (all-time): **15-8**
Super Bowl Championships: **2**
Retired Numbers: **None**
Passing (all-time): **Joe Flacco – 25,531 yards**
Rushing (all-time): **Jamal Lewis – 7,801 yards**
Receiving (all-time): **Derrick Mason – 5,777 yards**

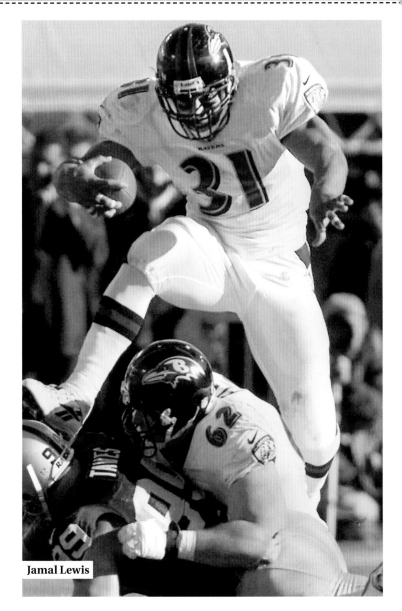

Jamal Lewis

DRAFT IMPACT

Jonathan Ogden (offensive tackle)
• drafted fourth overall from UCLA in 1996
• 11-time Pro Bowler and four-time First-Team All-Pro
• inducted into the Hall of Fame in 2013

Jamal Lewis (running back)
• drafted fifth overall from the University of Tennessee in 2000
• named Pro Bowler and First-Team All-Pro in 2003
• third player in NFL history to rush for over 2,000 yards in a season

Ed Reed (cornerback)
• drafted 24th overall from the University of Miami (Florida) in 2002
• nine-time Pro Bowler and five-time First-Team All-Pro
• career NFL leader in interception return yards (1,541)

Boomer Esiason

CINCINNATI BENGALS

TEAM ORIGINS: Legendary coach Paul Brown, who led the Cleveland Browns to seven conference championships and three NFL championships, decided that in 1962, it was time to move on. Fresh from a five-year hiatus, the coach, in partnership with a group of investors, was awarded an expansion team for the city of Cincinnati in 1967. Brown decided to name his new team the "Bengals" in honor of Cincinnati's old professional AFL team in the late 1930s, and on Sept. 15, 1968, Brown led his Bengals onto the field where they beat the Denver Broncos 24–10 in front of 25,000 fans. The next week, they followed up that win with another, this time over the Buffalo Bills. But after winning their first two regular season games, a rare feat for an expansion team, they won only one more game in 1968, finishing the season 3–11.

THE GLORY YEARS: The Cincinnati Bengals won two division championships in the 1970s, but didn't reach the pinnacle of professional football, the Super Bowl, until 1982, where they were defeated by the San Francisco 49ers, 26–21. Seven years later, the Bengals would chart an almost identical path to Super Bowl XXIII, defeating the Buffalo Bills in the AFC Championship (as they did in '82), only to again be defeated, this time in heart-breaking fashion, by the 49ers. The Bengals, who were leading Super Bowl XXIII with 3:20 left in the game, were left to watch as Niners' quarterback Joe Montana marched his team 92-yards down the field and capped off an 11-play drive with a touchdown pass to John Taylor. It is one of two plays in NFL lore known simply as "The Drive."

DRAFT IMPACT

Ken Anderson (quarterback)
- drafted 67th overall from the University Augustana (Illinois) in 1971
- named NFL MVP in 1981
- led the team to its first Super Bowl appearance in 1982

Boomer Esiason (quarterback)
- drafted 38th overall from the University of Maryland in 1984
- led the Bengals to their second Super Bowl appearance in the 1980s
- 1988 NFL MVP

RETIRED NUMBERS

BOB JOHNSON
54

ESSENTIALS (THROUGH 2014)
Founded: **1968**
Stadium: **Paul Brown Stadium**
Regular Season (all-time): **326-395-3**
Playoffs (all-time): **5-13**
Super Bowl Championships: **0**
Passing (all-time): **Ken Anderson – 32,838 yards**
Rushing (all-time): **Corey Dillon – 8,061 yards**
Receiving (all-time): **Chad Johnson – 10,783 yards**

CLEVELAND
BROWNS

Ozzie Newsome

TEAM ORIGINS: In 1946, a rival football league to the NFL known as the All America Football Conference (AAFC) was formed. The Cleveland Browns were one of seven teams to compete in the AAFC. After the league folded in 1950, the Browns joined the NFL. Under the guidance of head coach Paul Brown, they made their NFL debut on Sept. 16, 1950, with a dominant 35–10 victory over the Philadelphia Eagles. To everyone's surprise, the Browns ended up finishing their first season in the league by winning the NFL championship, defeating the Los Angeles Rams 30–28 on Christmas Eve, 1950.

THE GLORY YEARS: The Cleveland Browns won a total of four NFL championships between the years 1950 and 1964, including two back-to-back titles. In 1954, after losing two of their first three games, the club rallied to win eight straight, finishing the season with a 9–3 record. On Dec. 26, 1954, the Browns routed the Detroit Lions 56–10 to win their second championship of the decade. In 1955, Paul Brown led his team to a 9–2–1 regular season record, and quarterback Otto Graham had one of his best statistical years, throwing for 15 touchdowns and only 8 interceptions. The Browns dominated the St. Louis Rams in the '55 Championship, winning 38–14. It would also be Otto Graham's last game as a professional. In 1964, running back Jim Brown had one of his best seasons ever, rushing for over 1,400 yards and leading the Browns to a 10–3–1 record. On December 27, 1965, Jim Brown led the Browns to their fourth championship, by shutting out the Baltimore Colts 27–0.

ESSENTIALS (THROUGH 2014)

Founded: **1946**
Stadium: **FirstEnergy Stadium**
Regular Season (all-time): **505-442-13**
Playoffs (all-time): **16-20**
Super Bowl Championships: **0**
Passing (all-time): **Brian Sipe – 23,713 yards**
Rushing (all-time): **Jim Brown – 12,312 yards**
Receiving (all-time): **Ozzie Newsome – 7,980 yards**

DRAFT IMPACT

Ozzie Newsome (tight end)
- drafted 23rd overall from the University of Alabama in 1978
- played 13 seasons with the Browns
- three-time Pro Bowler and one-time First-Team All-Pro

Doug Atkins (defensive end)
- drafted 11th overall from the University of Tennessee in 1953
- eight-time Pro Bowler & one-time First-Team All-Pro
- inducted into the Hall of Fame in 1982

RETIRED NUMBERS

OTTO GRAHAM	JIM BROWN	ERNIE DAVIS	DON FLEMING	LOU GROZA
14	32	45	46	76

Lynn Swann

PITTSBURGH STEELERS

TEAM ORIGINS: The NFL's fifth oldest franchise was founded on July 8, 1933, by Arthur Joseph Rooney, and originally called the Pirates. In 1940, after seven years of struggling, Rooney decided to rename the team. Hoping a new blue-collar identity would change his team's fortunes, he decided on the "Steelers" in honor of the city's steel industry.

THE GLORY YEARS: Under the leadership of head coach Chuck Noll and quarterback Terry Bradshaw, the Pittsburgh Steelers became the NFL's first modern dynasty, winning four Super Bowls in the 1970s. The first Super Bowl victory came at the conclusion of the 1974 season, after going 10–3–1 in the regular season. Franco Harris rumbled for 153 yards and one touchdown, and the Steelers defeated the Minnesota Vikings 16–6. Harris took home the Super Bowl MVP. This would be the first of two Steelers' back-to-back championships.

The following year they defeated the Dallas Cowboys in Super Bowl X, 21–17, with Lynn Swann capturing the Super Bowl MVP.

The Steelers made their next Super Bowl appearance when they met rival Dallas in Super Bowl XIII at the end of the 1978 season. Terry Bradshaw put on a legendary performance, throwing for 318 yards and four touchdowns, en route to a 35–31 victory over the Cowboys. The next season, Bradshaw's encore was equally impressive, passing for over 300 yards and two touchdowns in a 31–19 romp over the St. Louis Rams. Bradshaw was named Super Bowl MVP for both games.

The Steelers recaptured some of their former glory by winning two Super Bowls in the 2000s, as quarterback Ben Roethlisberger marched his team to wins in Super Bowl XL and XLIII. A pair of receivers took home the MVP nods in those victories, Hines Ward in 2005 and Santonio Holmes in 2008.

DRAFT IMPACT

Franco Harris (running back)
• drafted 13th overall from Penn State in 1972
• a Super Bowl MVP and nine-time Pro-Bowl selection
• elected to the Hall of Fame in 1990

Lynn Swann (wide receiver)
• drafted 21st overall from USC in 1974
• played in three Pro Bowls and was named MVP in Super Bowl X
• elected to the Hall of Fame in 2001

RETIRED NUMBERS

ERNIE STAUTNER
70

JOE GREENE
75

ESSENTIALS (THROUGH 2014)
Founded: **1933**
Stadium: **Heinz Field**
Regular Season (all-time): **580-524-20**
Playoffs (all-time): **33-22**
Super Bowl Championships: **6**
Passing (all-time): **Ben Roethlisberger – 39,057 yards**
Rushing (all-time): **Franco Harris – 11,950 yards**
Receiving (all-time): **Hines Ward – 12,083 yards**

HOUSTON
TEXANS

TEAM ORIGINS: After the Houston Oilers left for Tennessee in 1997, the city of Houston was craving a team to fill their professional football needs. On Oct. 6, 1999, the NFL owners unanimously approved Bob McNair's application for an expansion franchise in Houston. The team began play in 2002.

On Jan. 21, 2001, Dom Capers was hired as the first head coach of the Texans. That February, the expansion draft took place and Capers began to build the franchise, selecting former first-round pick, offensive tackle Tony Boselli; Super Bowl champion linebacker Jamie Sharper; and former Heisman Trophy winning quarterback Danny Wuerffel.

Houston had the first overall pick in the 2002 NFL entry draft and took quarterback David Carr from Fresno State University. On Sept. 8, 2002, the Texans took the field against their state rivals, the Dallas Cowboys. In front of 69,604 fans, Houston defeated Dallas 19–10. David Carr led the attack, throwing for two touchdowns, one to tight end Billy Miller for the first touchdown in franchise history.

THE GLORY YEARS: The Texans, under head coach Gary Kubiak — who took over the reins from Capers in 2006 — finally made the playoffs for the first time as a franchise in 2011 with a 10–6 record. Winning their first game against the Cincinnati Bengals, the Texans advanced to the AFC divisional playoffs, only to lose 11–7 to the Baltimore Ravens. In 2012, riding the arm of QB Matt Schaub, the legs of Arian Foster and the hands of Andre Johnson, as well as the defense of rookie J.J. Watt, the Texans steamrolled to a 12–4 season and a first-place finish in the AFC South. Again they would defeat the Bengals, and again they would falter in the divisional round, this time losing to the New England Patriots 13–5.

ESSENTIALS (THROUGH 2014)

Founded: **2002**

Stadium: **NRG Stadium**

Regular Season (all-time): **88-120-0**

Playoffs (all-time): **2-2**

Super Bowl Championships: **0**

Retired Numbers: **None**

Passing (all-time): **Matt Schaub – 23,221 yards**

Rushing (all-time): **Arian Foster – 6,309 yards**

Receiving (all-time): **Andre Johnson – 13,597 yards**

J.J. Watt

DRAFT IMPACT

Andre Johnson (wide receiver)
- drafted third overall from the University of Miami in 2003
- nominated to his second Pro Bowl and named All-Pro in 2006
- caught career highs in receptions (103) and yards (1,147) in 2006

J.J. Watt (defensive end)
- drafted 11th overall from Central Michigan University in 2011
- led the NFL in sacks in 2012 with 20.5
- was named the 2012 NFL Defensive Player of the Year

Duane Brown (guard)
- drafted 26th overall from Virginia Tech in 2008
- named to the Pro Bowl in 2012
- named Second Team All Pro in 2011 and a First Team All Pro in 2012

Marvin Harrison

INDIANAPOLIS COLTS

TEAM ORIGINS: After playing in Baltimore for almost 40 years, the Colts moved to Indianapolis in 1984. Although the fans in Baltimore were outraged, the Indianapolis fans welcomed the Colts with open arms.

THE GLORY YEARS: After drafting Peyton Manning first overall, out of the University of Tennessee in 1998, the Colts built a solid franchise around their new quarterback. In 2003, after finishing the season 12–4, the Colts blew out the Denver Broncos in their wild-card match-up, 41–10. Manning, the 2003 NFL MVP, threw for five touchdowns. Carrying the momentum from their first-ever home playoff win in Indianapolis, the Colts took to the road to face the Kansas City Chiefs. Manning was cool under pressure throwing for over 300 yards and three touchdowns as the Colts defeated the Chiefs 38–31. The following week, in the AFC Championship game, they faced their playoff nemesis, the New England Patriots, and were defeated 24–14.

In 2006, the Colts claimed their ninth regular-season division title, going 12–4. After steamrolling through the early rounds of the playoffs, the Colts once again met the New England Patriots in the AFC Championship game. Trailing 34–31 late in the fourth quarter, Manning hooked up with Reggie Wayne for two big plays to get into Patriots territory. Running back Joseph Addai rushed up the middle for the score, sealing the 38–34 victory and sent the Indianapolis Colts to their first Super Bowl.

In Super Bowl XLI, Manning led the Colts to a 29–17 victory over the Chicago Bears and was named the game's MVP.

DRAFT IMPACT

Peyton Manning (quarterback)
- drafted first overall from the University of Tennessee in 1998
- 12-time Pro Bowler and six-time First-Team All-Pro
- three-time NFL MVP (2003, 2004, 2008); 2007 Super Bowl MVP

Marvin Harrison (wide receiver)
- drafted 19th from the University of Syracuse in 1996
- broke the NFL's record for most receptions in a season (144) in 2002
- eight-time Pro Bowler and three-time First-Team All-Pro

ESSENTIALS (THROUGH 2014)
Founded: **1944**
Stadium: **Lucas Oil Stadium**
Regular Season (all-time): **486-425-7**
Playoffs (all-time): **22-23**
Super Bowl Championships: **2**
Passing (all-time): **Peyton Manning – 54,828 yards**
Rushing (all-time): **Edgerrin James – 9,226 yards**
Receiving (all-time): **Marvin Harrison – 14,580 yards**

RETIRED NUMBERS

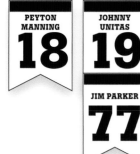

PEYTON MANNING	JOHNNY UNITAS	BUDDY YOUNG	LENNY MOORE	ART DONOVAN
18	19	22	24	70

JIM PARKER	RAYMOND BERRY	GINO MARCHETTI
77	82	89

JACKSONVILLE
JAGUARS

TEAM ORIGINS: With already two professional football franchises in the state of Florida, Jacksonville was a long shot to get a franchise when it applied for a team in 1991. The NFL defied the critics as it awarded Jacksonville a franchise on Nov. 30, 1993. Tom Coughlin, who was the head coach at Boston College, was hired as the team's first coach. On Sept. 3, 1995, the Jaguars played their first regular season game against the Houston Oilers and were defeated 10–3 in front of 72,623 fans at Jacksonville Municipal Stadium. The Jaguars would finish that first season 4–12, but had the building blocks for a strong future.

THE GLORY YEARS: The Jaguars' rise to success was a quick one. In 1996, in only their second year of existence, they made the playoffs, going 9–7 in the regular season. Quarterback Mark Brunell was starting to develop into a solid NFL pivot and complementing him was wide receiver Keenan McCardell. In 1999, going 14–2 in the regular season, it looked like this was going to be the season Brunell and company would not be denied.

The Jaguars were heavy favorites to represent the AFC in the Super Bowl going into the playoffs with a first-round bye. Sure enough, Jacksonville massacred the Miami Dolphins, their state rivals, 62–7 in the divisional round of the playoffs to advance to the AFC Championship. Coming off the big win, the Jaguars seemed primed to beat the Tennessee Titans and move on to the Super Bowl. Although Jacksonville led 14–10 at halftime, the Titans came out in the second half and shut down the Jaguars offense, and captured the AFC Championship with a 33–14 victory.

ESSENTIALS (THROUGH 2014)

Founded: **1995**
Stadium: **EverBank Field**
Regular Season (all-time): **147-173-0**
Playoffs (all-time): **5-6**
Super Bowl Championships: **0**
Retired Numbers: **None**
Passing (all-time): **Mark Brunell – 25,698 yards**
Rushing (all-time): **Fred Taylor – 11,271 yards**
Receiving (all-time): **Jimmy Smith – 12,287 yards**

Fred Taylor

DRAFT IMPACT

Fred Taylor (running back)
- drafted ninth overall from the University of Florida in 1998
- named to the Pro Bowl in 2007
- rushed for over 1,000 yards seven times in his career with the Jaguars

Tony Boselli (offensive tackle)
- drafted second overall from USC in 1995
- five-time Pro Bowler and three-time First-Team All-Pro
- retired after the 2002 season due to injury

Maurice Jones-Drew (running back)
- drafted 60th overall from UCLA in 2006
- three-time Pro Bowler and one-time First-Team All-Pro
- led the NFL in rushing yards (1,606) in 2011

Eddie George

TENNESSEE TITANS

TEAM ORIGINS: After decades as the Houston Oilers, the franchise to moved to Tennessee in 1997. The Tennessee Oilers made their debut on Aug. 31, 1997, at the Liberty Bowl Stadium in Memphis. Running back Eddie George ran for 216 yards on 35 carries and Al Del Greco kicked a winning field goal in overtime to defeat the Oakland Raiders 24–21.

The move to a brand-new stadium in Nashville in 1999 came with a brand-new name, too. The Oilers' moniker was shed in favor of a name that would allow Nashvillians to lay claim to their team, and so it would be that the team to represent Nashville, "The Athens of the South," would be the Titans.

THE GLORY YEARS: In 1999 the Titans won all of their home games, finishing the regular season 13–3. Eddie George rushed for 1,304 yards and was named to the Pro Bowl and "The Freak," Jevon Kearse, won the NFL's Defensive Rookie of the Year.

In their first playoff game at home in Tennessee, the Titans shocked the Buffalo Bills with a 22–16 last-second victory. Down by one point with 16 seconds left to play, and set to receive the ball from the kick-off, the Titans executed a special-team lateral play that saw Kevin Dyson race down the sidelines for the game winning touchdown. The play, which was surrounded by controversy (Buffalo insisted that the lateral was a forward pass), came to be coined "The Music City Miracle." The next week in the divisional playoff, the Titans upset the Indianapolis Colts, 19–16. In the AFC Championship game, trailing 14–10 at half time, the Titans came back and scored 23 second-half points en route to a 33–14 win.

In Super Bowl XXXIV, the Titans faced the high-powered offense of the St. Louis Rams. Despite a two-touchdown performance by Eddie George, the Titans came up short, literally. In one of the most exciting plays in Super Bowl history, Tennessee quarterback Steve McNair dumped a pass off to Kevin Dyson who was stopped one yard shy of the goal line as time expired.

DRAFT IMPACT

Eddie George (running back)
- drafted 14th overall from Ohio State University in 1996
- winner of the Heisman Trophy
- four-time Pro Bowler and one-time First-Team All-Pro

Jevon "The Freak" Kearse (defensive end)
- drafted 16th overall from the University of Florida in 1999
- first player to be drafted, developed and star in a Tennessee uniform
- three-time Pro Bowler and one-time First-Team All-Pro

RETIRED NUMBERS

WARREN MOON
1

EARL CAMPBELL
34

JIM NORTON
43

MIKE MUNCHAK
63

ELVIN BETHEA
65

BRUCE MATTHEWS
74

ESSENTIALS (THROUGH 2014)

Founded: **1960**
Stadium: **LP Field**
Regular Season (all-time): **401-429-6**
Playoffs (all-time): **14-19**
Super Bowl Championships: **0**
Passing (all-time): **Warren Moon – 33,685 yards**
Rushing (all-time): **Eddie George – 10,009 yards**
Receiving (all-time): **Ernest Givins – 7,935 yards**

DENVER
BRONCOS

TEAM ORIGINS: The Denver Broncos, founded by Earl Howsam and his two sons Lee and Bob, were one of the eight original American Football League (AFL) teams. The Broncos began their inaugural season by winning four of their first six games, but then took a slide, as they went on an eight-game winless streak, finishing their first season 4–9–1, last place in the AFL West.

THE GLORY YEARS: In 1987, the Broncos met the New York Giants in Super Bowl XXI and were soundly defeated 39–20. However, this proved to be a turning point for the franchise, as they were now looked upon as serious contenders in the NFL. The Broncos reached two more Super Bowls in the 1980s: Super Bowl XXII in 1988, where they were demolished 44–10 by the Washington Redskins; and Super Bowl XXIV in 1989 where they were hammered by the San Francisco 49ers, 55–10.

Denver quarterback John Elway was starting to get the reputation of never being able to win the big game. Nine long years later he would answer his critics. After defeating their AFC rivals, the Pittsburgh Steelers 24–21 in the 1998 AFC Championship, Elway would again be on his way to the Super Bowl, this time against defending champs Brett Favre and the Green Bay Packers. John Elway and power back Terrell Davis plowed their way through the Green Bay defense, scoring four rushing touchdowns on their way to a 31–24 win. Terrell Davis scored three of the four touchdowns and was named Super Bowl MVP.

The next year, the Broncos repeated as Super Bowl champions, defeating the Atlanta Falcons 34–19. Elway threw for over 300 yards and a touchdown, and ran for a score as well. Elway was named Super Bowl MVP. It was his last game.

ESSENTIALS (THROUGH 2014)

Founded: **1960**

Stadium: **Sports Authority Field at Mile High**

Regular Season (all-time): **444-382-10**

Playoffs (all-time): **20-19**

Super Bowl Championships: **2**

Passing (all-time): **John Elway – 51,475 yards**

Rushing (all-time): **Terrell Davis – 7,607 yards**

Receiving (all-time): **Rod Smith – 11,389 yards**

Terrell Davis

DRAFT IMPACT

Terrell Davis (running back)
- drafted 196th overall from the University of Georgia in 1995
- one of only seven players to run for over 2,000 yards in a season (1998)
- named the 1998 NFL MVP

Tom Jackson (linebacker)
- drafted 88th overall from Louisville University in 1973
- a key player on the "Orange Crush" defense
- three-time Pro Bowler and one-time First-Team All-Pro

RETIRED NUMBERS

JOHN ELWAY
7

FRANK TRIPUCKA
18

FLOYD LITTLE
44

Bobby Bell

KANSAS CITY
CHIEFS

TEAM ORIGINS: After three seasons as the Dallas Texans, owner Lamar Hunt (the man who started the AFL) moved his team to Kansas City in 1963. Under the leadership of Hank Stram, the Kansas City Chiefs won their first game over the Denver Broncos, dominating the contest 59–7. However, the Chiefs struggled during the remainder of the season, finishing 5–7–2. As well, the team had to deal with the tragic death of running back Stone Johnson, who fractured his vertebra in a preseason game against the Oakland Raiders, and died ten days later. The Chiefs retired his No. 33 in his honor.

THE GLORY YEARS: Success came early for the Kansas City Chiefs. After only three years in Kansas City, the Chiefs were the first team to ever play in the newly formed game between the NFL champion and the AFL champion — the game that would go on to be called the "Super Bowl." In 1966, Hall of Fame quarterback Len Dawson led the team to an 11–2–1 record. In the first-ever Super Bowl, Dawson threw for 211 yards and one touchdown, but it was not enough. The Green Bay Packers defeated the Chiefs 35–10.

In 1969, after going 11–3 in the regular season and defeating their arch rivals, the Oakland Raiders, in the AFL Championship game, the Kansas City Chiefs got another shot at Super Bowl glory when they faced the Minnesota Vikings in Super Bowl IV. The second time around, Len Dawson would not be denied. Despite being underdogs against the Minnesota defense, the Chiefs scored 16 points in the first half and never looked back, defeating the Vikings 23–7. Dawson completed 17 of 22 passes for 142 yards and one touchdown on his way to Super Bowl MVP honors.

ESSENTIALS (THROUGH 2014)
Founded: **1960**
Stadium: **Arrowhead Stadium**
Regular Season (all-time): **424-400-12**
Playoffs (all-time): **8-15**
Super Bowl Championships: **1**
Passing (all-time): **Len Dawson – 28,507 yards**
Rushing (all-time): **Jamaal Charles – 6,856 yards**
Receiving (all-time): **Tony Gonzalez – 10,940 yards**

DRAFT IMPACT

Bobby Bell (linebacker/defensive end)
• drafted 56th overall (AFL) from the University of Minnesota in 1963
• drafted 16th overall (NFL) by the Minnesota Vikings in 1963
• inducted into the Hall of Fame in 1983

Derrick Thomas (linebacker)
• drafted fourth overall from the University of Alabama in 1989
• nine-time Pro Bowler and two-time First-Team All-Pro
• inducted into the Hall of Fame posthumously in 2009

RETIRED NUMBERS

JAN STENERUD	LEN DAWSON	EMMITT THOMAS	ABNER HAYNES	STONE JOHNSON
3	16	18	28	33
MACK LEE HILL	DERRICK THOMAS	WILLIE LANIER	BOBBY BELL	BUCK BUCHANAN
36	58	63	78	86

OAKLAND
RAIDERS

TEAM ORIGINS: The Raiders, who were originally supposed to be located in Minnesota, were the AFL's eighth franchise. On Sept. 11, 1960, the Raiders played their first game, losing to the Houston Oilers 37–22 at Kesar Field in San Francisco (Raider home games would be held in San Francisco until 1962). The Raiders would not have a winning season until 1963 when Al Davis arrived from San Diego to take over both GM and head coaching duties.

THE GLORY YEARS: Under head coach John Madden, the 1976 Raiders posted a 13–1 regular season record. Oakland faced the New England Patriots in the divisional playoffs and were the beneficiaries of a controversial pass interference call that set up their game winning touchdown. The momentum from that 24–21 win carried through to the AFC Championship game where the Raiders easily defeated the Pittsburgh Steelers 24–7. In Super Bowl XI, the Raiders would play a talented Minnesota team who had visited the Super Bowl three times in the previous seven years. The Raiders handed the Vikings another Super Bowl loss with a dominating 32–14 victory.

The Raiders returned to the big show in 1981. After upsetting the San Diego Chargers in the AFC Championship game, 34–27, the Raiders rode into Super Bowl XV against the Philadelphia Eagles on the arm of quarterback Jim Plunkett. Plunkett threw for 261 yards and three touchdowns, and was named the Super Bowl MVP. The Raiders went on to beat the Eagles, 27–10.

After the team relocated to Los Angeles, the Raiders made another Super Bowl appearance, this time facing the Washington Redskins in Super Bowl XVIII. In arguably the best performance of his life, Hall of Fame running back Marcus Allen racked up 191 yards on the ground and two touchdowns. Allen was named the Super Bowl MVP, and the Raiders crushed the Redskins, 38–9.

ESSENTIALS (THROUGH 2014)

Founded: **1960**

Stadium: **O.co Coliseum**

Regular Season (all-time): **437-388-11**

Playoffs (all-time): **25-18**

Super Bowl Championships: **3**

Retired Numbers: **None**

Passing (all-time): **Ken Stabler – 19,078 yards**

Rushing (all-time): **Marcus Allen – 8,545 yards**

Receiving (all-time): **Tim Brown – 14,734 yards**

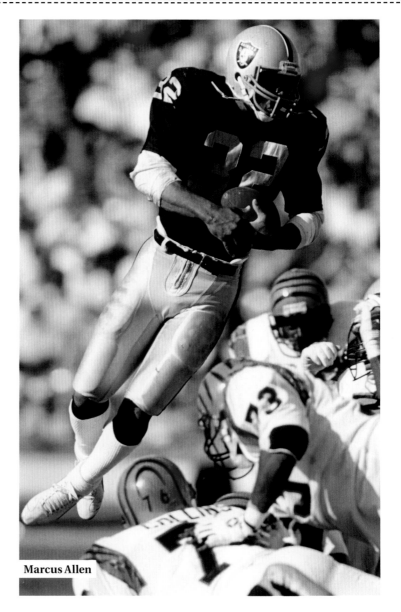

Marcus Allen

DRAFT IMPACT

Marcus Allen (running back)
- drafted 12th overall from USC in 1982
- winner of the Heisman Trophy in 1981
- named Super Bowl MVP in 1984 and NFL MVP in 1985

Fred Biletnikoff (wide receiver)
- drafted 11th overall from Florida State in 1965
- named Super Bowl MVP in 1977
- six-time Pro Bowler and two-time First-Team All-Pro

Nnamdi Asomugha (cornerback)
- drafted 31st overall from the University of California in 2003
- three-time Pro Bowler
- two-time First-Team All-Pro

Junior Seau

DRAFT IMPACT

LaDainian Tomlinson (running back)
- drafted fifth overall from Texas Christian University in 2001
- ranks second on the all-time rushing touchdown list with 145
- five-time Pro Bowler and three-time First-Team All-Pro

Junior Seau (linebacker)
- drafted fifth overall from Southern California University in 1990
- considered the face of the franchise in the 1990s and early 2000s
- 12-time Pro Bowler and six-time First-Team All-Pro

RETIRED NUMBERS

DAN FOUTS **14** LANCE ALWORTH **19** JUNIOR SEAU **55**

SAN DIEGO
CHARGERS

TEAM ORIGINS: The San Diego Chargers were originally slated to play in Los Angeles and did so for one year in 1960. In 1961, owner Barron Hilton moved the team to San Diego after the Greater San Diego Sports Association made a strong pitch for the professional football team. Under the guidance of head coach Sid Gillman, the Chargers made an impressive debut, beating the Dallas Texans 26–10 in Dallas. The Chargers followed up their debut victory with their first home win, defeating the Oakland Raiders 44–0 in front of a crowd of 15,000 people at Balboa Stadium. The Chargers captured the AFL West title in their inaugural year, but lost to the Houston Oilers 10–3 in the AFL Championship game on Dec. 24, 1961.

THE GLORY YEARS: In 1963, the San Diego Chargers, led by Hall of Fame receiver Lance Alworth, posted an 11–3 record and went on to take the AFL West division title. On Jan. 24, 1964, in front of 30,000 fans at Balboa Stadium, the Chargers trounced the Boston Patriots 51–10 in the AFL Championship game. Fullback Keith Lincoln scored two touchdowns and collected 206 yards on the ground and another 123 yards on receptions. To date it is the Chargers only professional football championship.

One of the most recognizable faces in San Diego Chargers' history is Hall of Fame quarterback Dan Fouts. Under Fouts, the Chargers would earn two trips to the AFC Championship game in 1980 and 1981, including the infamous –59 degrees Fahrenheit game in Cincinnati, in which the Chargers lost 27–7.

The Chargers would win the AFC Championship once, in 1994, when they defeated the heavily favored Pittsburgh Steelers 17–13 to advance to Super Bowl XXIX. They then lost to the San Francisco 49ers, 49–26.

ESSENTIALS (THROUGH 2014)
Founded: **1960**
Stadium: **Qualcomm Stadium**
Regular Season (all-time): **417-408-11**
Playoffs (all-time): **11-17**
Super Bowl Championships: **0**
Passing (all-time): **Dan Fouts – 43,040 yards**
Rushing (all-time): **LaDainian Tomlinson – 12,490 yards**
Receiving (all-time): **Antonio Gates – 10,014 yards**

DALLAS
COWBOYS

TEAM ORIGINS: Dallas was awarded an NFL franchise for the 1960 season. Originally named the "Steers," the team changed its name to the "Rangers" in honor of the local baseball club that was going to cease operations. However, the baseball Rangers decided to play in 1960, so "Cowboys" was adopted for the football team. On Sept. 24, 1960, the Cowboys opened to the Pittsburgh Steelers and were defeated 35–28.

THE GLORY YEARS: Under legendary head coach Tom Landry, the Cowboys first tasted Super Bowl success in 1972. The Cowboy defense, which held San Francisco to three points in the NFC Championship game, stymied the Miami Dolphins to set up a 24–3 victory in Super Bowl VI. Quarterback Roger Staubach passed for two touchdowns and was named MVP. Five seasons later in 1977, the Cowboys dominated the regular season with a 12–2 record. Dallas rolled into Super Bowl XII as the clear favorite over an inexperienced Denver Bronco squad and won easily, 27–10.

There was a 14-year draught of football success in the Lone Star State, but fortunes began to change when Dallas drafted quarterback Troy Aikman in 1989 and running back Emmitt Smith in 1990. The 1992 season saw the youthful Cowboys, now under head coach Jimmy Johnson, return to the Super Bowl. Led by Troy Aikman's MVP performance — an aerial attack of 273 yards and four touchdowns — the Cowboys defeated the Buffalo Bills in Super Bowl XXVII, 52–17. They would go on to do the same the next year, defeating Buffalo 30–13 at Super Bowl XXVIII, with MVP Emmitt Smith rushing for 132 yards and two touchdowns.

Dallas added one more Vince Lombardi Trophy to the mantle in 1996, defeating the Pittsburgh Steelers 27–17 in Super Bowl XXX.

ESSENTIALS (THROUGH 2014)
Founded: **1960**
Stadium: **AT&T Stadium**
Regular Season (all-time): **476-352-6**
Playoffs (all-time): **34-26**
Super Bowl Championships: **5**
Retired Numbers: **None**
Passing (all-time): **Tony Romo – 33,270 yards**
Rushing (all-time): **Emmitt Smith – 17,162 yards**

DeMarcus Ware

DRAFT IMPACT
Troy Aikman (quarterback)
- drafted first overall from UCLA in 1989
- led the Cowboys to three Super Bowl titles in the 1990s
- inducted into the Hall of Fame in 2006

Emmitt Smith (running back)
- drafted 17th overall from the University of Florida in 1990
- Named 1993 NFL MVP and the 1994 Super Bowl MVP
- Set the all-time rushing record with 18,355 yards over his career

DeMarcus Ware (linebacker)
- drafted 11th overall from Troy in 2005
- seven-time Pro Bowler and four-time First-Team All-Pro
- led the NFL in sacks in 2008 (20) and 2010 (15.5)

Frank Gifford

NEW YORK GIANTS

TEAM ORIGINS: New York businessman Tim Mara purchased the New York Football Giants for $500 in 1925, and the team made its debut with head coach Bob Folwell in October of the same year. The Giants lost their first contest 14–0 to the Frankford Yellow Jackets. It was an inauspicious start, but football has now been a New York tradition for more than 80 years.

THE GLORY YEARS: The Giants won four NFL championships before the NFL–AFL merger in 1966. Since then, the Giants have been Super Bowl champions four times.

In 1986, under legendary coach Bill Parcells, the Giants finished the regular season 14–2. In the divisional playoff, New York demolished the San Francisco 49ers to move on to the NFC Championship, where they faced the Washington Redskins. The Giants' defense carried the team, shutting out the Redskins 17–0. In Super Bowl XXI, quarterback Phil Simms threw for 268 yards and three touchdowns to lead the Giants past the Denver Broncos, 39–20.

The Giants were not absent from the big game for long, returning to football's grandest stage in 1991. This time their opponent would be the heavily favored Buffalo Bills. Ottis Anderson rushed for 102 yards and one touchdown, but it was a missed field goal in the dying seconds by Buffalo kicker Scott Norwood that sealed the deal for the Giants' second Super Bowl, as they hung on to win by one point, 20–19.

In 2007 and 2011 the Giants and the New England Patriots faced off for football's top prize. In 2007 the Giants pulled off one of the most electrifying upsets in modern sports' history, as they defeated the Patriots (projected as two-touchdown favorites), 17–14. A pass from Eli Manning to Plaxico Burress capped off the winning drive with only 38 seconds left on the clock. In 2011, again the Patriots were odds-on favorites to win, and again the Giants played giant killers, defeating the Patriots 21–17. Both times Eli Manning was named Super Bowl MVP.

DRAFT IMPACT

Phil Simms (quarterback)
- drafted seventh overall from Morehead State in 1979
- two-time Pro Bowler
- named MVP in Super Bowl XXI

Frank Gifford (wide receiver)
- drafted first overall from the USC in 1952
- named the NFL MVP in 1956
- inducted into the Hall of Fame in 1977

RETIRED NUMBERS

RAY FLAHERTY	TUFFY LEEMANS	MEL HEIN	PHIL SIMMS	Y.A. TITTLE	FRANK GIFFORD
1	4	7	11	14	16

AL BLOZIS	JOE MORRISON	CHARLIE CONERLY	KEN STRONG	LAWRENCE TAYLOR
32	40	42	50	56

ESSENTIALS (THROUGH 2014)

Founded: **1925**
Stadium: **MetLife Stadium**
Regular Season (all-time): **667-557-33**
Playoffs (all-time): **24-24**
Super Bowl Championships: **4**
Passing (all-time): **Eli Manning – 39,755 yards**
Rushing (all-time): **Tiki Barber – 10,449 yards**
Receiving (all-time): **Amani Toomer – 9,497 yards**

PHILADELPHIA
EAGLES

Donovan McNabb

TEAM ORIGINS: After moving the team to Philadelphia from Frankford, Pennsylvania, in 1933, owners Bert Bell and Lud Wray decided to change the name from the Yellow Jackets to the Eagles, in honor of the symbol of the National Recovery Administration. On Oct. 15, 1933, the Eagles made a less-than-stellar debut, being blown out 56–0 by the New York Giants. They finished the season 3–5–1.

THE GLORY YEARS: Before the NFL–AFL merger in 1966, the Philadelphia Eagles won three NFL championships (1948, 1949, 1960). Since then, the Eagles have been to two Super Bowls and to five NFC Championship games. In 1980, under the guidance of head coach Dick Vermeil and their strong-armed quarterback Ron "Jaws" Jaworski, the Eagles finished 12–4, top of their division.

Jaworski had a career year in 1980, passing for 3,529 yards and 27 touchdowns and being named to his first and only Pro Bowl. The Eagles would roll through the playoffs, beating the Minnesota Vikings 31–16, and then defeating the Dallas Cowboys in the NFC Championship game 20–7. In Super Bowl XV, the Eagles were grounded as the Oakland defense dismantled Jaworski and the Eagles offense, intercepting the quarterback three times. The Eagles were never a threat in the game, and lost 27–10.

In 2005, the Eagles made their Super Bowl return after falling one game shy of the Super Bowl for three consecutive years, from 2002–2004. Quarterback Donovan McNabb led the Eagles (without their star receiver Terrell Owens) to the promised land over the Atlanta Falcons, 27–10. In Super Bowl XXXIX, Owens made his return from a horrific ankle injury that had sidelined him for the latter part of the regular season and the playoffs. Although Owens caught a game-high 122 yards, and despite the Eagles having 357 total passing yards and three touchdowns, New England defeated Philadelphia 24–21.

ESSENTIALS (THROUGH 2014)

Founded: **1933**
Stadium: **Lincoln Financial Field**
Regular Season (all-time): **541-573-26**
Playoffs (all-time): **19-21**
Super Bowl Championships: **0**
Passing (all-time): **Donovan McNabb – 32,873 yards**
Rushing (all-time): **LeSean McCoy – 6,792 yards**
Receiving (all-time): **Harold Carmichael – 8,978 yards**

DRAFT IMPACT

Donovan McNabb (quarterback)
- drafted second overall from Syracuse University in 1999
- appeared in four NFC Championship games and one Super Bowl
- six-time Pro Bowler

Reggie White (defensive end)
- drafted fourth overall from the University of Tennessee in 1984
- 13-time Pro Bowler and eight-time First-Team All-Pro
- inducted posthumously into the Hall of Fame in 2006

RETIRED NUMBERS

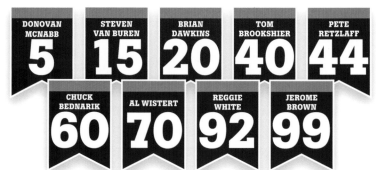

DONOVAN McNABB	STEVEN VAN BUREN	BRIAN DAWKINS	TOM BROOKSHIER	PETE RETZLAFF
5	15	20	40	44

CHUCK BEDNARIK	AL WISTERT	REGGIE WHITE	JEROME BROWN
60	70	92	99

Sammy Baugh

WASHINGTON REDSKINS

TEAM ORIGINS: On Feb. 13, 1937, team owner George Preston Marshall got approval from the NFL to move his team to Washington from the Boston area. On Sept. 16, 1937, the Washington Redskins played their first game and also recorded their first victory, defeating the New York Giants 13–3. That first season in Washington proved to be one of the most successful for an inaugural team as Hall of Fame quarterback Sammy Baugh led the Redskins past the Chicago Bears 28–21 for the 1937 NFL Championship.

THE GLORY YEARS: The Washington Redskins' most successful seasons (three Super Bowl wins in four appearances) came under the guidance of Hall of Fame coach Joe Gibbs.

The first Super Bowl win occurred in 1983. After a 7–1 regular season (shortened due to strike), the Redskins blew through their longtime rivals, the Dallas Cowboys, 31–17, in the NFC Championship game. In Super Bowl XVII against the Miami Dolphins (the Redskins first since 1973, also against the Dolphins) running back John Riggins dominated, rushing for 166 yards and one touchdown. The Redskins won 27–17 and Riggins was named Super Bowl MVP.

The Redskins returned to Super Bowl glory a few years later in 1988. In Super Bowl XXII, Doug Williams passed for 340 yards and four touchdowns as the Redskins pounded the Denver Broncos 42–10. Williams' performance earned him the Super Bowl MVP.

Super Bowl XXVI in 1992 marks the last time the Redskins have won the Vince Lombardi Trophy. Quarterback Mark Rypien led the Redskins to victory over the Buffalo Bills, 37–24. Rypien was named Super Bowl MVP. This victory marked the end of the Joe Gibbs era, as he left football to pursue his passion for NASCAR.

DRAFT IMPACT

Sammy Baugh (quarterback/running back)
- drafted sixth overall from Texas Christian University in 1937
- six-time Pro Bowler and four-time First-Team All-Pro
- inducted into the Hall of Fame in 1963

Art Monk (wide receiver)
- drafted 18th overall from Syracuse University in 1980
- three-time Pro Bowler and one-time First-Team All-Pro
- inducted into the Hall of Fame in 2008

RETIRED NUMBERS

SAMMY BAUGH
33

ESSENTIALS (THROUGH 2014)

Founded: **1932**
Stadium: **FedExField**
Regular Season (all-time): **569-558-27**
Playoffs (all-time): **23-18**
Super Bowl Championships: **3**
Passing (all-time): **Joe Theismann – 25,206 yards**
Rushing (all-time): **John Riggins – 7,472 yards**
Receiving (all-time): **Art Monk – 12,026 yards**

CHICAGO BEARS

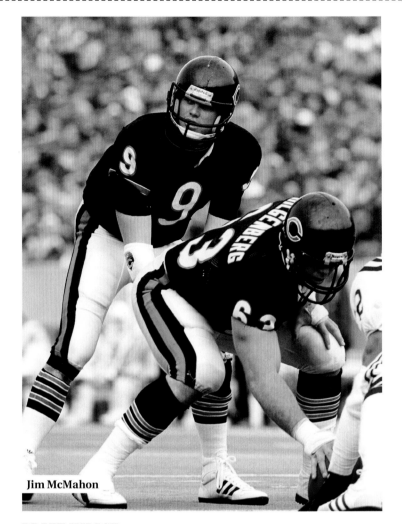

Jim McMahon

TEAM ORIGINS: The NFL's second oldest franchise was born as the Decatur Staley Football Club from Decatur, Illinois, in 1920, the same year the American Professional Football Association was formed. Led by George Halas, the team moved to Chicago in 1921, and by 1922, the same year the APFA changed its name to the National Football League, the team was named the Chicago Bears — partly in homage to the Chicago Cubs, who would share Cubs Park (Wrigley Field) with the Bears.

THE GLORY YEARS: Between 1920 and 1966, George Halas led his team to eight NFL championships, either as a player or as a head coach, or both. It would not be until the 1980s that the Bears were again champions. In 1984, two significant moments shaped the Bears. First, on October 7, Walter Payton became the NFL's all-time leading rusher, accomplishing the milestone in a win over the New Orleans Saints; second, on December 30, the Chicago Bears advanced, for the first time in franchise history, to the NFC Championship game with a 23–19 victory over the Washington Redskins. The Bears lost the game, but it would set the stage for huge success.

In 1985, defensive coordinator Buddy Ryan and head coach Mike Ditka formed "The Monsters of the Midway." Led by Hall of Fame middle linebacker Mike Singletary, the Monsters led the league in every major defensive category. Chicago finished the regular season 15–1. After shutting out the Los Angeles Rams in the NFC Championship game, 24–0, the Bears were on their way to Super Bowl XX.

A dominating defense and strong leadership on offense by Walter Payton and quarterback Jim McMahon led the Bears to a 46–10 rout of the New England Patriots, which even saw rookie defensive tackle William "The Fridge" Perry, rush for a one-yard touchdown.

ESSENTIALS (THROUGH 2014)

Founded: **1920**

Stadium: **Soldier Field**

Regular Season (all-time): **735-545-42**

Playoffs (all-time): **17-18**

Super Bowl Championships: **1**

Passing (all-time): **Jay Cutler – 18,725 yards**

Rushing (all-time): **Walter Payton – 16,726 yards**

Receiving (all-time): **Johnny Morris – 5,059 yards**

DRAFT IMPACT

Walter "Sweetness" Payton (running back)
- drafted fourth overall from Jackson State in 1975
- set the all-time rushing record (16,726) in 1987, since broken only by Emmitt Smith
- inducted into the Hall of Fame in 1993

Jim McMahon (quarterback)
- drafted fifth overall from Brigham Young University in 1982
- the first recipient of the Davey O'Brien National Quarterback Award
- nominated to the Pro Bowl in 1985

RETIRED NUMBERS

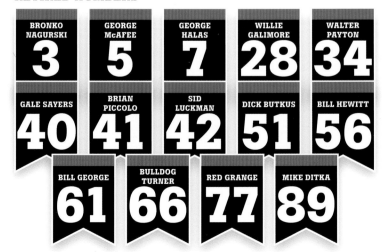

BRONKO NAGURSKI	GEORGE McAFEE	GEORGE HALAS	WILLIE GALIMORE	WALTER PAYTON
3	5	7	28	34
GALE SAYERS	BRIAN PICCOLO	SID LUCKMAN	DICK BUTKUS	BILL HEWITT
40	41	42	51	56
BILL GEORGE	BULLDOG TURNER	RED GRANGE	MIKE DITKA	
61	66	77	89	

Charlie Sanders

DETROIT LIONS

TEAM ORIGINS: Detroit radio executive George A. Richards purchased the Portsmouth Spartans for $7,952.08 in 1934 and moved them to Detroit. The Detroit Lions won their inaugural game over the New York Giants 9–0 on Sept. 23, 1934. In the same year, one of the NFL's oldest traditions was established as the Lions hosted the Chicago Bears on Thanksgiving Day — it was the first in a long tradition of Lions' Thanksgiving football games. Detroit finished the season with a 10–3 record.

THE GLORY YEARS: Detroit was an NFL powerhouse in the 1950s. Under head coach Buddy Parker, Detroit won back-to-back titles in 1952 and 1953, and would add another in 1957, the season Parker resigned. The 1950s also saw the emergence of a great rivalry as the Lions and the Cleveland Browns would face-off four times for the NFL Championship, with the Browns only win coming in 1954.

The Lions' first championship win against the Browns took place in Cleveland on Dec. 28, 1952. After a successful 9–3 campaign, the Lions were tied with the Los Angeles Rams for the NFC title. The Lions defeated the Rams easily in the conference championship game, 31–21, earning themselves a trip the NFL Championship. Although the Lions had the better record, the Browns were the more experienced team. Detroit, however, surprised Cleveland, 17–7, to claim their second NFL Championship (the first since 1935).

Hall of Fame quarterback Bobby Layne guided the Lions to a 10–2 regular season in 1953. The Lions met the Browns again in the championship game, and narrowly escaped defeat with a 17–16 victory. Detroit's third and final championship of the 1950s — a 59–14 shellacking of the Browns — came under head coach George Wilson, who took the reins upon Parker's departure. The Motor City has not had a professional football championship since.

DRAFT IMPACT

Barry Sanders (running back)
• drafted third overall from Oklahoma State in 1989
• Rookie of the Year in 1989; NFL MVP in 1991 and 1997
–inducted into the Hall of Fame in 2004

Charlie Sanders (tight end)
• drafted 74th overall from the University of Minnesota in 1968
• seven-time Pro Bowler and three-time First-Team All-Pro
• inducted into the Hall of Fame in 2007

RETIRED NUMBERS

DUTCH CLARK 7 — BARRY SANDERS 20 — BOBBY LAYNE 22 — DOAK CLARK 37 — JOE SCHMIDT 56 — CHUCK HUGHES 85

ESSENTIALS (THROUGH 2014)
Founded: **1930**
Stadium: **Ford Field**
Regular Season (all-time): **528-625-32**
Playoffs (all-time): **7-12**
Super Bowl Championships: **0**
Passing (all-time): **Matthew Stafford – 21,714 yards**
Rushing (all-time): **Barry Sanders – 15,269 yards**
Receiving (all-time): **Calvin Johnson – 10,405 yards**

GREEN BAY
PACKERS

TEAM ORIGINS: As far as legendary goes, the Green Bay Packers share company with sporting's elite: the New York Yankees, the Montreal Canadiens and the Boston Celtics. The Packers were founded in 1919 in a dingy editorial room at the *Green Bay Press-Gazette*. In 1921, they joined the NFL and finished their first season under head coach and owner, Curly Lambeau, 3–2–1.

THE GLORY YEARS: The Packers' long and storied history includes nine pre-Super Bowl NFL championships. Since the NFL–AFL merger, they have won four Super Bowls. Most notable are the victories in Super Bowls I and II, which have served to forever cement the legacy of the green and gold. In 1966, Green Bay posted a 12–2 regular-season record, and quarterback Bart Starr was named the NFL MVP. The Packers defeated the AFL Champion Kansas City Chiefs in Super Bowl I, cruising to a 35–10 victory. Starr was named Super Bowl MVP.

In 1967, Green Bay faced Dallas for the NFC title (as they had the previous year). On New Year's Eve in Green Bay, with temperatures dropping to –13 Fahrenheit and a wind chill of –43, the Cowboys and Packers played in what is now known as the "Ice Bowl." Bart Starr's last-minute quarterback sneak gave the Packers their second consecutive Super Bowl appearance, inching out the Cowboys 21–17. In Super Bowl II, the Packers faced the Oakland Raiders. Starr passed for over 200 yards and one touchdown to lead the Packers to victory. Starr was once again named the MVP.

In 1997, Brett Favre led the Packers back to the big game, defeating the New England Patriots 35–21 in Super Bowl XXXI. In his storied career with the franchise it would be his only Super Bowl victory. Aaron Rogers took over from Favre in 2008, and within two years brought the Packers back to the Super Bowl. His heroics in the Packers 31–25 victory over the Pittsburgh Steelers earned him MVP honors.

ESSENTIALS (THROUGH 2014)

Founded: **1921**
Stadium: **Lambeau Field**
Regular Season (all-time): **710-541-37**
Playoffs (all-time): **31-20**
Super Bowl Championships: **4**
Passing (all-time): **Brett Favre – 61,655 yards**
Rushing (all-time): **Ahman Green – 8,322 yards**
Receiving (all-time): **Donald Driver – 10,137 yards**

Sterling Sharpe

DRAFT IMPACT

Bart Starr (quarterback)
• drafted 200th overall from the University of Alabama in 1956
• led Green Bay to six division titles, five NFL titles and two Super Bowls
• inducted into the Hall of Fame in 1977

Sterling Sharpe (wide receiver)
• drafted seventh overall from the University of South Carolina in 1988
• five-time Pro Bowler and three-time First-Team All-Pro
• NFL receiving leader in receptions (108), yards (1,461), TDs (13) and yards per game (91.3) in 1992

RETIRED NUMBERS

TONY CANADEO **3** DON HUTSON **14** BART STARR **15** RAY NITSCHKE **66** REGGIE WHITE **92**

Carl Eller

MINNESOTA
VIKINGS

TEAM ORIGINS: In January 1960, the NFL awarded five Minnesotan businessmen the league's 14th franchise. The new franchise was originally to be a member of the AFL, but with news of the NFL's proposed expansion, the businessmen struck a deal with the more venerable league. The Vikings debuted on Sept. 17, 1961. Rookie quarterback Fran Tarkenton passed for 250 yards and four touchdowns and ran for a score as Minnesota upset the Chicago Bears 37–13. Unfortunately, the club finished the season 3–11.

THE GLORY YEARS: Minnesota has been successful throughout their history, but have yet to claim the top prize. In 1969, the Vikings won their second straight division title, finishing with a 12–2 record. Minnesota's defense, "the Purple People Eaters," held all opponents to just 133 points, and helped defeat the Cleveland Browns 27–7 in the NFL Championship. The win catapulted the Vikings to their first Super Bowl. However, Minnesota and the People Eaters would prove to be no match for the Kansas City Chiefs, as Kansas rolled to a 23–7 victory.

Fran Tarkenton and Minnesota originally parted ways in 1967 with a trade to the New York Giants. The Vikings, however, needed help at quarterback and decided to bring back the future Hall of Famer in 1972. Tarkenton led the Vikings to six division championships and three Super Bowl appearances in his second tour with Minnesota, yet, even the great Tarkenton would not be able to get the Vikings over the Super Bowl hump.

DRAFT IMPACT

Fran Tarkenton (quarterback)
• drafted 29th overall from the University of Georgia in 1961
• at retirement he owned every significant passing record including passing yards, passing touchdowns and pass completions
• nine-time Pro Bowler and one-time First-Team All-Pro

Carl Eller (defensive end)
• drafted sixth overall from the University of Minnesota in 1964
• foundation of the "Purple People Eaters" defense in the 1970s
• six-time Pro Bowler and five-time First-Team All-Pro

ESSENTIALS (THROUGH 2014)

Founded: **1961**
Stadium: **TCF Bank Stadium**
Regular Season (all-time): **438-374-10**
Playoffs (all-time): **19-27**
Super Bowl Championships: **0**
Passing (all-time): **Fran Tarkenton – 33,098 yards**
Rushing (all-time): **Adrian Peterson – 10,190 yards**
Receiving (all-time): **Cris Carter – 12,383 yards**

RETIRED NUMBERS

FRAN TARKENTON 10

MICK TINGELHOFF 53

JIM MARSHALL 70

KOREY STRINGER 77

CRIS CARTER 80

ALAN PAGE 88

ATLANTA FALCONS

Keith Brooking

TEAM ORIGINS: Rankin M. Smith, a successful insurance executive, was awarded the NFL's 15th franchise on Jun. 30, 1965. By Christmas Eve, 1965, the Falcons had already broken a franchise record by selling nearly 45,000 season tickets. On Sept. 11, 1966, the Falcons took to the field against the Los Angeles Rams. Although the Falcons kept the game close, the Rams prevailed, edging out the Falcons 19–14.

THE GLORY YEARS: The Falcons best year occurred in 1998, when they went 14–2 in the regular season, won their division and advanced well into the playoffs. The Falcons were led by running back Jamal Anderson as he rushed for 1,846 yards and scored 16 touchdowns.

In their divisional playoff showdown against the San Francisco 49ers, the Falcons jumped ahead to a 14–0 lead. Although the 49ers fought back, the Atlanta defense prevailed and they won the contest 20–18. The next week, the Falcons were heavy underdogs to the Minnesota Vikings in the NFC Championship. Behind 20–7 in the second quarter, it was the Falcons who needed to come from behind this time, and they did, tying the game 27–27 to force overtime. Veteran kicker Morten Anderson played the hero as his 39-yard field goal sent the team to Super Bowl XXXIII.

In Super Bowl XXXIII, the Falcons had to face Denver Broncos' John Elway, Terrell Davis and company, for football's ultimate prize. Hall of Fame quarterback Elway proved too much for the Falcons, as he guided Denver to a 33–19 win. Still, the 1998 season was deemed a major success for the franchise and helped the team take that next step in development.

ESSENTIALS (THROUGH 2014)

Founded: **1966**
Stadium: **Georgia Dome**
Regular Season (all-time): **322-424-6**
Playoffs (all-time): **7-12**
Super Bowl Championships: **0**
Passing (all-time): **Matt Ryan – 28,166 yards**
Rushing (all-time): **Gerald Riggs – 6,631 yards**
Receiving (all-time): **Roddy White – 10,357 yards**

DRAFT IMPACT

Keith Brooking (linebacker)
- drafted 12th overall from Georgia Tech in 1998
- recorded 887 tackles, 12 interceptions and 17 sacks over 11 years in Atlanta
- five-time Pro Bowler

Matt Ryan (quarterback)
- drafted third overall from Boston College in 2008
- 2008 NFL Rookie of the Year
- NFL leader in pass completion percentage (68.6) in 2012

Roddy White (wide receiver)
- drafted 27th overall from University of Alabama at Birmingham in 2005
- four-time Pro Bowler and one-time First-Team All-Pro
- NFL leader in receptions (115) in 2010

RETIRED NUMBERS

STEVE BARTKOWSKI 10

WILLIAM ANDREWS 31

JEFF VAN NOTE 57

TOMMY NOBIS 60

Steve Smith

CAROLINA PANTHERS

TEAM ORIGINS: On Oct. 26, 1993, the Carolina Panthers became the 29th team in the NFL, and the first expansion team since 1976. Carolina named former Pittsburgh Steelers defensive coordinator Dom Capers as head coach. After drafting quarterback Kerry Collins with the fifth overall pick in 1995, the Panthers took to the field against the Atlanta Falcons that September for their first game. The game went into overtime, but Carolina came up short and lost their debut 23–20.

THE GLORY YEARS: In only their second year of existence, the Panthers defied the odds and went 12–4 in the 1996 regular season and captured their first West Division title. In the franchise's first playoff game, the Panthers defeated the Dallas Cowboys (the defending Super Bowl Champions) 26–17. However, the magical season ended the next week in the NFC Championship, when the Panthers lost to the Green Bay Packers 30–13.

In 2003, quarterback Jake Delhomme came off the bench to lead the Panthers to an 11–5 regular-season record and an NFC South Division Championship. In the divisional playoff game against the St. Louis Rams, wide receiver Steve Smith sent his team to its second NFC Championship game by catching a 69-yard touchdown pass in the second overtime. This catch gave the Panthers the momentum they needed to advance to their first Super Bowl. In Super Bowl XXXVIII, the Carolina Panthers were up against the biggest challenge of their short existence: the New England Patriots, whose dynasty was in full swing. The teams fought like two heavyweight champions, punch for punch, throughout the whole game. Quarterback Jake Delhomme passed for 323 yards and three touchdowns, but in the end the Patriots got the final punch in. With four seconds left, Adam Vinatieri kicked the game-winning field goal, giving the Patriots a 32–29 victory and ending the magical run of the 2003 Panthers.

DRAFT IMPACT

Steve Smith (wide receiver)
• drafted 74th overall from the University of Utah in 2001
• four-time Pro Bowler and two-time First-Team All-Pro
• NFL receiving leader in receptions (103), yards (1,563) and TDs (13) in 2005

Julius Peppers (defensive end)
• drafted second overall from the University of North Carolina in 2002
• eight-time Pro Bowler and three-time First-Team All-Pro
• recorded 81 sacks in eight years with Carolina

Cam Newton (quarterback)
• drafted first overall from Auburn University in 2011
• NFL Rookie of the Year in 2011
• NFL leader in average yards per pass completion (13.8) in 2012

RETIRED NUMBERS

SAM MILLS 51

ESSENTIALS (THROUGH 2014)
Founded: **1995**
Stadium: **Bank of America Stadium**
Regular Season (all-time): **151-168-1**
Playoffs (all-time): **7-6**
Super Bowl Championships: **0**
Passing (all-time): **Jake Delhomme – 19,258 yards**
Rushing (all-time): **DeAngelo Williams – 6,846 yards**
Receiving (all-time): **Steve Smith – 12,197 yards**

NEW ORLEANS SAINTS

TEAM ORIGINS: On Nov. 1, 1966, the NFL awarded its 16th franchise to the city of New Orleans. The announcement was made on All Saints' Day, so the owners thought it appropriate to name the team after the day on which it was born. The New Orleans Saints first took to the field on Sept. 17, 1967, in front of 80,879 fans at Tulane Stadium. Despite a 94-yard kickoff return for a touchdown by rookie running back John Gilliam, the Saints were defeated 27–13 by the Los Angeles Rams.

THE GLORY YEARS: In 2000, head coach Jim Haslett led the Saints to a 10–6 record, their second division title and their first playoff victory. Quarterback Aaron Brooks passed for four touchdowns in the wild-card victory over the St. Louis Rams, three to wide receiver Willie Jackson. The fun was short lived, though, as the next week the Saints were beaten by the Minnesota Vikings, 34–16.

In 2006, one year after the devastating effects of Hurricane Katrina, the Saints returned home to New Orleans armed with a new quarterback, Drew Brees. It was one of the most inspiring seasons in the NFL's history, as the Saints, 3–13 in 2005, finished with a 10–6 record, and their third division title. The Saints marched all the way to the franchise's first NFC Championship game, but ultimately lost 39–14 to the Chicago Bears.

The Saints stumbled the next two years, and gave no indication that 2009 would be their best ever. Brees led the Saints to a franchise-best record of 13–3 (the three losses being the last three games of the season). The Saints shrugged off their slump, however, and demolished the Arizona Cardinals 45–14 in the divisional playoff before squeaking by the Vikings, 31–28, in the NFC Championship. In Super Bowl XLIV, Brees passed for 288 yards and two touchdowns to defeat Peyton Manning and the Indianapolis Colts, 31–17, and earn himself MVP honors.

ESSENTIALS (THROUGH 2014)

Founded: **1967**
Stadium: **Mercedes-Benz Superdome**
Regular Season (all-time): **324-409-5**
Playoffs (all-time): **7-9**
Super Bowl Championships: **1**
Passing (all-time): **Drew Brees – 43,685 yards**
Rushing (all-time): **Deuce McAllister – 6,096 yards**
Receiving (all-time): **Marques Colston – 9,239 yards**

Archie Manning

DRAFT IMPACT

Archie Manning (quarterback)
• drafted second overall from the University of Mississippi in 1971
• two-time Pro Bowler
• father of Super Bowl MVP quarterbacks Peyton and Eli Manning

Willie Roaf (offensive tackle)
• drafted eighth overall from Louisiana Tech in 1993
• 11-time Pro Bowler and three-time First-Team All-Pro
• inducted into the Hall of Fame in 2012

Jimmy Graham (tight end)
• drafted 95th overall from Miami in 2010
• name to the 2011 Pro Bowl
• NFL leader for receptions by a tight end (99) in 2011

RETIRED NUMBERS

ARCHIE MANNING
8

JIM TAYLOR
31

DOUG ATKINS
81

Warrick Dunn

TAMPA BAY
BUCCANEERS

TEAM ORIGINS: Tampa Bay was awarded the NFL's 27th franchise in 1976. A group of trustees bestowed the name "Buccaneers" on the team after a local pirate legend. John McKay was named the Buccaneers' first head coach. The 1976 season would go down in infamy as one of the worst seasons in professional sports, as the Buccaneers went winless for the season, finishing with a 0–14 record.

THE GLORY YEARS: The Bucs were the laughingstock of the NFL for most of their first 20 years in the league. In 1996, Tony Dungy was brought in as head coach and he made an immediate impact by emphasizing strong defensive play. In 1997, Dungy's charges allowed the second fewest points in the league, and the Buccaneers made the playoffs for the first time since 1982. That season proved to be the start of a great Buccaneers run, which lasted for the next ten years, with two appearances in the NFC Championship and one Super Bowl title.

In 2002, under the leadership of head coach Jon Gruden, the Buccaneers had one of their most successful regular seasons ever. The team finished 12–4 and after rolling over the San Francisco 49ers in the divisional playoffs, 31–6, the Bucs were ready to face their biggest challenge of the season — the Philadelphia Eagles. The Bucs defense was dominant on that day, allowing only ten points, winning the NFC Championship 27–10. In Super Bowl XXXVII coach Gruden faced his old team, the Oakland Raiders. The Bucs defense was well prepared and Raiders quarterback Rich Gannon threw five interceptions, two of those to safety Dexter Jackson, the game's MVP. Brad Johnson passed for two touchdowns and 215 yards, and in the end it was never close, as the Bucs toppled the Raiders 48–21 to claim their first-ever Super Bowl.

DRAFT IMPACT

Warren Sapp (defensive tackle)
- drafted 12th overall from the University of Miami in 1995
- seven-time Pro Bowler and four-time First-Team All-Pro
- inducted into the Hall of Fame in 2013

Warrick Dunn (running back)
- drafted 12th overall from Florida State University in 1997
- named Walter Payton Man of the Year in 2004 for his charity work
- three-time Pro Bowler

Ronde Barber (defensive back)
- drafted 66th overall from the University of Virginia in 1997
- five-time Pro Bowler and three-time First-Team All-Pro
- NFL interception leader in 2001 (10)

ESSENTIALS (THROUGH 2014)

Founded: **1976**
Stadium: **Raymond James Stadium**
Regular Season (all-time): **235-376-1**
Playoffs (all-time): **6-9**
Super Bowl Championships: **1**
Passing (all-time): **Vinny Testaverde – 14,820 yards**
Rushing (all-time): **James Wilder – 5,957 yards**
Receiving (all-time): **Mark Carrier – 5,018 yards**

RETIRED NUMBERS

DERRICK BROOKS
55

LEE ROY SELMON
63

WARREN SAPP
99

ARIZONA CARDINALS

TEAM ORIGINS: The Arizona franchise is one of the oldest in football, dating back to 1920 and the American Professional Football Association. Then they were known then as the Chicago Cardinals. The franchise moved to St. Louis in 1960, and after 28 years as the St. Louis Cardinals, owner Bill Bidwell moved his franchise out to the desert in 1988. On *Monday Night Football*, the Cardinals made their Arizona debut in front of 67,139 fans against their NFC East divisional rivals, the Dallas Cowboys, losing 17–14. The new Arizona Cardinals were competitive, and looked good starting the season 7–4, but stumbled and finished 7–9.

THE GLORY YEARS: The Cardinals have been haunted by mediocrity since day one, and their 522-721-39 franchise win-loss record is a testament to that fact. In 1998, riding the arm of quarterback Jake Plummer the Cardinals finished the season 9–7, good enough to advance to play the Cowboys in the wild-card game. Arizona won that contest, 20–7, the win breaking the longest postseason winless draught in professional sports, as the franchise had not won a playoff game since the 1947 NFL Championship.

The Cards did not post another winning season until 2008, where they again went 9–7. The roster featured the two-pronged wideout attack of Larry Fitzgerald and Anquan Boldin, with aging Super Bowl MVP Kurt Warner providing the tosses. The trio was the basis for the league's third best offense, and Arizona scored 30 or more points in the wild-card game, divisional playoffs and the conference championship to enter their first-ever Super Bowl. The heavily favored Pittsburgh Steelers got up early on the Cards, leading 20–7 going into the fourth quarter. But, two touchdowns by Fitzgerald in the final eight minutes of the game made it close, and if the Steelers hadn't manufactured a miracle go-ahead score with 42 seconds left on the clock, Arizona would have had their first Lombardi Trophy.

ESSENTIALS (THROUGH 2014)

Founded: **1920**
Stadium: **University of Phoenix Stadium**
Regular Season (all-time): **522-721-39**
Playoffs (all-time): **6-8**
Super Bowl Championships: **0**
Passing (all-time): **Jim Hart – 34,639 yards**
Rushing (all-time): **Ottis Anderson – 7,999 yards**
Receiving (all-time): **Larry Fitzgerald – 12,151 yards**

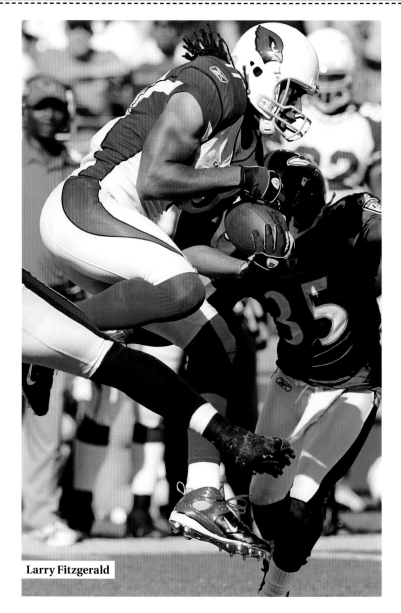

Larry Fitzgerald

DRAFT IMPACT

Larry Fitzgerald (wide receiver)
• drafted third overall from the University of Pittsburgh in 2004
• posted a career-high 103 receptions in 2005
• six-time Pro Bowler and one-time First-Team All-Pro

Anquan Boldin (wide receiver)
• drafted 54th overall from Florida State in 2003
• named Offensive Rookie of the Year in 2003
• three-time Pro Bowler

RETIRED NUMBERS

LARRY WILSON **8** — PAT TILLMAN **40** — STAN MAULDIN **77** — J.V. CAIN **88** — MARSHALL GOLDBERG **99**

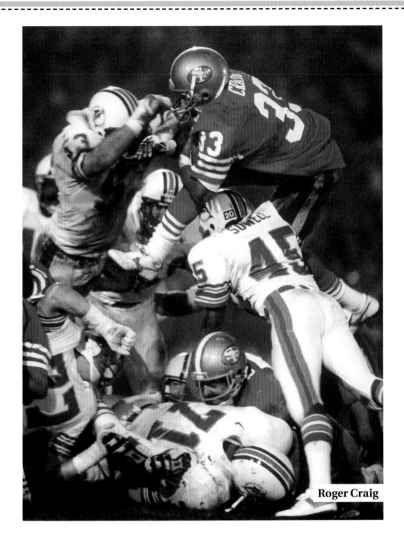

Roger Craig

SAN FRANCISCO
49ERS

ORIGINS: The San Francisco 49ers were established in 1946 after the city petitioned for five years to bring professional football to San Francisco. Its original owner was trucking executive Tony Morabito, who spent $25,000 to get charter into the All America Football Conference (AAFC). The first game took place against the New York Yankees at Kezar Stadium, in which the 49ers lost 21–7. However, the 49ers ended on a good note, going 9–5 in their first season of the AAFC. When the AAFC ceased operations in 1949, the 49ers joined the NFL the following year. Their first season in the NFL was tough under coach Lawrence T. Shaw, as the 49ers finished with a dismal 3–9 record.

THE GLORY YEARS: The San Francisco 49ers ended the 1970s by drafting two key players, one who would serve as the foundation of the team, and the other who would help establish the dynasty San Francisco enjoyed in the 1980s. Joe Montana, a third-round steal, and Dwight Clark and 10th-round pick, became the duo famous for the play simply known as "The Catch," which propelled the 49ers into their first Super Bowl appearance and victory in 1982.

That Super Bowl XVI victory was the first of four championship seasons in the 1980s for the 49ers, including Super Bowl wins in 1985, 1989 and 1990. For the 49ers, the 1980s were great draft years as well, as the club selected two Hall of Famers: Ronnie Lott (first round, 1981), and Jerry Rice, arguably the greatest player ever, (first round, 1985). The combination of solid drafting and signing of key free agents, along with acquiring Steve Young in a trade with the Tampa Bay Buccaneers in 1987, helped the 49ers carry their success into the early and mid-1990s. This run was highlighted by a then-record fifth Super Bowl win in 1995.

DRAFT IMPACT

Joe Montana (quarterback)
- drafted 82nd overall from the University of Notre Dame in 1979
- two-time MVP (1989, 1990)
- inducted into the Hall of Fame in 2000

Roger Craig (running back)
- drafted 49th overall from the University of Nebraska in 1983
- four-time Pro Bowler and one-time First-Team All-Pro
- collected a career-high 1,502 yards in 1988

RETIRED NUMBERS

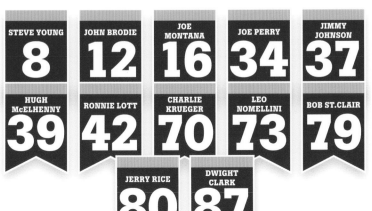

STEVE YOUNG	JOHN BRODIE	JOE MONTANA	JOE PERRY	JIMMY JOHNSON
8	12	16	34	37
HUGH McELHENNY	RONNIE LOTT	CHARLIE KRUEGER	LEO NOMELLINI	BOB ST.CLAIR
39	42	70	73	79
JERRY RICE	DWIGHT CLARK			
80	87			

ESSENTIALS (THROUGH 2014)

Founded: **1946**
Stadium: **Levi's Stadium**
Regular Season (all-time): **553-439-16**
Playoffs (all-time): **31-21**
Super Bowl Championships: **5**
Passing (all-time): **Joe Montana – 35,124 yards**
Rushing (all-time): **Frank Gore – 11,073 yards**
Receiving (all-time): **Jerry Rice – 19,247 yards**

SEATTLE
SEAHAWKS

Shaun Alexander

TEAM ORIGINS: On Jun. 4, 1974, the NFL announced that Seattle would have a professional football team by 1976. In 1975, a year before the Seahawks would play their first game, 59,000 season ticket applications were received. Finally, after two years of waiting, the Seattle Seahawks stepped onto the field, led by head coach Jack Patera, to play the St. Louis Cardinals. The Seahawks were competitive, but their last-second Hail Mary was intercepted, and they lost 30–24.

THE GLORY YEARS: In 2005, the Seahawks dominated the NFC with a 13–3 record. Running back Shaun Alexander led the offense on his way to being named the NFL MVP. In the Seahawks' divisional playoff against the Washington Redskins, quarterback Matt Hasselbeck rallied the team after losing Alexander to a concussion. Seattle won the match 20–10, and in doing so ended the franchise's 21-year playoff winless streak. In the NFC Championship game, the Seahawks thrashed the Carolina Panthers 34–14 and advanced to their first Super Bowl in franchise history. Despite losing in Super Bowl XL to the Pittsburgh Steelers, the season was a success story for the Seahawks.

Nearly a decade later, the Seahawks were back in the hunt for a Super Bowl title. Coach Pete Carroll, quarterback Russell Wilson and running back Marshawn Lynch led the charge as the club went 13–3 in 2013, establishing the first 4–0 start in franchise history. Wilson threw for 26 touchdowns and Lynch rushed for 12 touchdowns to lead the league. The Seahawks decimated the Denver Broncos to win Super Bowl XLVIII with a score of 43–8. The win was the largest margin of victory in the Super Bowl since the Dallas Cowboys defeated the Buffalo Bills by 35 points in 1992. Seattle, proving their title was no fluke, was back in the Super Bowl the next year to face off against the New England Patriots in Super Bowl XLIX. The game, however, came down to a hotly debated play call that resulted in a Seattle turnover and ended any chance of a repeat title.

ESSENTIALS (THROUGH 2014)

Founded: **1976**
Stadium: **CenturyLink Field**
Regular Season (all-time): **305-307-0**
Playoffs (all-time): **14-13**
Super Bowl Championships: **1**
Passing (all-time): **Matt Hasselbeck – 29,434 yards**
Rushing (all-time): **Shaun Alexander – 9,429 yards**
Receiving (all-time): **Steve Largent – 13,089 yards**

DRAFT IMPACT

Walter Jones (tackle)
• drafted 6th overall from Florida State University in 1997
• nine-time Pro Bowler (eight straight from 2001 to 2008)
• four-time First-Team All-Pro

Shaun Alexander (running back)
• drafted 19th overall from the University of Alabama in 2000
• named NFL MVP (2005)
• NFL leader in rushing yards (1,880), touchdowns (27) and yards per game (117.5) in 2005

RETIRED NUMBERS

WALTER JONES 71
STEVE LARGENT 80
CORTEZ KENNEDY 96

Isaac Bruce

ST. LOUIS
RAMS

TEAM ORIGINS: The Rams have called Cleveland, Los Angeles and St. Louis home over their 71-year history. In 1988, the St. Louis football faithful were trying to get another team to call the Midwest home in the wake of the Cardinals departure. In 1995, they got their wish as the Los Angeles Rams relocated after being unable to get funding for a new stadium. In their first season in St. Louis, under head coach Rich Brooks, the Rams finished a sub-par 7–9.

THE GLORY YEARS: In 1999, after signing quarterback Trent Green, the Rams were set to make their first playoff push in St. Louis. Green tore his ACL in preseason action and was out for the year. In a classic case of "blessing in disguise," Green's injury opened the door for an undrafted free-agent quarterback named Kurt Warner.

Kurt Warner shocked the NFL, as the former the Arena Football League star passed for 4,353 yards and 41 touchdowns on his way to an MVP award. Warner and company: veteran receiver Isaac Bruce, explosive rookie receiver Torry Holt and running back Marshall Faulk, finished the regular season 13–3, booking their first playoff appearance in 10 years.

In the divisional playoff, the Rams showed no signs of playoff rust and steamrolled over the Minnesota Vikings 49–37. The NFC Championship against the Tampa Bay Buccaneers was a battle of defenses as the Rams persevered, 11–6 for a berth in Super Bowl XXXIV.

In one of the most memorable Super Bowls in the modern era, Kurt Warner would pass for 467 yards, and two touchdowns against the Tennessee Titans. But it was the defense that would again shine for the Rams, as linebacker Mike Jones stopped Tennessee star receiver Kevin Dyson at the one-yard line as time expired to give the Rams their first Super Bowl victory. Warner was named the game's MVP, capping off one of the most remarkable individual seasons in NFL history.

DRAFT IMPACT

Orlando Pace (offensive tackle)
- drafted first overall from Ohio State in 1997
- helped lead the team to two Super Bowl appearances
- seven-time Pro Bowler and three-time First-Team All-Pro

Isaac Bruce (wide receiver)
- drafted 33rd overall from the University of Memphis in 1994
- four-time Pro Bowler
- NFL leader in receiving yards (1,338) in 1996

ESSENTIALS (THROUGH 2014)

Founded: **1937**
Stadium: **Edward Jones Dome**
Regular Season (all-time): **533-533-21**
Playoffs (all-time): **19-24**
Super Bowl Championships: **1**
Passing (all-time): **Jim Everett – 23,758 yards**
Rushing (all-time): **Steven Jackson – 10,138 yards**
Receiving (all-time): **Isaac Bruce – 14,109 yards**

RETIRED NUMBERS

BOB WATERFIELD
7

MARSAHLL FAULK
28

ERIC DICKERSON
29

MERLIN OLSEN
74

DEACON JONES
75

JACKIE SLATER
78

ISAAC BRUCE
80

JACK YOUNGBLOOD
85

SUPER BOWL HISTORY

Super Bowl I — Jan. 15, 1967
Memorial Coliseum, Los Angeles, California
Green Bay Packers   35
Kansas City Chiefs   10
MVP: Bart Starr, QB, Green Bay

Super Bowl II — Jan. 14, 1968
Orange Bowl, Miami, Florida
Green Bay Packers   33
Oakland Raiders   14
MVP: Bart Starr, QB, Green Bay

Super Bowl III — Jan. 12, 1969
Orange Bowl, Miami, Florida
New York Jets   16
Baltimore Colts   7
MVP: Joe Namath, QB, New York

Super Bowl IV — Jan. 11, 1970
Tulane Stadium, New Orleans, Louisiana
Kansas City Chiefs   23
Minnesota Vikings   7
MVP: Len Dawson, QB, Kansas City

Super Bowl V — Jan. 17, 1971
Orange Bowl, Miami, Florida
Baltimore Colts   16
Dallas Cowboys   13
MVP: Chuck Howley, LB, Dallas

Super Bowl VI — Jan. 16, 1972
Tulane Stadium, New Orleans, Louisiana
Dallas Cowboys   24
Miami Dolphins   3
MVP: Roger Staubach, QB, Dallas

Super Bowl VII — Jan. 14, 1973
Memorial Coliseum, Los Angeles, California
Miami Dolphins   14
Washington Redskins   7
MVP: Jake Scott, S, Miami

Super Bowl VIII — Jan. 13, 1974
Rice Stadium, Houston, Texas
Miami Dolphins   24
Minnesota Vikings   7
MVP: Larry Csonka, RB, Miami

Super Bowl IX — Jan. 12, 1975
Tulane Stadium, New Orleans, Louisiana
Pittsburgh Steelers   16
Minnesota Vikings   6
MVP: Franco Harris, RB, Pittsburgh

Super Bowl X — Jan. 18, 1976
Orange Bowl, Miami, Florida
Pittsburgh Steelers   21
Dallas Cowboys   17
MVP: Lynn Swann, WR, Pittsburgh

Super Bowl XI — Jan. 9, 1977
Rose Bowl, Pasadena, California
Oakland Raiders   32
Minnesota Vikings   14
MVP: Fred Biletnikoff, WR, Oakland

Super Bowl XII — Jan. 15, 1978
Superdome, New Orleans, Louisiana
Dallas Cowboys   27
Denver Broncos   10
co-MVP:Randy White, DT, Dallas
Harvey Martin, DE, Dallas

Super Bowl XIII — Jan. 21, 1979
Orange Bowl, Miami, Florida
Pittsburgh Steelers   35
Dallas Cowboys   31
MVP: Terry Bradshaw, QB, Pittsburgh

Super Bowl XIV — Jan. 20, 1980
Rose Bowl, Pasadena, California
Pittsburgh Steelers   31
Los Angeles Rams   19
MVP: Terry Bradshaw, QB, Pittsburgh

Super Bowl XV — Jan. 25, 1981
Louisiana Superdome, New Orleans, Louisiana
Oakland Raiders   27
Philadelphia Eagles   10
MVP: Jim Plunkett, QB, Oakland

Super Bowl XVI — Jan. 24, 1982
Pontiac Silverdome, Pontiac, Michigan
San Francisco 49ers   26
Cincinnati Bengals   21
MVP: Joe Montana, QB, San Francisco

Super Bowl XVII — Jan. 30, 1983
Rose Bowl, Pasadena, California
Washington Redskins   27
Miami Dolphins   17
MVP: John Riggins, RB, Washington

Super Bowl XVIII — Jan. 22, 1984
Tampa Stadium, Tampa, Florida
Los Angeles Raiders   38
Washington Redskins   9
MVP: Marcus Allen, RB, Los Angeles

Super Bowl XIX — Jan. 20, 1985
Stanford Stadium, Palo Alto, California
San Francisco 49ers   38
Miami Dolphins   16
MVP: Joe Montana, QB, San Francisco

Super Bowl XX — Jan. 26, 1986
Louisiana Superdome, New Orleans, Louisiana
Chicago Bears   46
New England Patriots   10
MVP: Richard Dent, DE, Chicago

Super Bowl XXI — Jan. 25, 1987
Rose Bowl, Pasadena, California
New York Giants   39
Denver Broncos   20
MVP: Phil Simms, QB, New York

Super Bowl XXII — Jan. 31, 1988
Jack Murphy Stadium, San Diego, California
Washington Redskins   42
Denver Broncos   10
MVP: Doug Williams, QB, Washington

Super Bowl XXIII — Jan. 22, 1989
Joe Robbie Stadium, Miami, Florida
San Francisco 49ers   20
Cincinnati Bengals   16
MVP: Jerry Rice, WR, San Francisco

Super Bowl XXIV — Jan. 28, 1990
Louisiana Superdome, New Orleans, Louisiana
San Francisco 49ers   55
Denver Broncos   10
MVP: Joe Montana, QB, San Francisco

Super Bowl XXV — Jan. 27, 1991
Tampa Stadium, Tampa, Florida
New York Giants   20
Buffalo Bills   19
MVP: Ottis Anderson, RB, New York

Super Bowl XXVI — Jan. 26, 1992
Metrodome, Minneapolis, Minnesota
Washington Redskins   37
Buffalo Bills   24
MVP: Mark Rypien, QB, Washington

Super Bowl XXVII — Jan. 31, 1993
Rose Bowl, Pasadena, California
Dallas Cowboys   52
Buffalo Bills   17
MVP: Troy Aikman, QB, Dallas

Super Bowl XXVIII — Jan. 30, 1994
Georgia Dome, Atlanta, Georgia
Dallas Cowboys   30
Buffalo Bills   13
MVP: Emmitt Smith, RB, Dallas

Super Bowl XXIX — Jan. 29, 1995
Joe Robbie Stadium, Miami, Florida
San Francisco 49ers   49
San Diego Chargers   26
MVP: Steve Young, QB, San Francisco

Super Bowl XXX — Jan. 28, 1996
Sun Devil Stadium, Tempe, Arizona
Dallas Cowboys   27
Pittsburgh Steelers   17
MVP: Larry Brown, CB, Dallas

Super Bowl XXXI — Jan. 26, 1997
Louisiana Superdome, New Orleans, Louisiana
Green Bay Packers   35
New England Patriots   21
MVP: Desmond Howard, KR-PR, Green Bay

Super Bowl XXXII — Jan. 25, 1998
Qualcomm Stadium, San Diego, California
Denver Broncos   31
Green Bay Packers   24
MVP: Terrell Davis, RB, Denver

Super Bowl XXXIII — Jan. 31, 1999
Pro Player Stadium, Miami, Florida
Denver Broncos   34
Atlanta Falcons   19
MVP: John Elway, QB, Denver

Super Bowl XXXIV — Jan. 30, 2000
Georgia Dome, Atlanta, Georgia
St. Louis Rams   23
Tennessee Titans   16
MVP: Kurt Warner, QB, St. Louis

Super Bowl XXXV — Jan. 28, 2001
Raymond James Stadium, Tampa, Florida
Baltimore Ravens   34
New York Giants   7
MVP: Ray Lewis, LB, Baltimore

Super Bowl XXXVI — Feb 3, 2002
Louisiana Superdome, New Orleans, Louisiana
New England Patriots   20
St. Louis Rams   17
MVP: Tom Brady, QB, New England

Super Bowl XXXVII – Jan. 26, 2003
Qualcomm Stadium, San Diego, California
Tampa Bay Buccaneers   48
Oakland Raiders   21
MVP: Dexter Jackson, FS, Tampa Bay

Super Bowl XXXVIII – Feb 1, 2004
Reliant Stadium, Houston, Texas
New England Patriots   32
Carolina Panthers   29
MVP: Tom Brady, QB, New England

Super Bowl XXXIX – Feb 6, 2005
Alltel Stadium, Jacksonville, Florida
New England Patriots   24
Philadelphia Eagles   21
MVP: Deion Branch, WR, New England

Super Bowl XL – Feb 5, 2006
Ford Field, Detroit, Michigan
Pittsburgh Steelers   21
Seattle Seahawks   10
MVP: Hines Ward, WR, Pittsburgh

Super Bowl XLI – Feb 4, 2007
Dolphin Stadium, Miami, Florida
Indianapolis Colts   29
Chicago Bears   17
MVP: Peyton Manning, QB, Indianapolis

Super Bowl XLII – Feb 3, 2008
University of Phoenix Stadium, Glendale, Arizona
New York Giants   17
New England Patriots   14
MVP: Eli Manning, QB, New York

Super Bowl XLIII – Feb. 1, 2009
Raymond James Stadium, Tampa, Florida
Pittsburgh Steelers   27
Arizona Cardinals   23
MVP: Santonio Holmes, WR, Pittsburgh

Super Bowl XLIV – Feb. 7, 2010
Dolphin Stadium, Miami, Florida
New Orleans Saints   31
Indianapolis Colts   17
MVP: Drew Brees, QB, New Orleans

Super Bowl XLV – Feb. 6, 2011
Lambeau Field, Green Bay, Wisconsin
Green Bay Packers   31
Pittsburgh Steelers   25
MVP: Aaron Rodgers, QB, Green Bay

Super Bowl XLVI – Feb. 5, 2012
Gillette Stadium, Foxboro, Massachusetts
New York Giants   21
New England Patriots   17
MVP: Eli Manning, QB, New York

Super Bowl XLVII – Feb. 3, 2013
Mercedes-Benz Superdome, New Orleans, Louisiana
Baltimore Ravens   34
San Francisco 49ers   31
MVP: Joe Flacco, QB, Baltimore

Super Bowl XLVIII – Feb. 2, 2014
MetLife Stadium, East Rutherford, New Jersey
Seattle Seahawks   43
Denver Broncos   8
MVP: Malcolm Smith, LB, Seattle

Super Bowl XLIX – Feb. 1, 2015
University of Phoenix Stadium, Glendale, Arizona
New England Patriots   28
Seattle Seahawks   24
MVP: Tom Brady, QB, New England

ADDITIONAL CAPTIONS

Pg 9: Bart Starr lines up to take the snap in the 1966 NFL Championship game against the Cleveland Browns. Green Bay won the game 23–12.

Pg 11: O.J. Simpson sidesteps a New York Jets defender at Shea Stadium in 1973.

Pg 13: Thurman Thomas takes a break between downs in 1997, during a 22–13 victory over the Detroit Lions.

Pg 15: The New York Giants celebrate winning Super Bowl XLII, a 17–14 upset of the New England Patriots.

Pg 26: Sweetness runs the ball against the Oakland Raiders in 1977 preseason action. Payton would lead the league in regular-season rushing yards with 1,852.

Pg 29: Terry Bradshaw watches the defense work in a 24–13 victory over the Oakland Raiders in the 1974 AFC Championship game. The Steelers went on to win their first Super Bowl.

Pg 32: Jim Brown powers through a pile of Giants in his 1963 MVP season.

Pg 35: Dick Butkus flies through the air to make a crushing stop on the Los Angeles Rams on Dec. 8, 1968. The Bears won the game 17–16.

Pg 38: John Elway looks to pass in a 21–20 loss to the Los Angeles Raiders on Dec. 4, 1988. Elway tossed two touchdowns, three interceptions and was sacked three times in the game.

Pg 41: Brett Favre rolls out of the pocket against the Seattle Seahawks during an NFC divisional playoff game at Lambeau Field on Jan. 12, 2008. The Packers beat the Seahawks 42–20.

Pg 44: Forrest Gregg yells from the sidelines during a 13–0 victory over the San Francisco 49ers on Dec. 10, 1960.

Pg 47: Deacon Jones on the sidelines in 1970, one of his eight Pro Bowl seasons.

Pg 50: Dan Marino drops back to pass on Dec. 5, 1999. Despite a three-touchdown performance from Marino, the Dolphins lost 37–34 to the Indianapolis Colts. It was Marino's last season.

Pg 53: Joe Montana warms up for a game against the Los Angeles Raiders on Sept. 12, 1982. The 49ers lost 23–17 on the way to a 3–6 record in the nine game strike-shortened 1982 season.

Pg 56: Walter Payton rushes against Los Angeles Rams defensive back LeRoy Irvin during the 1985 NFC Championship game on Jan. 12, 1986. The Bears won 24–0 on their way to crushing the New England Patriots 46–10 for their first Super Bowl.

Pg 59: Jerry Rice heads downfield during a game against the Chicago Bears on Dec. 17, 2000. The 49ers won the game, 17–0.

Pg 62: Barry Sanders rushes for a total of 75 yards on the day in a 26–17 loss to the Green Bay Packers on Nov. 21, 1993. Despite only playing 13 games in 1993, Sanders still rushed for over 1,100 yards.

Pg 65: Deion Sanders runs against the San Francisco 49ers in the Cowboys' 20–17 overtime win on Nov. 10, 1996.

Pg 68: Gale Sayers carries the ball in 1967 at Wrigley Field. He appeared in 13 of 14 games that season.

Pg 71: Emmitt Smith collects crucial yards in a tight game against the San Francisco 49ers in 1996. Smith's Cowboys won in overtime, 20–17.

Pg 74: Roger Staubach runs with the ball against the Washington Redskins in 1977, his fourth Pro Bowl season.

Pg 77: Fran Tarkenton, looking downfield for the pass, scrambles out of the pocket to collect a few of his 3,674 career-rushing yards.

Pg 80: Lawrence Taylor and cornerback Mark Collins have a reason to smile: the Giants won 55–24 over the Green Bay Packers, giving the team their best season record of 14–2.

Pg 83: Johnny Unitas poses for photographers at Colts training camp in the mid-1960s.

Pg 86: Reggie White gets ready to play in a game during the 1996 season, the same season he won his only Super Bowl.

Pg 88: Malcolm Butler intercepts a pass intended for Seattle Seahawks' Ricardo Lockette during Super Bowl XLIX. The play clinched the game for the Patriots, who won 28–24.

Pg 100: Tom Brady passes the ball under pressure from Kamerion Wimbley of the Cleveland Browns on Oct. 7, 2007. Brady passed for 265 yards and three touchdowns as the Patriots crushed the Browns 34–17, on the way to a perfect season.

Pg 162: Calvin Johnson dives for a pass in a game against the New England Patriots on Nov. 23, 2014. He finished the season in seventh for all-time receiving yards for active players with 10,405.

Pg 206: Green Bay wide receiver Ruvell Martin celebrates the Packers NFC North division title with fans after a 34–14 drubbing of the Detroit Lions in the last regular season game of the year. The Packers would advance to the NFC Championship game where they would lose to the eventual Super Bowl champion New York Giants.

ACKNOWLEDGMENTS

Steve Cameron of Firefly Books was the driving force behind this project. Not only was he a tactful editor but a beacon of encouragement, especially when he sent e-mails that read, "Good job. You only have 18 more biographies to go." Thanks, Steve. It's your turn to buy the next round of beers, though.

George Johnson and I have shared many laughs over the years covering sports. He is delightfully skeptical; a wickedly funny guy who can recite every Monty Python skit ever done. The *Calgary Herald* is lucky to have him as its main sports columnist, as was I to have him as a contributor on this book.

A special thanks goes to Derek Iwanuk for his Joe Montana like deftness when compiling both the statistical information and the franchise stories. As well, designer Jamie Hodgson deserves a special thanks for his ability to plow through revisions — much the way Reggie White plowed through offensive lines — and, of course, a great design.

I forced a lot of people to listen as I bounced names, storylines and ideas off of them, but David Naylor and Matthew Sekeres, my *Globe and Mail* colleagues, did more than their share when it mattered, and it was appreciated. A special thanks also goes to *Globe and Mail* sports editor Steve McAllister for allowing me to adjust my work schedule so I could spend time researching what receiving records Jerry Rice didn't hold.

Without those people, this book never would have happened.

Photo Credits

Getty Images:
B. Bennett 96; Bruce Bennett Studios 20, 213; Peter Brouillet/NFL 117, 211; Scott Cunningham 230; Jonathan Daniel 56, 94; David Drapkin 228; Stephen Dunn 103, 137; Elsa 100, 216, 233 (Allsport); Focus on Sport 68, 77, 147, 151, 229, 235; James Flores 232; George Gelatly/NFL 227; George Gojkovich 6, 111, 125, 127, 143; Bob Gomel/Time & Life Pictures 33; Andy Hayt 221; Stephen Jaffe/AFP 218; Allen Kee 39; John Kelly 226; Kidwiler Collection/Diamond Images 69; Jeff Kowalsky/AFP 63; Ron Kuntz Collection/Diamond Images 212; Don Lansu/NFL/Bears 153; Gene Lower 234; Andy Lyons/Allsport 159, 224; John Mabanglo/AFP 210; Ronald C. Modra/Sports Imagery 53, 57, 119, 121; John Orris/New York Times Co. 18; Joseph Patronite/NFL 217; Doug Pensinger 14; Mickey Pfleger 5; Robert Riger 9, 17, 32, 44, 84, 157; George Rose 38, 54, 60; Robert Skeoch/NFL 12; Jamie Squire 215; Rick Stewart 51, 66, 155, 209, 220; Tony Tomsic 11, 36; Rob Tringali/Sportschrome 113, 208; John Vawter/Diamond Images 105; Ron Vesely 50, 145; Charles Aqua Vida/NFL 19; Michael Zagaris 24, 26, 29, 75, 92, 115

Associated Press Images:
AP Photo 109, 131, 223; Bettman/Corbis 16, 78, 107, 139; Vernon Biever 21, 95, 219
Cal Sport Media 162; Mark Cowan/Icon Sportswire 98; David Drapkin 93, 204; John Froschauer 236; Kevin Higley 206; Al Messerschmidt 30, 71, 86, 99, 123; NFL Photos 35, 45, 47, 48, 72 (Paul Spinelli), 83, 90, 91, 129, 135, 149, 161, 207, 231 (Kevin Terrell); Todd Ponath 87; Pro Football Hall of Fame 225; Todd Rosenberg 2; Paul Spinelli 65, 80, 81; David Stluka 41, 62, 237; Charles Tasnadi 74; Greg Trott 59
Kathy Willens 88

Icon Sports Media:
Justin Berl 167; Zach Bolinger 173, 183; Ray Carlin 179, 222; Andrew Dieb 187; Manny Flores 214; Rich Gabrielson 199; Rich Kane 189; Todd Kirkland 181; Kellen Micah 197; MSA 165, 185; Doug Murray 195; Orlando Ramirez 203; John Rivera 77, 201; Ric Tapia 171; Joshua Weisberg 169; Zumapress 175 (Kansas City Star), 191, 193 (Fort Worth Star-Telegram)

Front Cover:
Scott Boehm/AP Photo (Aaron Rodgers)
Tom DiPace/AP Photo (Barry Sanders)
Peter Read Miller/AP Photo (Larry Fitzgerald)

Back Cover:
Cliff Welch/Icon Sportswire (Walter Payton)

Further Reading

Bradshaw, Terry, and Colin P. Cohn. *No Easy Game*. Chicago: Fleming H. Revell Co., 1979.

Curran, Bob. *The $400,000 Quarterback or: The League That Came in From the Cold*. Toronto: Signet Books, 1969.

Fleder, Rob, editor. *The Football Book*. New York: Sports Illustrated Books, 2005.

Fitzgerald, Ed. *The Johnny Unitas Story*. New York: Tempo Books, 1968.

Grimley, Will, editor. *The Sports Immortals: 50 of Sports' All-Time Greatest as Selected by the Sports Staff of The Associated Press*. Eaglewood Cliffs, New Jersey: Stratford Books, 1972.

Kramer, Jerry, and Dick Schaap. *Distant Replay*. New York: G. P. Putnam's Sons, 1985.

Kramer, Jerry. *Instant Replay*. Edited by Dick Schaap. Toronto: The New American Library of Canada Ltd., 1968.

Taylor, Lawrence, and David Falkner. *LT: Living on the Edge*. New York: Random House, 1987.

MacCambridge, Michael. *America's Game: The Epic Story of How Pro Football Captured a Nation*. New York: Random House, 2004.

Maramiss, David. *When Pride Still Mattered*. New York: Touchstone Books, 2000.

Montana, Joe, and Dick Schaap. *Montana*. Nashville: Turner Publishing, 1995.

Nielsen, Nancy J. *Eric Dickerson*. Mankato, Minnesota: Crestwood House, 1988.

Paolantonio, Sal. *The Paolantonio Report: The Most Overrated and Underrated Players, Teams, Coaches & Moments in NFL History*. Chicago: Triumph Books, 2007.

Rand, Jonathan. *300 Pounds of Attitude: The Wildest Stories and Craziest Characters the NFL Has Ever Seen*. Connecticut: The Lyons Press, 2006.

Rice, Jerry, and Brian Curtis. *Go Long! My Journey Beyond the Game and the Fame*. New York: Ballantine Books, 2007

Rushin, Steve. 1954-1994: *How We Got Here*. New York: Time Inc., 1994.

Sahadi, Lou. *The Long Pass*. New York: Bantam Book, 1969.

Sanders, Deion, and Jim Nelson Black. *Power, Money & Sex: How Success Almost Ruined My Life*. Nashville, Tennessee: Word Publishing, 1998.

Sayers, Gale, and Al Silverman. *I Am Third*. New York: Bantam Books, 1970.

Vancil, Mark, editor. *Marino: On the Record*. San Francisco: Collins Publishers, 1996.

Wiebusch, John, editor. *Lombardi*. Chicago: Follett Publishing Co. 1971.

Zimmerman, Paul. *A Thinking Man's Guide to Pro Football*. New York: Warner Paperback, 1972.

Additional resources include the network of NFL.com websites,
Sports Illustrated/SI.com, *The Sporting News*/TSN.com, ESPN/ESPN.com,
as well as pro-football-reference.com, sportsencyclopedia.com and drafthistory.com.

INDEX